HOW
TO TALK
SO PEOPLE
LISTEN

Also by Sonya Hamlin

What Makes Juries Listen

What Makes Juries Listen Today

How to Talk So People Listen: The Real Key to Job Success

HOW TO TALK SO PEOPLE LISTEN

CONNECTING IN TODAY'S WORKPLACE

New for Business Now

SONYA HAMLIN

Collins

An Imprint of HarperCollinsPublishers

A previous edition of *How to Talk So People Listen* was published in hard-cover in 1988 by Harper & Row, Publishers. A paperback reprint edition of that book was published in 1989 by Perennial Currents.

HOW TO TALK SO PEOPLE LISTEN: CONNECTING IN TODAY'S WORKPLACE. Copyright © 2006 by Sonya Hamlin. All rights reserved. Printed in the United States of America. No part of this book may be used or reproduced in any manner whatsoever without written permission except in the case of brief quotations embodied in critical articles and reviews. For information, address HarperCollins Publishers, 10 East 53rd Street, New York, NY 10022.

HarperCollins books may be purchased for educational, business, or sales promotional use. For information, please write: Special Markets Department, HarperCollins Publishers, 10 East 53rd Street, New York, NY 10022.

Designed by Nancy Singer Olaguera

Library of Congress Cataloging-in-Publication has been applied for.

ISBN-10: 0-06-073406-X
ISBN-13: 978-0-06-073406-0

06 07 08 09 10   ISPN/RRD   10 9 8 7 6 5 4 3 2 1

For Bernie
who has completed my life

Contents

Hello. I'm Sonya Hamlin.

How can I start talking to you without some personal greeting?

Here I am, a total stranger, about to tamper with such an instinctive, spontaneous, and very personal process as how you communicate and present yourself. I'm going to upend some things you've been doing and ask you to try some new ones. Which is why I'd like to at least reach out my hand and greet you, smiling (which I'm doing right now), *before we start*. To get us going in a relaxed and personal way.

You see, I'm going to talk very directly and openly to you throughout our journey together. Person to person, me to you. Now, since this book is all about what will make anyone pay attention to you and also like and be persuaded by you, I face that same challenge:

You're my audience! How I talk to *you* throughout this book must demonstrate that I can do that!

I'll use an approach slightly different from the just-the-facts, do-this list found in many business presentations. You'll get both facts *and* the reasons why they work. Just listing how-to's without some basic understanding of what happens when you do them and what's a good reason for doing them—that won't give you the kind of solid information, or even the motivation, that you need to try them out.

What We'll Cover

This book is about getting what you want at work. You'll learn about:

- **<u>Pre-thinking:</u>** Gaining an organized, fail-safe method for strategizing any communication encounter; analyzing your audience so you can predict what they'd respond to and how to pitch your message

- **<u>Motivating your audience:</u>** How to get people to listen by understanding any audience's self-interest enough to make them *want* to hear your message; discovering how to customize and personalize it

- **Today's basic communication principles:** What it takes to get and keep attention today; new ways to explain and persuade and make messages clear, concise, and *visual*
- **The most common obstacles:** What gets in the way as we interact at work; strategies and skills for solving them
- **Learning to give and take:** How to listen, support, and disagree constructively, while making colleagues out of potential opponents along the way
- **How to handle presentations:** How to deal with one-on-one encounters and meetings

and lots more . . .

Some Ways I'll Communicate with You

My style is, and will be, informal and colloquial. And since I can only do this for you on black-and-white pages, without the extra persuasive powers of voice, gesture, energy level, and personal presence, I'll resort to many *visual devices* to get my message across. You've already seen some of them:

- *Italics,* so you can read certain words with a louder internal voice
- *Bullets and lists* to organize and explain a group of connected ideas
- *Indented one- or two-line paragraphs* for emphasis, to make you slow down and think about each new idea
- *Exclamation points and ellipses* (those . . . things), to make you stop, notice, and go "Hmmm" or, hopefully, "Wow" about certain statements
- *Layouts* that show you where we're going and what's extra important and memorable with bold letters and different type sizes

- *Headings, sections, and subsections* designed to make the book visually pleasurable, succinct, clear, and organized for you
- *Illustrations and charts* to speak to you by showing, not telling

I'll talk to you personally, one-on-one, as I would if we could see each other. I really do imagine each of you as I write—reading, thinking about what you just read, wondering, musing, trying it on, objecting sometimes, and hopefully, saying "Aha" a lot.

Sounds like a lot of "I" stuff but this is all to get you comfortable with the form of this book—and with the writer.

How to Use this Book

I know you bought this book to give you answers and new ideas, ASAP. Since we can truncate time so well now, technologically, and since today's average attention span in the United States is 1½ minutes, you'll probably want to jump right into the chapters that most represent your personal needs.

Fine. Feel free to skip around, but . . . The first two chapters are designed to give you the base—the cornerstones—on which *all* the chapters will stand. They tell you what's changed and what kind of new, overriding issues you face and what to factor into *every kind* of communicating you do today.

So do try to read it chronologically (which is how the book is constructed). Take the time to read Chapters 1 and 2 *before* you dash off to find out about your specific, practical workplace needs. And keep this book nearby at work as a ready reference, so I can be your own personal coach, on call.

But before getting under way, there's one more thing . . .

Why Should You Listen to Me?

I've worked as a conscious and aware communicator all my life, continually trying to solve the puzzle of getting people interested, keeping them tuned in and absorbing what I mean.

as a dancer and musician, creating as well as per-
e challenge was always this:
dience doesn't yet know (or care) about my message
or why i m dying to give it. What can I do to make them want it?"

As an adult, I was challenged by the toughest audience of
all—the television audience. As the first cultural reporter on
nightly television news in the country (WBZ-TV, Boston), I
learned how to interest my audience in material basically unfamiliar to most of them. To capture them *before* they reached for
the remote. Secrets learned? Everyone must find a way to answer
people's automatic internal question: "Why should I listen to
this?" "What's in it for me?" So I learned to intrigue them and tell
my audience how my material connects with their lives in some
way—a basic principle that you'll hear throughout this book!

Next came hosting my own one-hour live daily talk show for
eleven years. The letters, phone calls, personal contact (and the
ratings!) gave me instant feedback about what worked and what
went astray, even with the best of intentions. Covering serious,
controversial, unpopular as well as scientific, factual, and hard-
to-hear issues gave me a virtual Ph.D. in getting people to listen
and stay tuned, even when it wasn't always charming and fun!

I looked next for one of the *hardest* places in our world to get
people to listen and pay attention: the courtroom. So I set myself
the task of teaching trial lawyers how to communicate with
laypeople—jurors.

I developed a course at the Harvard Law School, *Communication in the Courtroom,* and I've been teaching and consulting on
cases with lawyers ever since, showing how to explain complex
facts and simplify issues visually and verbally. I also do this on
television, as an ongoing contributor, analyzing famous cases
from the jury's point of view: the entire O. J. Simpson case, the
Oklahoma City bomber case, the Clinton impeachment case, the
2004 presidential debates, and the Michael Jackson case.

Writing *What Makes Juries Listen* and *What Makes Juries Listen
Today* made me think through and condense this information
into useful basic principles for trial lawyers—which brings me to
you and the business world.

For the past twenty years I've been coaching and consulting with Fortune 100 CEOs and senior executives as well as giving workshops and lecturing about how to talk so people on any level *listen* and get what you're saying.

Enter *How to Talk So People Listen Today: The Real Key to Job Success,* previous editions of which have gone through nine printings. But over the last years I've seen such large changes in how we communicate and what new challenges we face that I had to write another book and tell you how to deal with them. Even with today's "electronic talking," you must *still* give verbal messages and present yourself personally to succeed in this fast-paced business world. To do that effectively now, you need new skills and a new understanding of what's happened.

Bottom line: I think I know your goals, needs, and general hang-ups because I've spent a lifetime figuring out what makes people listen, understand, and become persuaded. So I also know what makes lots of folks *ineffective* communicators and how to get people at many levels to change and become *much better* speakers.

Which is not so hard because when it comes to communicating, we're so connected to each other. All you have to do is tune into yourself to discover how many basic human foibles and weaknesses we share; how many of the same mistakes we make. That's why it won't be hard for you to understand your listeners. And for me to show you how to get your messages across brilliantly.

I'm excited about sharing those concepts and techniques with you. Let's find out what you need to know about what's changed in how we communicate now. Here comes Chapter 1!

1

ENTER TECHNOLOGY, EXIT TALKING

WHAT'S NEW IN COMMUNICATING

Everything—and I'm about to tell you about it. But the absolute *core* of great communicating hasn't changed at all.

It's not about you and your skills.

It's not about your subject.

It all starts from this basic principle:

KNOW YOUR AUDIENCE!

Talking so others listen *starts* with understanding those others, *first!* Then basing any presentation, one-on-one encounter, meeting, or negotiation on what the audience wants, needs, and cares about.

Now, this audience orientation comes in two flavors.

1. What you should know about any *specific* audience you're going to talk to so you can adapt your approach each time

and

2. What basic facts you should know about *any* audience you're communicating with *today* to learn how they listen now.

In order to build a great repertoire for you as supercommunicator, you need to learn these two approches. They are the foundation for building *any* kind of communication, especially at work.

WHAT YOU NEED TO KNOW FIRST

The rest of the book will show you how to analyze any *specific* audience and what techniques to use to reach *them*. But we must begin, in the first two chapters, wth the same basics—truths that exist now for *all* the audiences you'll talk to.

Understanding what's happened to us as a society and how we've changed our communication with each other—this is a *cornerstone* for building successful communication on any level today. Another is understanding more about the disparate groups in today's workplace and what they each need. You'll be surprised by lots of this, recognize yourself, and say "never thought about that," about others.

So let's begin gaining some perspective on where we are now, to give you a base for going forward and learning the new skills I'll show you. Let's now discover:

- How we currently listen and learn, and where talking still fits in
- What motivates us to listen; what's important
- What else is happening in the workplace that affects how you'll communicate with each other successfully

WHAT'S NEW IN THE TWENTY-FIRST CENTURY

Let's start with how we communicate with each other. Wow, has *that* changed in recent years!

To really nail this, here's an email I got recently that says it all:

You know you're living in 2005, when . . .

1. You haven't played solitaire with real cards in years.

2. You have a list of 15 phone numbers to reach your family of three.

3. You email the person who works at the desk next to you.

4. Your reason for not staying in touch with friends and family is that they don't have email addresses.

5. You make phone calls from home and accidentally dial 9 to get an outside line.

6. You've sat at the same desk for four years and worked for three different companies!!

7. You pull up in your own driveway and use your cell phone to see if anyone is home to help you carry in the groceries.

8. Every commercial on television has a website at the bottom of the screen.

9. Leaving the house without your cell phone is now a cause for panic.

10. You get up in the morning and go online before getting your coffee.

True?
See what we have to work with, or against, when we want to *talk so people listen?*
Well, let's get started finding out the kind of work we have to do to make this happen.

EVEN HELLO HAS CHANGED

Just take how we greet each other—that "Hello, I'm Sonya Hamlin" thing I did at the beginning of the book. That's how we usually do it when we meet someone, isn't it? Picture a typical first encounter and what goes with it.

the look
　　the name
　　　the handshake
　　　　the smile
　　　　　the noticing
　　　　　　the visceral response
　　　　　　　the face-to-face *human* contact

That opening moment helps us evaluate and decide at what level to relate and, most of all, how we instinctively feel and respond to the other person. Personal contact has always been the number one way we start any relationship.

But is it, anymore?

We now live in a world where online meeting and greeting and email and text-messaged "conversations"—with no sound, touch, feel, sight, or smell—are substituting for the old in-person ways. We're trading *senses* for *technology*. Today's standards are *speed* and *ease*, *not* human contact and personal perception.

Is that good? Bad? Costly? As effective as the old way? Can we really totally eliminate the old way?

That look-in-your-eyes-to-see-if-I-really-trust-you way?

That notice-how-shifty-he-looks, why-can't-she-stand-still way?

That what-a-warm-smile, how-nice-this-feels way?

That's today's communication dilemma, and the issues we now need to deal with are:

- How recent advances have affected how we now communicate and how we get to know each other
- What else we need to do now to sell and persuade, to develop trust and confidence, and to explain and be understood

THE BIGGEST ISSUE

We're incredibly more efficient now. We can do just about anything business requires—worldwide—by just hitting the keyboard, sending email and searching the Web.

Except . . .
Except the ultimate: *selling ourselves.*
That means the ability to convince

- Potential customers
- Fellow workers
- Upper management
- The people in power

about the validity and trustworthiness of your ideas, your plan, your product, your abilities—*yourself.*

Would anyone hire you simply because you send in a great résumé complete with PowerPoint diagrams and pictures of ads and ideas you created? Would you hire someone on that basis?

In order to close *any* deal, people want to know "Who am I dealing with?" "Can I trust him?" " Would I like to work with her?" "Do I want this person to represent my company?" "Does she seem quick on the draw?"

Can any of that ever be decided by email? Doesn't it always need the old face-to-face, every time?

Where Do People Skills Now Fit

Even with our incredible inventions, twenty-first century business still needs great personal, live communication skills from you to get any message across and make it stick—and to make you, the deliverer effective and memorable.

My task in this book is to show you how to reclaim and enhance those more traditional communication techniques and create your own memorable, get-to-the-point-and-don't-lose-'em style.

So here's your challenge:

- You've got a workplace audience that is *forever* imprinted with speedy, easy technologies for finding out anything, just *visually.*

- You've got an exceedingly *impatient* population. Sit still and just listen? We can get our *own* information, with a mouse!
- You need new tools and approaches to satisfy today's demand for tightly edited and *visual* rather than just *oral* communication.

Here comes the good news.

It's not either-or! The technology is here to help *enhance* your original people skills. You can use it to *support, emphasize, and shorten* your message to help you get and hold the attention of your tech-conditioned audience.

What We Need to Know Now

First, we must recognize, absorb, and accept what's really happened to us, communicationwise. We all compete with technology for people's attention.

Then, we must recapture and develop those personal communication skills that have come to seem secondary.

HOW COMMUNICATING HAS CHANGED

How did we used to communicate and learn from each other? As we fly into the future, let's take just a moment to consider those personal skills and what's happened to them.

THE COMMUNICATION REVOLUTIONS

The world has lived through two major communication revolutions. One began more than 50 years ago and the other around 1985.

Revolutions that changed human behavior forever.

Revolutions no one seemed to notice or be alarmed by.

Revolutions whose implications were never really recognized, analyzed, or warned about very much, even now.

We just absorbed them and were changed and conditioned by them without ever realizing that we had moved onto a new plane of human communication and how we relate to each other.

The revolutions? First television. Then computers and the Internet.

And the changes?

Listening and verbal communication are now becoming much less important, less respected, and less used.

What used to be the accepted way of imparting information from the beginning of time—talking, telling, narrating, explaining, one human being to another (or others)—is not our first choice anymore.

The process of passing on our history—our knowledge, morals, and ethics—used to be elders *telling* the next generation, wise men *telling* the throngs, professors and masters *telling* apprentices and students.

Oral communication was the major means for imparting knowledge and wisdom and skills right up to the middle of the twentieth century. But that process is essentially going, going . . .

What's taken its place is the world of electronic communications, where information is delivered free and convenient, fast and easy. With no effort. Just send it over.

Yes, people still make speeches, politicians still hold forth, grandparents still tell stories—but it's no longer the coin of the realm as far as what we want and expect from communicating.

What makes us pay attention now? What do we do now instead of listen?

We *look*.

At TV screens.

At computer monitors.

At multimedia, hit-all-the-senses-at-once attention grabbers.

Learning this way is surely faster. It's more independent and more entertaining. Contrast this with the time and effort required to just listen to a talker, not to mention the possible boredom! To give people the floor—and all the power—to talk at will, at their own pace, while we wait for *them* to develop an idea . . . *verbally*.

We learn with much less effort now. The *visual* transmission of ideas—with no one else involved—gives us great freedom. Pictures and text are fast and self-explanatory. People can read many times faster than you can talk. We can search for what we want, whenever we want it, mechanically. In an instant.

This is especially important since there are now at least two generations whose daily learning experiences and exposure to new ideas and concepts of the past have been mainly electronic and visual. They have had much less contact with that earlier world of verbal communication, where personal contact and oral teaching were the order of the day and people naturally learned, persuaded, and sold ideas, and themselves, orally.

So, before we learn how to talk to our audiences—the Baby Boomers who grew up before, or on the cusp of, these revolutions, and the generation Xers and Yers who grew up with technology as mother's milk—let's find out what we *don't* do much anymore that we used to do so naturally.

Because no matter how different things become, some things stay the same. We all still need to know how to present ourselves and our ideas personally and verbally, using those original communicating skills to do it.

Come with me on a little visual-verbal journey. Let's visit how we used to do it and how it all worked, so we can add it to today's repertoire.

HOW IT USED TO BE

We used to delight in *words*. For centuries, they were our primary means of exchange. Skillful orators and complex, evocative, even flowery written language were widely admired and actual sources of pleasure. We were accustomed to learning from teachers, masters, and gurus in live exchange. Next to that was reading.

Family entertainment meant talking, telling stories, and reading aloud in the evening. Everyone listening with rapt attention, using his or her own imagination to transform the words into personal pictures. In the United States, elocution teachers were the rage one hundred years ago. Just plain folks recited, and even wrote, poetry to express their deepest emotions.

And for solo entertainment? No movies, television, or other outside elements. We used to just *read;* to go quietly inside ourselves and let someone spin a web and take us with them. Slowly. We would let our imaginations take off from the springboard of another's words and then do the rest ourselves. Get *involved.* (Remember that. It's a major issue in getting any message across.)

Now, this slower, patient way to convey ideas or develop a mood was all about our sense of time. About the rhythm and pacing of our lives. You see, listening and reading or saying words took time.

Time to listen.

Time to think.

Result? We were accustomed to *waiting* till we got what we wanted. Audiences were really good listeners. They expected to wait until they heard the whole story. They used time to actually enjoy the detours and nuances that someone "telling" could provide—the little asides, the descriptive phrases that triggered our imagination to hum along and become an active part of the story ourselves.

Think about this for a minute: the use of time then and now explains a lot about today's problems with communicating. Personal, verbal communication skills, like presenting ourselves, still means that other people must take the *time to listen.*

But we're in a place in history where we're in control of our own time as never before! Think of the *speed* of our own lives and everything we can accomplish now—especially learning and gathering information—in no time at all! And so easily. With so little effort. Verbal presentation, on the other hand, still requires effort. Effort we were used to making.

But time passed and the world and its timing surely changed.

And we were on our way toward the future.

Toward television.

THE NEW TECHNIQUES OF TELLING

TELEVISION

The most important aspect of television for us is that it can impart information *visually*. Words are a secondary adjunct.

We now no longer really *need* to listen.

Television, from its earliest days, has conditioned us to communicate with each other with much more than mere words. We've learned to stop just listening while someone else just talks. What for? It's too slow and boring, waiting while someone gets to the point!

We know we can now get information quicker and more easily, and surely with more entertainment, by viewing information or stories electronically, while an amorphous voice-over fills in the details. And it's more fun to be personally, actively engaged in seeing for oneself, rather than ceding center stage passively to someone *just talking* (and too often talking too long and disjointedly!).

By allowing electronic pictures to become the first line of communication, we've actually changed our relationship to each other. We no longer learn from each other. Instead we now get our information independently, from an anonymous third source that communicates information visually, using words only secondarily.

Now visually transmitting information is not new.

Communicating Visually

From the prehistoric cave painters on, artists have "talked" to us through icons and images. And we always found visual messages the most arresting, the most stirring and instantly eloquent.

But the difference between then and now is *effort*. It took effort to view those images, just as it takes effort to process words alone. People had to *travel to see* them for the pictures or statues to give their message.

But television requires little or no effort.

- Television gets its messages across with amazing efficiency.
- It gives pleasure without requiring any effort from the viewer.
- You're home when you watch it. Just turn on a knob.
- The subjects and material covered are designed to be explicit and reach out to the broadest population.

To find out where speed and ease are taking us and what kind of effect it's having on our work life, we'll look at television from a totally new perspective—how it has affected how we communicate with each other.

How Television Has Changed Us

Here are some "telling" facts:

- 77 percent of all Americans get about 90 percent of their news from television.
- 47 percent get *all* their news from television.
- Major U.S. corporations have their own television studios.
- Video and web conferencing are replacing those big on-site face-to-face sales meetings.
- Digital video recording systems are becoming commonplace in homes and offices.
- Children now log about 22,000 hours watching television by age 18, more than twice the time spent in school.

The Effect on Business Communication

Since television created tremendously effective techniques for giving hard information like the news, there's real value in analyzing how these techniques work. These are the same kinds of data you offer in any business communication—facts, numbers, ideas, strategies. And your audiences are conditioned to receive such material quickly and easily.

WHAT TELEVISION NEWS HAS TAUGHT US

The ever-changing daily news forces us to process information anew every day. Let's see how TV news delivery systems have conditioned us to learn, and from whom. How people absorb this *nonfiction* part of television is a great example of how they expect you to deliver your factual information.

TV News Stories Are Short and Graphic

One and a half minutes long, they're designed for short explanations, not an in-depth analysis with background material. Basically, they deal with what's *new,* not what is or was. So we're already trained to expect that we can get enough information on a subject to be satisfied, with skimming off the top in only *a minute and a half.* We've learned that's about enough to understand what happened without learning much about the context of *why* or *how* or *what if.*

Real Time Is Not Reality Now

Natural time—how long it actually takes to do anything or go anywhere—has disappeared on television, making us an even more impatient audience. Just think of the illogical time frames displayed in an average news story:

- Anchor person intros story from studio. (That seems OK.)
- *Zip!* Instant appearance of reporter at scene of fire. (How

did he get there? Who saw him go?) Shots of fire from ground and helicopter. (Oh yes, anyone can go from the ground to the air in one second!)

- *Zip!* Shots of ambulance arriving at hospital. (How did they get *there* in one second? When did we see that jump in time?)

- *Zip!* Reporter wraps up and *Zip!* back to the studio and anchor desk. (Wow!)

And we never question all this magic. It seems normal, since we've technologically *mastered time!* Result? We want—nay, *expect*—information the same way. To collapse time and get it fast and easy.

How can you, as a speaker, fulfill this capturing of multiple perspectives, *zip zip*, while you're just speaking?

This is what you're competing with, since you're talking to an audience that's very used to this process.

Visuals Carry the Message

Words and people are no longer the primary message givers. Now pictures tell and affect us more directly. Human tellers introduce, comment a little, and do voice-overs, but they're not as powerful. Television has taught us to expect *visual proof*, not to take anyone's word for it. And to be entertained by pictures, not talking.

The Talking-Head Taboo

A "talking head"—a close-up of a person just talking—is considered so boring now that it's only given 6 seconds of unadulterated exposure—called a *sound bite*—on the air. Then we immediately go to "lip flap": the person's picture remains but a reporter's voice gives the audience the highlights of what else the talking head said, abbreviating a whole speech or interview into just 30 seconds of shorthand explanation.

Result? We now believe that listening to any talking head—any person speaking—is to be carefully avoided. We expect we can get the gist of it all in 30 seconds. . . .

It's Really All So Simple!

The biggest challenge for TV networks and program producers is to get and keep the largest audience, to net the top dollar for the network's airtime. More people watching means more money per minute for commercials. So news programs and TV content in general are geared to the broadest audience with the least challenging intellectual content, to keep the most people watching, and interested.

Reinforcing and Visual Support Are Expected

Since the major goal is to keep you tuned in, television news teaches us that "if you don't catch on, we'll help you till you do"— by means of graphics and voice-overs to reinforce whatever is happening. We've grown accustomed to repetition and support since we're not paying much attention anyway.

Here's how it works. See if you recognize this:

ANCHOR PERSON *(in studio):* "There's a big demonstration at City Hall about the rezoning of the downtown area. Let's go right to Joe Jones, live at City Hall Plaza, reporting from the demonstration."

JOE JONES *(on camera, in front of masses of people, carrying signs and shouting angry slogans):* "Hi, I'm Joe Jones, coming to you live at the scene of this large demonstration at City Hall Plaza."

OK. So far we've heard the same intro *twice*—once verbally, once verbally and visually. But, assuming that we probably didn't get it yet (since they know we don't pay attention very well), we next see the following:

- Words written at the bottom of the screen under the picture of Joe Jones talking, with the *same* folks demonstrating, still carrying signs and shouting slogans.
- The words on-screen say "Joe Jones live at City Hall."
- And underneath *that* it says "XYZ Eyeball News," while in

the bottom right-hand corner shines the logo of the network. Right?

Why all this repetition? To keep you informed, in case you
forget or don't listen well enough in the first place. TV producers
know we don't bother to do that much anymore.

And what does all this dumbing-down do to any audience's
tuning in to an intense, or not so interesting, or just plain ordinary
business presentation or sales pitch? How does this supersimpli-
fying and repetitive technique affect the way we listen to the
usual business presentation?

Television's Effect on How We Listen, Learn, and Concentrate

Passivity

We want information delivered quickly and easily. Unlike the
time and effort listening, talking, and reading takes, television
does the work for us with its edits, visuals, and graphics.

Inattention

We've learned to listen with half an ear. The television is on at
home, competing for your attention with phone calls, kids
yelling, trips to the fridge, and other chores.

TV now teaches us it's OK—actually *normal* —to listen just a
little, from time to time, instead of making us concentrate and
focus.

Interruption

Commercials have taught us that no matter how important,
dramatic, or engrossing a subject is, the mood and concentration will always be broken every 5 to 8 minutes by commercials.
This conditions us not to get too involved in any subject—emotionally or otherwise—and not to expect anything to go on for
too long.

Lack of Continuity

We're OK with coming in on the middle of a show or event. Others fill us in with an even more edited version than the television show itself presents. We either ask "What's this about?" or bumble along till things come clear or click the remote control and move on to something else.

This Is Boring! Click

Those wonderful remotes give us the power to click off communication in midsentence, switching subjects at will when the first hint of boredom or disinterest hits us. This bodes ill for anyone wanting to impart new, unfamiliar, necessary-though-difficult information to an audience. We don't even need a remote control! We just tune you out.

Individual Imagination Is Suppressed

MTV's music videos have preempted unique *personal* visions with universal visuals-for-all interpretations. The prepackaged images tell us that our own imaginations can't, won't, or don't need to come up with visions of our own.

This conditioning encourages a sameness of thinking and a need to fit in with the crowd, affecting our desire to discover, imagine, and explore on our own.

How does this affect management's goal of motivating individuals to step out and perform new tasks, find original solutions, and press ahead of the crowd?

Television's Communication Legacy

- Just listening to someone talking is no longer in our experience.
- The pace of television precludes taking time for ideas to unfold.
- Technology has taught us how to get anything with speed and ease, now we expect to learn that way, too.
- Our attention span has now shrunk to 1½ minutes of

total, uninterrupted focus before we drift off. (Recognize the length of a news story?)

- We need not just a reason but instant recognition that there's something of interest to get us and keep us listening.
- Television has shown us much more direct and faster ways to get information, without any personal effort on our part.
- The visual is now the message. Without pictures, graphics, diagrams, designs, color, we no longer tune in and stay tuned—either to television or to talking. Visuals are so easy, so direct and explicit, so captivating, and so easy to understand. And they're entertaining!
- We also need visual support for any new idea. Accustomed to things being very explicit, we can't picture what we haven't seen. Our imagination is down; we now have the habit of passively absorbing what's given—shown—to us.

In Defense of Television

Since I've spent most of my life working in television, I see two sides to this picture.

We can't un-invent it. It's a mixed blessing, providing pollution as well as power. But there's much we can now learn from television about communicating.

Television gurus really analyzed our natural tendencies and what makes us listen and pay attention. And they've definitely figured out how to get messages across to us in our new fast-time zone.

Though TV's techniques have taught us impatience and the quick fix, as practical folks in a speeding world we've got to take what's here and run with it.

You're as challenged to hold on to your audience as TV was and is. I plan to help you use the best techniques we've learned from TV to become great *live* communicators in this electronic world.

Now, remember that I said there were two revolutions at the beginning of this chapter? Well, it's time to talk about that other revolution and what it has done to complete the massive change in how we reach each other now.

COMPUTERS AND THE INTERNET

How has the Internet, this brilliant, totally pervasive invention, affected us and how we learn? Especially since this is now our ultimate business communication tool? Let's find out what effects the Internet has had on how we communicate and what we therefore expect from communicating now.

MAJOR EFFECTS ON COMMUNICATING

On Our Own

Information giving and getting is now a solitary act, from anonymous sources. No one, other than ourselves, is involved at all—neither speaking nor affecting us in any way. Just me to machine and machine to me.

Control and Power

We now have total control and power over how and when we get any information. We can go to the Web whenever we wish and it serves us at the click of a mouse. We get answers to questions instantly, just sitting at our desks. We cut and paste, transpose, delete at will, and send reams of documents, music, pictures anywhere in the world. No dependency on *anyone*. And no *waiting!* We can get instant replays of any show or news broadcasts we missed earlier.

No Personal Contact

The getting-to-know-you game is now relegated to our invisible chat rooms and Match.coms. We're losing our old sensory ways of evaluating people and what they say to us. Without seeing, hearing, or just sensing the new people we meet in the network match-up world, we can only accept or reject what they choose to tell us and what they want us to know or believe. That instinctive editing and questioning we've always done in person—those first-impression judgments we're so capable of making—aren't our first line of defense or attraction anymore.

Judging Responses

We don't even know what the people we *do* know truly think or feel about the things we or they communicate by email. These are carefully edited to be as short and to the point as possible. And without our ability to respond to how they'd be delivered *in person,* we have to try to read between the lines and guess at how they might really *feel* about what's in those emails.

Speed and Ease

Nothing in history has ever delivered requested information faster. This is today's basic litmus test and how we measure whatever is being communicated. We can, and do, demand email, Instant Messaging, everything the Internet has to offer, since it's possible and available and getting better, easier, cheaper, faster, and more efficient every day. Who needs to use patience in developing ideas? Or ruminate? Or look too much at both sides?

OK. That's just a little about our second communication revolution, because we're still in it. . . .

Think about how profoundly the Internet has affected our communications skills and style.

And it continues to blow our minds with ever more astonishing capabilities. Who knows what's next out of that pipeline and how profoundly that will affect our giving messages to each other?

We'll only keep moving on, because we can and our strides forward are so monumental and useful. But let's also stay aware of what effect all these great strides have on us as people who still need to communicate verbally, face-to-face, no matter what we invent.

WRAP-UP: HOW COMMUNICATING HAS CHANGED

- We're living in the early stages of a new period in human history. Communication has changed forever.
- The attention span of the American public is now 1½ minutes. To lengthen that, there are many new techniques to learn.

- People are in control of getting their own information, customizing, and editing to suit their exact needs.
- Electronic media and the need for speed and ease are today's coin of the communications realm.
- Time is a major issue. Succinct, clear, and to the point is today's imperative.
- We expect to get information super-fast and super-easily, in small bites, highly organized and lean, with much variety and multimedia input.

IMPLICATIONS FOR BUSINESS COMMUNICATION

All of the above truths affect how you'll communicate from now on. These facts must be your *number-one guidelines* for any planning and presenting you do.

- Audiences need to visualize your ideas to bring clarity, interest, and credibility to them.
- You must be challenging, interesting, surprising, alive, energized, and original to get and hold the audience's attention today.
- You need to involve your audience and interact with them to keep them with you.

These facts must be your number one guidelines for any planning and presenting you do.

Ready to go on to discover the techniques that can do that best? Not quite . . .

WHAT ELSE CAN AFFECT YOUR AUDIENCE

There are two more areas you must know about that deeply affect how people will receive and process your messages in the workplace: generational differences and multicultural diversity, particularly as they manifest themselves in the workplace. Read on to complete your orientation to today's communication issues.

2

GENERATION GAPS AND DIVERSITY IN TODAY'S WORKPLACE

Besides the *external* factors, like technology, that affect how your audience listens today, there are also *internal* factors. The personal beliefs and attitudes of your audience also define how they're going to hear and interpret what you say. And these are determined very much by what generation people belong to, where they came from, and how recently.

We now live in the most heterogeneous, diverse, and multi-ethnic society in the history of our country. This makes it harder to communicate effectively across many kinds of borders. Borders that affect not only how groups communicate and gather information but also how they hear you.

We used to expect our audience would be Tom, Dick, and Harry. Then we added Tina, Dina, and Harriet. And now it might be Astrid, Zayeed, and Juan, LaShawna, Jawaharlal . . . *and* Harry.

That's the *multicultural* factor.

And then there's the *generational* factor.

We have three distinct groups at work today: Baby Boomers, Generation Xers, and the new, incoming Generation Y. And they are different from each other—*very* different.

You must become aware of *all* these differences to communicate and strategize successfully with your colleagues at work.

HOW ARE BOOMERS, GEN XERS, AND GEN YERS DIFFERENT?

Here are the general categories of the generations in the workplace now. These groupings are my synthesis of current thinking about generational cohorts.

- <u>Seniors</u>: Born before 1946: ages 60 and up. Not many left in corporations: many retired; others still working part-time or on their own.
- <u>Baby boomers</u>: Born 1946 to 1960: ages 46 to 60.
- <u>Generation Xers</u>: Born 1961 to 1978: ages 30 to 45.
- <u>Generation Yers</u>: Born 1978 to 2000: ages 6 to 29. Sometimes called Echo Boomers or Millennials.

THE ISSUES

To understand how they differ, we need to consider how the three generations think, work, act, and prioritize.

- What motivates them? What do they expect and care about?
- How has each generation been conditioned to communicate?
- What's different in their goals, standards, influences, and assumptions? How does that affect their work?

DIFFERENCES IN FAMILY AND LIFE EXPERIENCES

To begin, let's just consider the changes in American family structure since 1960.

- 1960: 88 percent of all children grew up in a traditional two-parent household.
- 1988: 60 percent of all children grew up in a traditional two-parent household.
- 1997: Less than 50 percent of all children grew up in a traditional two-parent household.

What effect would the breakdown in the family structure—the first social institution we all get exposed to—have on the attitudes of Gen X and Gen Y as they grew up?

Although the Boomers grew up during the Vietnam War and the civil/women's/gay rights movement, the nuclear family was still intact and that basic piece of their world still looked pretty solid and predictable. But Gen X and Gen Y children grew up in a volatile, changeable family structure. Their very roots were shaken. What could these groups learn to depend on?

If even the nuclear family can disintegrate before their eyes, consider what this taught them about survival as they grew up and developed.

Gen Xers needed to develop self-reliance: "Don't count on anything. You're on your own. You better learn to improvise, to figure it out for yourself. Nothing's getting handed to you anymore. Make up your own rules. Adapt the world to suit *your* needs."

Gen Yers simply supplanted family with friends and peers. That became their structure and support group, their fail-safe haven, along with their families.

DIFFERENT VIEWS OF THE ESTABLISHMENT

If the fundamental family, that closest, most personal, most needed social institution, is so precarious and undependable, what can Generations X and Y look to in other parts of the "establishment"? What other institutions represent stability? Businesses and corporations? Schools, governmental institutions, authority figures, police, courts, laws? What can they depend on from any of them?

What these young people saw instead was:

- Familiar corporate names, great competitors, now merging and sailing off together. Don't they even care about old loyalties?
- Banks, national chain stores, newspapers all going under.
- Corporate leaders standing trial.
- Schools with metal detectors, and teachers being beaten up.

- Police charged with violations and crimes.
- Governors and congressmen going to jail.

Nothing's very dependable or built that solidly in the establishment, is it?

CULTURAL ICONS TELL IT

A quick retrospective on how the nuclear family has been depicted in pop culture over the years can show us the very different belief systems these three generations grew up with.

Boomers

Baby Boomers grew up believing in family, seeing traditional roles defined in TV sitcoms like *Leave It to Beaver, Father Knows Best, The Donna Reed Show,* in which all the old traditions were reinforced. Mom was the homebody. Dad was the breadwinner and ultimate authority. Kids knew their place and knuckled under to the rules.

Just a step to believing in the orderly way the world seemed to work. The expectations? You grow up, marry, have kids, work your way up the ladder of the place you started at, visit Grandma around the corner. The institutions would be there for you.

Gen Xers

A very different message about marriage, family, relationships, and the so-called inviolate institutions of our society came through to *this* group. What Gen Xers saw on TV reflected the new approaches to what constitutes family.

All in the Family told the truth behind the "nice" façades of the 1950s and '60s, revealing prejudice, generational differences, and a father who was irascible and ignorant. *My Three Sons* gave us a new "normal family structure" and *One Day at a Time* certainly portrayed the divorced mother raising her children alone as normal and unsurprising.

Married—with Children and *The Simpsons* gave some pretty satirical, dystopian views of family life: a whole new view of the "nuclear family."

But here's a very important change. *The Mary Tyler Moore Show* and *Alice* showed us a new set of truths. Work was becoming the center of our lives, supplanting the traditional nuclear family with a much looser, more open, but still crucially important "family"—*friends* who were connected to and dependent on each other. There for each other, no matter what.

So, for Gen X, the message was—anything goes. Make it up yourself and make it work for you. No prescribed basic structure to automatically slide into. And that goes for other established institutions as well. . . .

Gen Yers

Let's see what this generation grew up seeing as the norm on TV. What was now reflected as society's accepted norms for family? *The Simpsons* are still there. *Seinfeld* shows us how to be single and applauded for getting by with it. *Everybody Loves Raymond* shows us—actually kind of *exposes*—intergenerational issues in one kind of family. Seniors are irascible, not able to communicate or work things out; Gen Xers, very outspoken, with the *wife* solving most of the problems, eventually do. Whatever happened to *Father Knows Best*?

Friends: Any question about their being a family to each other? Much closer than their families of origin? This reflects the new major *family* role that peers now play for each other: how they understand life from such a different perspective than their original, older-generation family members do, and how judgmental and rather shocked by their choices this older generation is.

The Nanny: How many families now have one version or another of child care? Mom's at work, no more apron or flour on her hands.

And if they watched *The Golden Girls,* they saw old women—independent, sexual, working or not, bossing each other around, judging and giving opinions. Certainly a new family grouping, reflecting our time.

When I talked to Gen Yers about marriage and family, this is what I heard:

"Y'know, there's so much expected from a relationship now. Such an idealized, all-fulfilling version that *nothing* could satisfy that. That's why so many people end in divorce. It's never enough." They also can't picture the long haul: "Who can sustain a romantic relationship for 25 or 30 years?" And when they talked about parenting, there was some agreement that there's a lack of boundaries and that their major do's and don'ts come from their peer group.

Research shows that many Gen Yers have real and solid relationships with their parents—much more open than those of previous generations, though the typical dysfunctional families still exist in large numbers. But Gen Y has developed a new, normal family-type connection. Rather than simply getting *born* into one, they've made one out of their peers.

BASIC DIFFERENCES IN PRIORITIES AND ATTITUDE

Now, aside from all of the above being an interesting analysis of what's happened to us as a society, how does it all affect your communication in the workplace?

Here's a chart I've put together for a bird's-eye view of the generation gaps, comparing how the changes I've just described have affected the generations' attitudes toward some key aspects of our lives.

Just *look* at the entirely different choices of each generation! How their priorities not only don't mesh but are actually in *opposition* to each other! See how trying to address each group, let alone trying to address an audience with all *three* groups, needs some special thought and adaptation?

And each of you reading this belongs to only *one* of these generations, so your instincts take you in one, not three directions. . . . That's why all of this matters. And there's more coming.

PRIORITIES AND ATTITUDES

	BABY BOOMERS	GENERATION XERS	GENERATION YERS
I get most information from . . .	Network news, mainstream newspapers, traditional magazines, my friends	Cable news, alternative newspapers, niche magazines, my friends	Websites, e-zines, blogs, my friends
I can be persuaded with . . .	Traditional perks, public recognition, participative decision making	Insiders' benefits, private recognition, responsibility for decision making	Moral payoff, respect for authority figures, clear expectations, freedom
My career goals are . . .	To have a stellar career with increasing status	To have a movable career where I'm in charge	To have parallel careers with jobs I love
I resent . . .	Disrespect, being passed over	Politics, trade-offs	Stereotyping, limits
My preferred work day is	Not over until I'm done with what I set out to accomplish	Getting the job done on my terms	Lots of fun and working with people
I am motivated by . . .	Recognition, being valued and appreciated	Trust, getting to do things my way	Results, the opportunity to make tangible changes
In the media I trust those who . . .	Give full analysis, are in a prestigious position	Are irreverent, pushing the envelope	Are online or books, not TV or newspapers

CAREERS AND WORK

Now I know I'm generalizing about the generations and that can get me into lots of trouble and disagreement. But to clarify some basic differences between them, I have to resort to some boiled-down stereotypical snapshots. Let's discuss each of these snapshots in terms of how they would affect that generation's attitudes toward careers and work.

Boomers

Boomers inherited the model of working *vertically*. Starting from the bottom, they committed to one company as a loyal team member, expecting to grow, develop, and achieve in a steady climb to the top, or close to it. Work and career, getting ahead, making money, and being recognized came first. These were lessons learned from the previous generation. "Do better than Dad" was the motto. "Get out there and make it" was the goal.

Personal considerations were still secondary since Boomers saw how little concern the previous generation seemed to give to things like being fulfilled, following one's muse, or spending time on other things. Work, money, and success basically came first.

So it's only a step to understanding their attitude toward what they expected from themselves and from work. Being a team player, loyal to the firm and viewing the company as family— these were the existing standards everyone accepted. That's how Boomers started out.

They *did* want to make a difference in society and felt that they could. They looked to distinguish themselves in their work life, to be leaders, to try to change the old approaches. They were also the Woodstock, flower-children generation who worked for civil rights and against the Vietnam War. They were there in the vanguard of the women's movement. But those were the mavericks. The majority of the Boomer generation still stayed connected to the values, family systems, and priorities of the seniors before them.

At work, the models for success and the styles and norms of work were already established by the previous generation of management. They were so deeply rooted and apparent in the workplace that all the newcomers could do was take on the style and work habits that were already there. To act like the men who ran the establishment. Women even "dressed for success" in navy blue suits (skirts, not pants!), white blouses, and dainty ribbon bow ties. And women worked twice as hard as the men in order to prove their worth. They were very much under suspicion, being dismissed by the old guard as unqualified interlopers, of questionable value, in their new, unrecognizable roles.

Gen Xers

Gen Xers work in a more *horizontal* pattern, going sequentially from job to job, rather than vertically climbing upward on one path as Baby Boomers did.

Their major goal, first and foremost, is a *good life*. For them, it's not just about money and recognition for their work and status or even making much of a difference societally. Gen Xers value independence and carving their own design for what they do, rather than knuckling under to authority in order to get ahead. And they enter the workforce as individuals, not as team players with a desire to "belong."

This concept of putting "the good life" first, before the needs of the organization and the independence it implies, is in direct opposition to the underpinnings of how Baby Boomers generally work. And Baby Boomers are Gen Xers' bosses! The chasm between these two orientations made for much misunderstanding in the workplace when Gen Xers came to work.

Now here's a curious turn of events: Boomer managers' total dedication to "work comes first" was threatened when women entered the workforce. Feeling that women would have babies and want to leave for a while or want more flexible hours, they said: "You can't hire a woman for this management position, invest in her executive training, or choose her for a serious career climb. They do not have real dedication to the job; you can't count on them for the long haul." Even college professors believed this as they chose which students to invest in. But here's the shocker.

It was discovered that young Gen X men also saw work as only one of the things in their life! *They* wanted to go home and parent their children, too!

Law firms, whose Boomer partners had been willing to work 90 hours a week for years to make partner, couldn't understand this new generation. "They're so *lazy*! They want to go home at five o'clock? How do they think they'll ever make partner that way? When I was their age . . ."

Well, Gen Xers certainly added some new thinking to the workplace. Their goals—the quality of life at work and beyond; to be personally original and innovative; to gain some control over what they did—all these flew directly in the face of existing systems and accepted norms of how people worked until that time. It began to raise some questions in *everybody's* mind.

Results? The workplace began adapting to these new ideas. The old formal suit-and-tie look gave way to "office casual." Informality became the new order of the day, as closed offices changed to an open room with cubicles, everyone visible to each other.

Corporations began adding employee services, responding to the total needs of the person in their employ, as executives, well trained by one company, started leaving, without too much regret, for others that suited their life needs better. Being "the best place to work" became the new mantra for corporations. Joining the traditional bottom line as a measure of success, "quality of life in the workplace" became a major goal, and is evaluated and reported on annually by all the business magazines.

Great forward strides have been made as a result of the stimulus Gen X brought, based on the reality of employees' total lives and needs. Companies now support graduate work, child (even elder!) care, Alcoholics Anonymous, gay and lesbian networks, multicultural groups, and so on.

The workplace has become a surrogate supportive "family" (interesting in the light of the family discussion above). Starting with the effort to build loyalty and keep their employees, especially Gen X employees, happy, companies have really been trying to add more to people's work lives.

Based on what you've just read, look at the major differences between Boomers and Gen Xers and what motivates them. Can you see how you'd have to adapt what you use to persuade both groups when you plan to present an idea? You'd really have to think about what would turn each group on.

Gen Yers

Now these newcomers to the workforce are making Gen X go through what Baby Boomers went through when Gen X came on the scene! Again, I hear the same complaints: "They don't know how to work hard!" Gen X is amazed, not only because Gen Yers don't work the way *they* did but also because they have an attitude: "Gen Yers seem to think they already know it all. No need to learn, study, pursue, follow up, ask questions. What's that about?"

Well, here's an interesting angle. In a new book about how video games are affecting Gen Y work habits, *Got Game: How the Gamer Generation Is Reshaping Business Forever* (Harvard Business School Press 2004), John C. Beck and Mitchell Wade establish that "Game Boy and PlayStation . . . are a central, defining part of growing up for millions of people." They go on to say, "This new generation is completely different from the Baby Boomers [and nongamer Gen Xers] in the way they think and work, and all of this is entirely attributable to gaming."

They further describe the generation gap by reporting that Gen Xers, walking into a videogame expo, will discuss the games with developers, but rarely step up to play in public! Gen Yers, however, will routinely go right for the controller mouse. Why? For the Gen Xer "the learning is an investment, a personal risk, maybe even a chore," while for the Gen Yers, "jumping in to play, even a totally new game, even in front of peers, is as natural as breathing."

According to Beck and Wade's research, gamers in general take a more adventurous approach toward work. Here are a few examples:

- "If you get there first, you win."
- "Trial and error is the best strategy and the fastest way to learn."

- "Elders . . . can't help; they don't understand even the basics of this new world."
- "You will confront surprises . . . but the sum of these risks and dangers . . . cannot make the quest foolish."
- "Once you collect the right 'objects' (business plan, prototype, customers, maybe even profits), you'll get an infusion of gold to tide you over."

Can you see the implications for this group entering the workforce? What *their* expectations and resultant work habits would be?

Here's a surprise, however: though gaming seems like such an individual pursuit, gamers have highly developed teamwork skills and a strong desire to be part of a team, probably from their deep and constant connection to, and need for, their peers, growing up. They also care more about the organization they work for than other groups do.

On another note, though, more than 50 percent are more likely than nongamers of the same age to describe themselves as "a deep expert in my work." Picture how *that* level of arrogance from newcomers in their twenties goes down with the folks they come to work for, the ones who paid their own heavy dues to get where they are! And what issues it creates as management tries to incorporate them into the ongoing systems. Quite a dichotomy between what Boomer/Gen Xers expect of them and what Gen Y thinks it can already deliver.

And the dot-com industry gave them another view of what it takes to make it. Talking to a number of Gen Yers, I heard, "You get a job for a few years, come up with something great, and are set for life at 26. You don't have to pay any dues." And many of them expect to do something just like that. Not too much effort. Not impossible. "Just do it!"

Of course, these are generalizations but they're an interesting start in trying to understand Gen Y's work attitudes as they enter the workforce.

Here's a set of comparative responses by all three generations showing their attitude toward work. Again, just a snapshot, but they will give you some interesting viewpoints. Each generation that reads these will surely recognize themselves.

The Generations at Work

	BABY BOOMERS	GENERATION X	GENERATION Y
Getting ahead	My job has defined me. Now that I've gotten where I wanted to be, I want more balance. I am the expert—let others do the work.	I'll end up in a good place if I stick to my beliefs and get lots of diverse experience—but work isn't everything without a "life."	I'm going to work hard and learn what it takes to get ahead. Mainly I think authority isn't too difficult to earn.
Communications	Formal vertical systems in organization —don't copy me on everything, just keep me informed.	I need continuous flow, back and forth—don't keep things from me.	I need to be in touch constantly. I know what's going on, so don't hold back. My friends and I talk about everything.
I trust and listen to those who . . .	Give a full analysis.	Push the envelope.	Are cool, totally connected, and easygoing
Team building	It's OK to have a team, but individual contribution is what makes things happen. You can't build a team with games and exercises.	I like having a sense of family—let us hang loose together, have fun together, then we'll get the work done.	If we can all put our skills together, we can take collective action that will truly be more powerful than just our individual contributions.

THE GENERATIONS AT WORK (CONTINUED)

	BABY BOOMERS	GENERATION X	GENERATION Y
Speaking of respect,	I expect to be listened to.	I don't think anyone listens to me, so I'll use my own ideas!	I think people listen to me.
Someone's experience and credentials	I am either really impressed or not at all.	You have to prove to me you're legit.	Not assumed, but I'll listen.

Bottom Line in Generational Differences

Gen X and Gen Y had to learn to improvise institutions; to make it up as they went along; to create structures, like families, to suit themselves. No models to follow.

Gen X broke with previous work models and tried crafting the workplace to suit their needs and priorities.

It's only a step to understanding why Gen Y also expects to "make it up as you go along" and *to design how they'll work,* based on how and what they like to do, rather than any established system. They have no experience in simply accepting an established system . . .

Now let's look at how each group likes to get information and use technology.

GENERATIONAL DIFFERENCES IN GETTING INFORMATION

We all follow the conditioning of our growing up—how we got news and entertainment, what was the norm at that time. Here's how this plays out.

Boomers

Boomers are not very aggressive in how they get information. They're likely to read local and national news in their newspapers and the big general magazines, which they consider reliable, like *Time, Newsweek, Fortune, Business Week, Money.* They look through the pages for something of particular interest to them. They sit still and watch network news broadcasts, with their reliable and familiar anchors. They may also add cable for variety or a more in-depth look, but none of it takes much effort. They may not find much of what they're interested in but click around till they do. The essence is: "Present it to me; make it happen."

Gen Xers

Gen Xers are highly selective and proactive. They don't wait for the six o'clock network news to get their information. They make self-determined choices, waiting for nothing. Their news comes from cable (which they record for viewing at their convenience) or they get it online. Theirs is the world of *narrowcasting*, seeking out specialized media for what they specifically care about. They don't read features in general newspapers (too much time wasted on things they don't care about). They seek out specialty magazines for particular information that deals with subjects they do care about: success, parenting, men's concerns, women's issues , sports, fitness, health, travel and adventure, good living, food, and look for more about these areas on the Internet.

As Karen Ritchie writes in *Marketing to Generation X:*

"Control" is the key word. Far from being passive viewers of television, Xers are active channel surfers, who view with remote control in hand, searching among hundreds of options for whatever suits the impulse of the moment [selecting] among broadcast programs, cable, prerecorded videos rented . . . shows they taped . . . and video games. Programming dictates selection.

Gen Yers

The computer is well on the way to markedly diluting the old systems of learning from a teacher, an elder, a specialist, a mentor, and the library. Unlike Boomers, where gathering information always involved an identifiable person, the new motto is "I can do it myself." As one Gen Yer put it, "Why go from book to book when you can get all the information at once, print it out, and you're ready to go!"

Depending on what you're looking for, a dependable source on the Internet is always important. "I can find stuff out by Googling but then I look for the reliability of the source: how the website is set up, how legitimate it looks, etc."

How do they get their news? Print rarely; mostly from the Web. TV is strictly entertainment—*not* a source of news and information at all, either network or cable. After 9/11 the number one complaint among Gen Yers was: "All the TV stations are showing *news* all the time!"

Many Gen Yers use their cell phones to surf the Web but the biggest use is for keeping in touch at the drop of a hat. Text messaging is now the prime method on cell phones but calling for instant communication is still there. And of course there are always IMs.

Although all three generations receive their information from different sources, using different equipment, the common thread for what gets them to listen is still how the info is presented. "How well does the presenter capture my attention? How does the material fulfill any of my needs—this is the only way I'll listen to anyone or anything."

PERCEPTION OF TIME

Boomers

They grew up with talking teachers, not computers, as the major sources of information in their classrooms. They took time-consuming trips to the library to get information.

Gen Xers and Gen Yers

They're both, especially Gen Y, accustomed to creating and controlling reality and manipulating time through video games, IMs, and sci-fi movies. "Old movies are so literal and chronological. Not like *Memento,* where it all got told backwards!"

So the real-time clock that ticks as you deliver your message is a time trap they don't particularly want to be in. And their fund of patience runs out fast when it comes to listening to words and explanations in real time.

THOUGHTS ABOUT INFORMATION TECHNOLOGIES

To wrap this up in a true twenty-first-century time-warp way, let me put all three generations together again, comparing their thoughts about the most dramatic twenty-first-century thrust—information technologies. And do read this thinking about how relevant their different approaches and responses are to you *as speakers.*

	BABY BOOMERS	GENERATION X	GENERATION Y
Email is . . .	One more place to check, another method to learn.	The best way to stay in touch.	Not nearly as good as instant messaging and blogging.
Voice mail is . . .	Convenient; more personal than email but what's safe to say on tape?	A slow alternative to email.	Passé; a mere substitute for IM.
Text messages are . . .	For techie kids.	Too much work but good for short messages.	What I do all day.
Landlines are . . .	Essential!	For real conversations.	Expensive, and why bother—I've got my mobile and VoIP.

	BABY BOOMERS	GENERATION X	GENERATION Y
Mobile phones are . . .	So handy but also really intrusive. And taking pictures???	The only way to stay in touch and be continually available.	My lifeline.
PDAs (like palm pilots) are . . .	Another gadget. But really useful.	Where I used to keep my life before data phones.	For old people. We don't need them.
Conference calls are . . .	Formal performances.	A way for everyone to stay involved.	Rare—used them for school projects.
Videoconfer-ences are . . .	Painful, expensive, never really work.	Not much better than conference calls.	Haven't tried them. Sounds cool.
Web conferences are . . .	How does it work? How can I talk to someone? How do I use it?	Great, but a little slow.	Super cool, especially if I can do it myself. Love chat rooms.
Face-to-face meetings are . . .	The way to get everyone tuned in. How can you do it without being in the same room?	Key. I need to know people understand what is important.	Uncomfortable, confrontational, and overly for-mal.
Memos are . . .	A great way to communicate to everyone when there is something important to say.	Totally out of date and out of touch.	So lame.

	BABY BOOMERS	GENERATION X	GENERATION Y
PowerPoint is . . .	A little intimidating but so effective and impressive!	My right arm.	A necessary evil; they're pretty boring in a speech. Hard to make interesting.
Flip charts are . . .	Easy and comfortable.	Very 60s.	Preachy, old-fashioned, cumbersome; you have to type it to record it, don't you?
Books are . . .	Still great—love to read, especially nonfiction.	Great but take so much time.	Too time consuming and take too much thinking. For learning, not entertainment.
Search engines are . . .	I use them but still don't like them—who knows where the info is from?	How did we ever survive without them?	My super tool. My home page and lots more.
Libraries are . . .	For research, the best place.	Where they keep all the books if I ever, for some reason, might need them.	Good places to hang out (College years). Boring. Too quiet (H.S. years).
Overhead projectors are . . .	Much better than a slide projector! Easy to use.	Just fine but charmingly old-fashioned.	Retro; used them in school.

WHAT ALL THIS MEANS TO YOU

The generational differences you've just read about make it hard for everyone to be on the same page, when you talk to them on any subject. They're not automatically in tune with each other, sharing one set of values and approaches to work and one set of motivations.

These goals, needs, belief systems, and priorities are key to reaching and motivating each group. And the rest of the book is all about the various ways to capture and hold such diverse audiences.

But now, let's turn to the other issue that can affect how people hear your message today.

OUR MULTICULTURAL WORKFORCE AND COMMUNICATING NOW

We now work around the globe with people whose traditions and background cause them to communicate in very different ways from our familiar American lingo and style. And many of those global groups now live here, bringing with them their ethnic roots, their culture and religious observances, their mores and standards, all unfamiliar to native-born Americans.

We must also realize that we are such a diverse country, regionally, even within our own borders. The cultures and speech of native-born Americans from urban ghettos, rural areas, the suburbs, small towns, or cities present vast differences, making us unfamiliar to each other, although we all were born here.

So communicating with each other at work now needs another level of awareness.

THE MIXED-POPULATION PHENOMENON

Our many new immigrants have created a number of subcultures within our own society. In most cities, even towns, you can now hear foreign languages spoken. Public signs and telephone answering machines attest to the fact that Spanish has become a second language in most of the United States. There are now more Muslims in this country than Episcopalians. And this multicultural diversity in the United States, and our workplace, will continue to grow.

Here is a chart from the U.S. Census of the year 2000, predicting the population changes our country will undergo for the next 50 years.

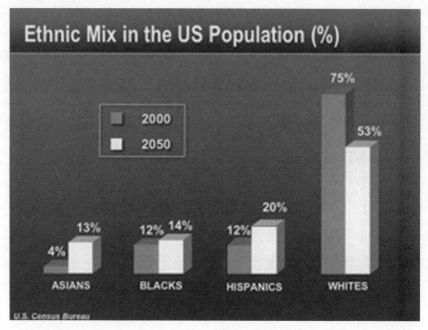

Ethnic Mix in the US Population (%)

- 2000
- 2050

75% / 53% — WHITES
20% / 12% — HISPANICS
12% 14% — BLACKS
4% 13% — ASIANS

U.S. Census Bureau

Actually, these numerical changes are expected to take place even *before* 2050. We need to think about what kinds of issues this raises about people from other cultures working side by side with us. And how these migratory waves do and will affect successful communication at work and in our communities.

BECOMING AMERICANIZED

Since we werealways the "land of opportunity," our country, from its earliest days, has been a landing place for immigrants. The goal of incoming immigrants at each juncture in our history, especially the ones at the beginning of the twentieth century, was to lose their "foreignness" as soon possible. To fit in, to integrate, and to become "American."

But the great immigration influx that began after the immigration laws were changed in the 1960s has brought major differences in how new immigrants *now* relate to our country.

Unlike their early-twentieth-century predecessors, many feel no driving need to become "Americanized" at once. Immigrants seem to hold on to their own national identity longer, resisting total absorption into our culture. It takes about two generations for full assimilation now, even when the parent generation is naturalized.

And so the old immigrant goal of leaving the old culture behind and speaking only English is no longer the case. People don't seem to *want* to erase their differences.

The communication issues this raises go far beyond just adjusting to and understanding a new language. Immigrants also need to learn and understand a new way of life and adapt to new work standards, technologies, and new styles of communicating. And our assuming that these adjustments have been made is incorrect.

WHAT IMMIGRANTS BRING: ISSUES AND OBSTACLES

Think about the experiences and conditioning people from other lands and cultures have had; what they learned about life and how to live it. This affects not only what belief systems they bring to the United States. It affects their families, that are born here, because the old world attitudes, stories, strictures, and concerns also influence them.

To bring it home to you, imagine the attitudes immigrants bring with them about these key issues of our way of life.

- Work: what's expected: how do you move up the ladder?
- Technology: its challenges and differing experiences
- Money, power, influence: how to get them
- Education: How important it is, who could get it, what it took to get it
- Success: what that means, who can achieve it, and how

- Social and class structure
- Religious beliefs and the role those played in their lives
- Government; its systems, its regulations, and the law
- Acceptable behavior for groups and individuals
- Independence and human rights
- Individuality and the right to exercise it

We assume that Western Europe's cultures are more like our own, but now picture how those issues are handled and how people experienced them in the following countries of origin. What access did they have, what conditioning did they get; what did they learn to respect and/or fear in these countries?

- The Pacific Rim: China, Japan, Korea, Malaysia, Indonesia
- Former Soviet Union and the Iron Curtain satellite countries
- The Middle East
- Mexico, Central and South America, and their many cultures
- Various Caribbean islands
- India, Pakistan, and Bangladesh
- Africa and its widely different countries and cultures

Here's an example of how deeply rooted are the belief systems immigrants bring and how strange ours are to them.

In Los Angeles, a number of Latino Americans who recently became U.S. citizens responded to being summoned for jury duty in a curious way.

They asked if they could pay a fine and *not* serve on a jury. When asked why, they said: "If the United States government has accused someone of doing something wrong, who are we to say they are innocent and that the *U.S. government* is wrong? They have our names. We could be deported!" The idea of talking back to—even finding fault with—the reigning government was incomprehensible!

In some countries this kind of freedom is not only unknown but talking back to the people in power is very dangerous and everyone knows that. Who dares to say the government is wrong? What reprisals can there be? Who wants his or her name connected with such an act?

Expand this story to include all those way-of-life subjects listed above, the various areas of our lives we take so much for granted. See how many assumptions we live with daily that are very different from the experiences immigrants from other countries have?

HANDLING ALL THIS AT WORK

What new skills and responses do we need at work? I don't mean to sound like a preacher, but let me offer these ideas for facilitating contact and filling gaps between us, the "entrenched natives" and the new arrivals to our workplace.

The overall concept is to reach out and make yourself available, to offer your knowledge and experience, trying to be "someone to go to."

Just start considering how the experiences and expectations of people from other cultures and even regions within America differ from yours.

It helps to get curious. Finding out how long ago your immigrant colleagues arrived can tune you into what to expect of them and how to reach out to help them enter the fold at your workplace. Here are some ideas: Ask about:

- Contrasts and changes between their old life and ours.
- How they used to do the job they're doing now: did they ever do it before?
- What did they like and not like about their old jobs?
- What else they need and how you can help them.

As I write this, I hear your voices saying "What? Isn't that rude? How would people feel about my asking them personal questions like that?"

It all depends on your intention. Are you *really* curious? Check out your own preconceived notions. That's what will come through as you pose your questions. If you generally respect that their lives were as legitimate and all-encompassing as yours and you'd really *like* to find out more about what people's lives are like in other parts of the world, then your questions will be welcomed.

It's flattering for people to be asked about themselves. And of course, you'll instantly pick up signals if they don't want to talk. But always preface your questions with why you're asking. What purpose will their answers serve? How will it help you to help them solve a problem or get more comfortable in their job.

Then think of the many ways you can bridge the gaps you hear by finding out:

- What background or context could you offer before you ask someone to do something?
- What orientation should you provide in implementing a new system?
- How can you encourage speaking up and asking questions?
- How will you stimulate individuality and creative thinking and create a safe environment in which to do that?
- How will you explain the why of critiques, of fixing and changing things?

People respond eagerly when they feel an open door, a respectful attitude toward differences, and a genuine interest in bridging gaps and helping. And there's so much to learn from them, too!

Here's one more idea:

TRANSCENDING LANGUAGE BARRIERS

Even if the person you're speaking to has learned to speak English, we need to recognize that we're all still not necessarily speaking the same language. We must become more aware of our unconscious use of historical and pop-culture reference points and colloquial expressions that have no meaning to new Americans—that English and our style of speaking and formulating ideas isn't native and natural to new Americans. Nor are our mores, standards, and ways of life.

Talking to people for whom English is a second language, sometimes a *distant* second, there is an important way to help make things clear and memorable. It's to make your message visual.

Spoken language needs instantaneous understanding since the words go right by. Visuals stand still. They don't talk fast, like native-born Americans do. Therefore, making messages visual is extremely helpful for people from other cultures. They can understand and remember by having your messages reinforced *while you're talking,* but at their own pace. This is even more true for doing global business.

Does all of this adjusting sound like lots of communication obstacles? Does any of it make you feel anxious about the "right way" to handle people from other cultures?

Please look at it this way: the problems evaporate as *problems* when you become conscious of them and examine their components. *Awareness* is step one in helping you figure out how to deal with them.

My plan, as the coming chapters unfold, is to show you many new techniques you can use to make people of any generation, background, or ethnicity feel more comfortable—to anticipate people's needs, encourage dialogue, and make what you want to say clear and easy to understand.

So we come to the end of Chapter 2.

Now let's move on to Chapter 3 and find out the basic truths about *what makes anyone listen to anything, ever.* Do people ever really listen? Can they? Will they? What does it depend on? And what can you do to make that happen?

3

HOW TO GET ANYONE TO LISTEN TO ANYTHING

GETTING ATTENTION IS HARD

Chapters 1 and 2 gave you the new challenges you face in trying to get people to listen to anything you wish to get across.

But it's always been a struggle to get people to listen, pay attention, and stay tuned while you deliver your message. This chapter is all about the basics of what can motivate *anyone* to listen to you.

Why is making people listen such a struggle? Just consider what listening requires.

The Me-First Factor

Listening requires giving up our favorite human pastime—involvement in *ourselves* and our own self-interest. It's our primary, entirely human focus. And it's where our motivation to do anything comes from. With this as a base, can you see what a problem is created when we're asked to listen to someone else?

So, here's a cardinal rule:

To make anyone listen while you try to get your message across, you must always answer the listener's instinctive question: "Why should I listen to you? What's in it for me if I let you in?"

To reach anyone with your message you have to start with them. You have to motivate listeners; to make them *want* to hear you talk. Especially now, when our visual world of instant information is instantly available to all, it's harder than ever to make people sit still and just listen!

WHAT MAKES PEOPLE LISTEN

These are the three basic motivating factors that stimulate anyone to listen to any speaker.

- What's in it for me?
- Who's telling?
- How do you tell it?

To help you absorb just how powerful these three motivating factors are, let's just look at you for a moment: what basically motivates *you* to do anything?

WHAT'S IN IT FOR ME?

What's your prime motivator? How do you decide whom to call back, what to do over the weekend, or whom to have lunch with?

You decide based on what best serves your needs. "Do *I* want to do that? What could *I* get out of it? Is it good for me? Helpful to me? Important or pleasurable to me, me, *me?*"

Just test yourself.

- <u>The newspaper:</u> What do you read first and why? What gets you past the headlines or makes you turn to the follow-up page? Isn't it "*I* want to or need to know that"? or "Hey, that could help *me* at work, to look good, to be healthy, etc."

- <u>The weekend:</u> How do you choose what to do? Even when you go somewhere you'd rather not go just to keep the peace, your voluntary activities always come from your deciding what's the best move for *you*.

- <u>At work:</u> Whom do you call back and how quickly? Whose email do you read? What assignments do you finish first? It's all about self-interest here, too.

The me-first instinct is so basic to our human nature. From prehistoric times to the present, our main motivating factor is still "What's best for me?"

So here's your first step in becoming a compelling speaker:

In order to make people listen to your self-interest, you must first tap into _their_ self-interest.

How to Find Anyone Else's Self-Interest

It's all about focus. Whenever you start to talk, you first need to focus on your potential audience, whether it's one-on-one or a large group—and answer their basic question: "What's in it for me if I listen to this?"

"Uh-oh," I hear you saying. "Where's the crystal ball? How do I find out _what's_ in somebody else's self-interest?"

It's not nearly as hard as you think. To understand your audience's goals, needs, and expectations, recognize first how much we all have in common.

What You Know Already

Sure, our daily lives may be different, but when it comes to work—no matter what your position is—you'd be amazed to learn how many similar goals we share. Just check this out.

No matter what level you're at and what it takes you to feel that way, who doesn't want to:

- Feel secure in oneself?
- Feel competent, effective, and on the move at work?
- Learn some new skills to make work a little easier and more efficient?
- Understand something about what it takes to get along with others?

See how much more compelling any of your speeches or requests would be if you started by hooking into one of these commonly held goals or made us see how your message could help us accomplish any of them?

Knowing Your Audience at Work

Just look at the many ways anyone's self-interest at work is already apparent to you. Look at the common denominators you share here.

- You have a common workplace culture.
- You know the mechanics and the problems of how to get things done.
- You interact with the same cast of characters and know their habits.
- You're aware of the latest issues the business or your department faces.

See how much information you can tap into already to motivate your workplace audience to listen?

So you don't need a crystal ball. You already know a lot. What you need is to start with the self-interest principle: the first reason anyone listens.

Let your audience know, right up front, that what you have to say does indeed fit their needs, their concerns, their desire for information, guidance, or getting what they want. That's where the motivation for listening starts. That's what makes an audience want to hear your message.

A word of caution: Telling them "This will be good for you" or "You should do this" *never* works. Has it ever worked for you? Diet? Exercise? Studying? Making the tough phone call?

Now, on to the second motivation for listening.

WHO'S TELLING?

When you begin to listen, you cede power to someone else. Although it's temporary, and you keep an active, internal debate going with the speaker, basically, you, as listener, are no longer in control. You're letting something be done to you.

Paying attention to just anyone is not something you do willingly. Attention is a hard-won prize and not given freely.

So if you are the speaker, your audience needs to know who you are. You have to relate to them as a human being, not just as a message giver. People want to listen to someone they like, trust, respect, admire, feel good about, and recognize as a fellow human being.

Here's some of what we instinctively look for and how we respond to any speaker.

Trust

From our earliest days, we've always been wary of strangers, instinctively looking for their intentions before letting them in.

Just think about a salute. An open right hand over the eye—angled in the United States, flat-palmed in the UK and elsewhere. Ever think about that gesture, why we use it and what it could have meant?

It comes from medieval times when men in armor lifted the visor of their helmet with an empty right hand to identify themselves as friend, not foe. To show their face and that they had no weapon in their right—the generally predominant—power hand. And we still do it! Don't we generally shake hands (right hands) and make eye contact when we meet a stranger? We still look for "Who's this and what do I see so far?"

So, whether it's showing our face, knowing the password, speaking the lingo, or wearing the right clothes, first impressions are *always* about trust: "How do I feel about you? Should I trust you, at least enough for me to sit still and listen to you?"

But there's more.

Admiration

You're in an audience. Ever notice how the person introducing the speaker always goes on and on about the upcoming speaker's background—the business title, the degrees and awards, the job experience, the books written? Why? To bring up expectations: "Something of substance will surely be coming, so please stay tuned. This'll be good."

And the speaker had better show you very early on that he or she not only knows what you care about (back to self-interest), but is knowledgeable enough about the subject to make it worth your while to stay tuned. And this need to believe, admire, or at least assume someone's knowledge about a subject is true whether it's someone making a speech, coming into an office to sell something, or just speaking up at a meeting.

But that's just the first part of getting your audience to listen. The real test, the one that pushes anyone into becoming a willing listener, is much more subjective.

Likeability, Openness, and Outreach

We instinctively need to *relate* to any speaker. We always look for some kind of identifiable kindred spirit, for the human qualities in any speaker. That's the much more powerful trigger for making people listen. Most of us don't think first; we feel. We like, trust, believe, or follow someone because our sensory antennae, our instincts, tell us we should.

Unconsciously, we question:

- "Who are you when you leave here and go home?"
- For the powerful: "Are you the kind of person that knows anything about life as I know it—who cares at all about my issues or has ever experienced them? Ever get yelled at by Mom or Dad? Lose at anything, fail, or get scared?"
- For peers: "How tough are you really? Are you unsure of yourself or open to another's ideas? What else interests you?"

The search here is for identifiable human characteristics, for finding some comfort level on the recognizably human —not just the intellectual—scale.

But this can sometimes be tough to convey.

There's a built-in problem whenever you're speaking, especially in a formal presentation setting. You automatically present a slightly forbidding visual image to an audience:

- You're up there, on the platform or in front of us.
- Your audience is sitting below or before you.
- You're active; we're passive.
- You're the sole authority figure; we're anonymous, a group.
- You have the mike and everyone can hear you; we're silent.

These signals are isolating, no matter how much you intend to reach out and come across to your audience.

But what if you, as speaker, present yourself with remoteness, formality, superiority, and power, holding back personal glimpses of yourself? What response does *that* create in a group of people who are asked to give their time and attention? Whether it's a staff meeting, a one-on-one encounter, or a large audience, have you ever noticed how turned off you get by the teacher style, slightly superior, imbued with bringing the word to us misguided, less knowledgeable folks? Does that encourage anyone to become a listener?

What else do we look for in deciding whether to give a speaker our attention. To feel if we like him or her.

Personal Style

Certain basic, personal qualities immediately capture your attention and make you want to spend more time with certain people. Whether it's in a formal speech setting or at a mix-and-mingle cocktail party, just think for a moment about what qualities you respond to.

Here are two lists describing some typical speaker styles for quick associations. What do you feel as you read the words? What do you imagine and with whom would you rather be involved? Who would you listen to and who would you resist?

List 1

Warm	Honest
Friendly	Exciting
Interesting	Knowledgeable
Organized	Creative
Confident	Inspiring
Open	Authentic
Informal	Funny

List 2

Pompous	Vague
Flat	Complex
Patronizing	Nervous
Formal	Irrelevant
Stuffy	Monotonous
Intense	Closed

Depending on your own personality, preferences and peeves will vary somewhat. But I think we can agree that list 1 is much more appealing than list 2, right?

Now, did you ever wonder *why* you like some styles and not others?

In an effort to help release more of your positive, appealing qualities as a speaker (and also help you unload the negative ones), let's analyze that a little. And, as you're reading, think about *your* basic style and approach and how it might affect others.

What Appeals to Listeners and Why

Letting go of our own reserve and besting our own personal demons is hard. But here's why relaxing and reaching out to express the qualities in list 1 has such a great payoff.

Warm, friendly, open, honest speakers put us at ease. They invite us to feel closer to the speaker, to relax and dare to relate more directly and openly ourselves. They're a welcome alternative to the guarded way most of us behave, and tell us how comfortable and secure someone must be to behave this way.

Exciting, creative, interesting speakers promise pleasure and make us lose ourselves in a feeling of anticipation and curiosity about what comes next.

Knowledgeable, confident speakers are very reassuring. The speaker has obviously done his or her homework. We listen with trust and the assumption that listening will be both beneficial and definitive.

Organized speakers satisfy the brain's need for order and logic. We welcome material delivered in an easily absorbed and recognizable format. We need to see, hear, and picture the structure and order that underlies the message, especially in today's technological world.

Authentic speakers show us that what we see is indeed what we get. A truthful person speaking from the heart is without subterfuge or hidden agendas.

Inspiring speakers appeal to our deeply rooted willingness to follow a leader, to be carried by another's enthusiasm and innovation.

Informal speakers move right into the comfort zone of casual conversation: no orating, lecturing, or heavy-handed instruction. The message becomes digestible, in bite-sized pieces. And so relaxed.

Funny: This does not mean opening with a joke and never showing another drop of humor after that! It's important to know that not everyone can do this. Don't ever *try* to be funny. If you are naturally funny, with a powerful, built-in "appropriateness" filter as your monitor, we really welcome this dimension.

What Doesn't Appeal and Why

The qualities on list 2 have one thing in common: they make us feel uncomfortable. Of course no one sets out to make an audience uncomfortable or turn people off! But speakers who are anxious or hide behind what they think is professionalism can assume a persona or present an image that works against them. You might recognize any of the following as the kind of posture you fall into. Learning what effect it has can help you be more aware and motivate you to consciously change it, since the results are such a turnoff to listeners.

Formal, stuffy styles show us someone operating from a rigid set of rules unrelated to the situation at hand. This speaker doesn't reach out to us but hides behind prescribed behavior, thinking this looks dignified and serious.

Closed, synthetic demeanors are worrisome. Who *is* this person? How can I predict anything about what he or she means, feels, or believes in?

Pompous behavior sets the speaker apart from and above the listener. This creates two problems. First, the listener resents the speaker. Second: who wants to look up to someone before you yourself have designated him or her as worthy?

Monotonous tellers turn our already passive state into one of torpor. Remember the nature of listening? It takes work to keep our attention focused, since we're not doing anything active. Remember, we're now personally in control of getting information all by ourselves, quickly and easily. Why waste a minute with someone who drones on and on and never gets to the point, with a one-level voice, no pace, no nuance, and no emphasis to help us get the message?

Flat, unenergized speakers make us mad! If you move into my life but don't seem to make much effort to *connect* with me or be sure I get your message, why should I allow you in or listen to you? How can you ask for any of my time and attention if you don't give me the most of yourself by showing me a full-fledged, pumped-up desire to help me understand?

Vague, complex explainers create anxiety in the listener. We *hate* to know that we don't understand. A talker who confuses or doesn't help us "get it," clearly and succinctly, betrays the attention we have given him so far and we remove that concentration ASAP.

Irrelevant messages betray the first rule of getting people to listen—their own *self-interest!* Who needs to hear something that matters only to someone else, or maybe not even that?

Patronizing is insulting. If you, the teller, know what we don't know, you should be in the position of working hard to share your knowledge, not berating us for not knowing it yet!

Unsure, nervous speakers make us *really* uncomfortable! Since we've all been there and hated it, we recognize and feel it keenly when we see it in others, and don't want to be a part of it again.

Intense starts us out at too hot a level. The speaker, passionate about his or her subject, is already at a full gallop, while we—the blank-slate audience—can only begin at a walk. Your intensity presumes that we're at the same level of passion and information as you. You need to start us just walking with you. Then, as you develop your material and back it up with hard facts, we'll rise with you, getting as irate or passionate as you are. But start from where we are, not where you are.

Obviously these are clearly only primary-color descriptions, thumbnail sketches of much more complex personal styles each of us develops and presents whenever we communicate. But they help you see how people who are asked to listen, respond. We have visceral, subconscious reactions to what persona and style you present, and extrapolate your intentions and your attitude toward us based on your body language and tone of voice as well as your words.

Consider these responses. They're here to alert you, to encourage you to explore the role you present, and to get to know audiences a little better.

Now I can hear many of you thinking: "Sure, I see what turns people off. But change? Hah, that's easy for *you* to say, Sonya. How do I get out of these habits? I get so uncomfortable, or scared, or defensive, when I talk to a group that that's what comes out!"

I also hear: " Y'know, I do fine one-on-one or just sitting and talking or answering questions. But when I have to stand up and generate the whole thing, uh-uh. I do so want them to take me seriously, so I get really stiff or stage fright takes over and I can't find the next word or even get comfortable, let alone be open and warm and friendly!"

Sound familiar to some of you? I understand completely. Especially about stage fright, which is such a common problem. (You'll find the route to fixing this in Chapter 7).

But for everyone, the goal of this book is to give you tools and understanding so there will be *no difference* between your persona at the kitchen table, having coffee with two buddies, speaking up at a meeting, or telling a large group about your ideas. They should all be the same—you asking for attention and making yourself understood. Learning some basics, like what makes people listen, can give you the comfort to do that.

So, let's summarize this section before we go on to the third way we judge whether to listen or not.

How Do Audiences Decide About You?

The process of deciding who's telling is visceral first, then cerebral. People's decision to listen is filtered first through their feelings. Those supersensitive, subconscious instincts were there long before we started learning cerebrally. They're our first line of defense as we deal with the world.

First comes Stop. Look. Listen. I don't like this.

Then comes I'll think about it.

That's why we process who's telling and how we feel about a person *before* we think or process their message.

So before you get to the heart of your message, and right after you've tapped into the audience's self-interest, you must "lift your visor" to let your audience in so they can see and feel who you are, what you intend to do, and how you relate to them.

If you don't, your audience will do it for you. They're looking for those labels and categories (like the ones spelled out above) to relate to you. They need those recognizable signals they'll absorb through your personal approach to them, to decide who's telling and if they'll let you.

HOW DO YOU TELL IT

The Techniques of Telling

Now that you've engaged their self-interest and related to them as an open and real person, what techniques do you use to deliver your message so that people will listen and stay tuned?

Here's what today's audience needs from you in order to pay attention. You must:

- Be succinct and clear.
- Hit your point first and *then* explain it.
- Stimulate us by providing some juice and excitement along the way.
- Make us feel like fellow participants, not passive listeners.
- Approach subjects in a new and challenging way, not just by talking.
- Grab us right at the beginning, before we zone out on you.
- Pause and recap after each section, in order to be sure we're all still on the same page.
- Establish credibility through objective sources and back-up data.
- Remind us of our own experiences.

Using a myriad of "telling" techniques—some old, some new—is a major key to successful professional communication. Here are some basic concepts to begin the process:

Make It Visual

The first order of business in the new techniques of telling is making what you want to say visual. Here's why.

People now need to absorb messages through our most direct and powerful sense—sight. As a species, we remember 85 to 90 percent of what we see but less than 15 percent of what we hear. That means that if you want me to learn and remember, you must also support your words by *showing* your ideas to me. And that means not only showing me lists and facts and numbers and diagrams (absolutely essential for impact, clarity, and accuracy) but also making concepts and ideas visual too.

You now need to use the power of the visual to help sustain your audience's interest and bring it to new levels of understanding.

And that means not just showing ideas visually. It also means learning to think and talk in visual terms. It means no longer relying on just words or jargon or lingo alone to make others understand you. It means finding ways to *speak visually,* using word pictures, to get your audience to picture what you're saying, to go there with you and get involved. That's how you need to tell it now so that your audience truly understands what you mean by internalizing and actively participating.

Consider how dependent we have become on the visual in our daily lives.

- 77 percent of the American population gets almost all its news from television or the Internet. Mainly pictures, not words.
- Hundreds of newspapers have disappeared from our communities in the last two decades.
- Most homes are now equipped with at least one TV and at least one VCR. Many now have a DVD player as well.
- Computers? Who's talking? It's all visual.
- Generations X and Y get most of their information electronically.
- Video games, not Lincoln Logs, are today's toys.
- Text messaging comes through on cell phones and PDAs—visually.
- Phoning now includes speakers' pictures.
- Shopping? Online with no talking!

The fact is, people today need and expect the visual approach to explain any new idea, to be able to picture something they haven't experienced, and even to just get interested.

Whether it's teaching someone a new system, justifying change by showing the results of a bad move, or convincing people about something that's lacking in their work, visualizing is the most direct, compelling route.

How else to measure and compare yesterday and today? Would you respond as quickly, or be as convinced if I just *told* you that "Yesterday we used to do this and today we don't," rather than demonstrating and comparing numbers and performance?

How Making Ideas Visual Works

Let's have *you* experience it. Let's demonstrate several ways to tell the same idea and see how eloquent, effective, or persuasive each approach is.

Suppose I wanted to comment on the effects that the changes in family structure have had on our society.

First Approach

I could say, "You know, the family structure in our country has undergone vast changes. There was a time when the nuclear family was the basic element of our society. Now there's a rise in the divorce rate, and it's much more common for family units to be dissolved and either re-formed differently or to continue with single parents."
Audience response: Unmoved. They could hear it, maybe feel some concern, but I haven't led them to understand much else. I haven't shown any relevance to them or why I feel this is important. You, as an audience member, would surely not yet feel how pervasive or significant this problem is or what effect it has on you.

Second Approach

I could say, "The nuclear family has changed" and then *show* you some statistics.

U.S. Children's Family Structure

1966 - 88%:   2 Parents

1988 - 60%:   2 Parents

1997- over 50%: 1 Parent

Source: 2000 U.S. Statistical Abstract

Audience response: More involved. This moves the audience to a quantitative "how much" response to the issues. Just looking at the numbers as hard information might engender a visceral response: "Wow. Never realized that. Wonder what personal or economic effects that could have?"

I've at least had *some* impact on my audience and gotten them a little concerned. Showing the facts as objective, documented statistics gives them more impact, makes them more real and trustworthy. It also engages the audience in doing its own work—reading—while I talk about the chart and what else it means. See how much more effective my message becomes?

Third Approach

I could start by saying, "There have been many changes in our society that have affected how we live our lives now, but none are more important than the changes in the nuclear family and the effect it's having on how children grow up," setting them up for what's to follow. Then show them these slides, in succession.

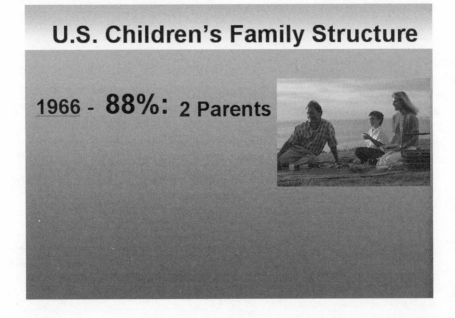

U.S. Children's Family Structure

1966 - **88%:** 2 Parents

1988 - **60%:** 2 Parents

U.S. Children's Family Structure

1966 - **88%:** 2 Parents

1988 - **60%:** 2 Parents

1997- **over 50%:** 1 Parent
for at least
a year

No extra comment from me needed here, right? By the way, it's important to use pacing here, to get the maximum effect:

- Show the first line with the picture.
- Then reveal the second line, keeping the picture showing.
- Then show the last line in three sections: first "1997"; then "over 50 percent"; and only then the picture of a single mother and child plus the rest of the text.

Audience response: Totally involved, cerebrally as well as emotionally. Here I've opened the *visceral, emotional* reaction as well as the *intellectual, cerebral* one. The pictures—not words or numbers—evoke feelings and become the most effective way to tell a complete story about the family, making audiences *feel* the loss and the painful consequences for the single mother (or father) and child. The contrast with the full family pictured above them moves us more than any mere words could do. How?

By causing people to *internalize* the scene and respond to it from their hearts and their own experience, rather than listening to me simply give them words and numbers. And these pictures can be shown without saying a word. They stand on their own, creating credibility and impact. Succinct and punchy, affecting and clear—just what today's audience needs.

So learn to be much more effective, simply by rethinking how you present your information. There will be many more examples of visual techniques for you to use throughout the book. Just get used to the idea that this is now a major focus in learning how to reach today's audience.

Bottom Line: Remember what makes any audience listen:

- What's in it for me?
- Who's telling?
- How do you tell it?

Now let's go back to another basic—a natural form of communication that still underlies how we communicate with each other.

VERBAL AND NONVERBAL COMMUNICATION

HOW THEY WORK; WHAT THEY DO

Picture this scene.

You're walking down a corridor at work and you see your friend Jack coming toward you:

YOU: *(walking up to him, smiling):* "Hi, Jack, haven't seen you in a while. How's everything going?"

JACK: *(backs away a little, avoiding eye contact):* " Fine, fine."

YOU: "What's up? Are you OK?"

JACK: *(dropping his papers, scrambling for them, getting up and quickly looking past you as he shifts his feet from one foot to the other):* "Yeah, sure. I'm fine. Everything's just fine."

YOU: "Gee, you seem a little distracted."

JACK: *(Stepping back, finally looking at you):* "No, no, everything's just—uh . . . great *(looking off)*. Yeah, great . . ."

Do you believe Jack? Would you accept what he says about everything being fine, just fine? What do you think is really going on: Just been fired? Messed up on the job? Trouble at home?

And what makes you think this? What clues do you use to give you the answer?

Go back and read the scene again, but ignore the directions in parentheses.

The words alone don't tell you what you need to know to get at the truth, do they? Actually, the truth emerges only in what Jack *does*, in contrast to what he *says*. And if you turned off the sound and just watched this, you'd get a much clearer message, wouldn't you?

By the way, do you realize that you just learned all of this through mental pictures you created just by reading the words about Jack? This is the kind of visual approach you need to adopt when speaking, too. You need to use words that make ideas visual and allow your audience to experience them totally.

Multimessaging

We all share a primary human need to evaluate, not just accept, what is communicated. We automatically filter incoming messages: "What does this mean?" "Do I trust or believe him?" "Why is she saying this?"

By putting things in context, we look for as much information as we can get. And the most authentic information we get is nonverbal language. Why?

Nonverbal language is unedited, unfiltered, and totally unconscious. We don't even know we're doing it! But it tells you, the observer, how I'm *really* feeling, not just what I'm saying for your benefit.

Let's go back to that scene with Jack. Look at how much you automatically pick up from his nonverbal signals alone and how quickly you can process and understand it.

- *Body language:* Jack shifts his feet. He can't seem to hold his ground. He twitches, nervously drops his papers, scrambles hastily for them. He can't seem to stop moving, seems uncoordinated in a simple task.
- *Eye contact:* Jack can't look at you. Why is he avoiding eye contact? He looks off, thinking. About what? What's he hiding?
- *Space relationship:* You get closer, and he backs away. He's avoiding contact. He wants to distance himself from me and my questions.
- *Speech rhythm:* Jack speaks hastily. He's trying to get this exchange over with. There are long pauses between words. He's distracted, thinking of something else. He sighs as he speaks. Is this an expression of inner feeling: disappointment? sadness?

And the words?

He says, "Fine . . . Sure, I'm fine. . . . No, no, everything's great. . . . Yeah, great."

WORDS VS. BODY LANGUAGE

Words are the basic currency of communication but body language is the other, much more powerful dictionary we use. Each is powerful and eloquent, but nonverbal messages have much more impact on how we process information and relate to the teller.

- **Words are cerebral. Body language is visceral.**
Words are very specific symbols that require us to mentally translate them into meaning. Body language is absorbed instinctively, through the gut, not the head. We *feel*—we don't think—about what it means.

- **Words are self-edited. Body language is unedited and spontaneous.**
From our earliest days, we learn to choose what we say. We filter and edit our words as a self-protective measure, verbalizing only what seems fitting, safe, or not too revealing. Words are *consciously* manipulated, whereas posture, gesture, pausing, sighing, and tone of voice all happen *unconsciously*. They're involuntary and totally uncontrolled and therefore much more revealing. Unlike edited words, body language is a more reliable source for understanding what's really happening, how people really feel, and what any communicated message really means. Remember the scene with Jack?

- **Words are specific. Body language is universal.**
Words mean very specific things to anyone using the same language. But movement, posture, and gesture are universal and can be understood pretty quickly by anyone the world over. Just think of yourself in a foreign country, trying to make yourself understood. Asking where something is becomes you turning your palms and eyebrows up. Wanting to find a place to eat becomes your hands gesturing toward your mouth. And conflict is instantly clear based on what two people are *doing*. People everywhere understand body language because we all share the common human experience and life makes us do some of the same basic things. It's true

that there are cultural nuances, but basic human emotion comes through wherever you are.

- **Words are extravagant. Body language is succinct.**
  Though words can eventually describe and tell, you'd need to use several to get depth of feeling across. But body language evokes "feeling" responses in us very quickly. How quickly did you know a parent was angry with you? Or that you've lost the sale or made a hit (or not) on a first date? Just think of—actually try to do—the gestures that say:

  "It's three o'clock! Oh, I'm late!"

  "It's three o'clock? What, already?"

  "It's three o'clock. Finally!"

  See how little you have to do to make yourself understood without words?

Words and body language *together* create a dialogue. If they *match*, they strengthen and underscore any message. If they *don't match*, they tell us you're saying two different things (like Jack's words and movements). The viewer disregards the words and takes the body language as the real truth.

For example, if you report that "The outlook for this quarter is very positive" while avoiding eye contact, clearing your throat, and shuffling your papers, you've convinced us of only one thing: you're trying to hide that there's trouble ahead.

CHOOSING YOUR WORDS

Since words are a key ingredient in any form of communication, let's focus on words alone and the many ways in which they can help or hinder people understanding you.

Since words are exact, you need to state facts or concepts precisely. Once we know a language, we expect its words to be accurate and clear to us, to make the same immediate image for everyone. We depend on processing words easily. We don't expect to get stuck and, when we do, we're challenged and rather uncomfortable.

Therefore, how you use words to put forth your message can make you a welcome teller, giving us comfort and confidence as we plow through what you're saying, or it can turn us off very quickly when you confuse us and give us words we don't understand.

When We Don't Understand the Words

- **We stop listening.**
  We put on the brakes when we hit an unintelligible word-snag, we lose concentration, and we also lose the momentum built up by the speaker. We start ruminating instead, scanning our storehouse of language, looking for possible meanings:

  "Sounds like . . ."

  "It might mean x (or maybe y) in that context."

  "Wonder how it's spelled. Wish I could see it."

  But while we're doing that, we're not processing any more of your data! Of course that makes us miss something, perhaps even the essence of what you're trying to tell us.

- **We discover our ignorance.**
  The deeper consequence of using a word that is not in the audience's vocabulary is discovering what we don't know and what you *do* know. "This feels over my head. I don't get it. Maybe I *won't* get it." Whenever you use unfamiliar words to inform or persuade, you widen the gap between yourself and your audience.

- **We learn how you feel about us.**
  Subconsciously we also feel that if you persist in using words we don't understand, you don't know or care much about whether we're getting your point or not! You haven't plugged

into our self-interest but are only into yours. This taints your whole message and turns us off to you, the messenger.

Words That Work

- **Use the simplest, clearest words you can.** For example, say "before" and "after" instead of "prior" and "subsequent." Use real talk rather than fancy words and insider expressions. And if you hear yourself using obscure words, explain them at once, with a little laugh about getting too technical or fancy.

- **Less is more.** In these times when messages can be delivered with laser speed, you need to cut down your verbiage to the essence of what you mean. Get to the point right away and then explain, or we'll get bored very quickly.

- **Recognize what your audience already knows** and what else they need to learn before you launch into your sales pitch. Give them background and context first to get them grounded in your subject. Then tailor your language accordingly to keep them with you at all times.

- **Don't simply depend on people asking questions** if they don't understand. This is too embarrassing and exposing for most people in a group. *Do the editing yourself, in advance.*

  Let's now look at one last set of obstacles to getting others to hear you.

HOW PEOPLE FEEL ABOUT LEARNING

Explaining new information or introducing ideas that challenge existing beliefs presents problems for any communicator. Most of us are grounded in the familiar and what has worked for us in the past. Exploring is only for the relative few.

Even questioning existing beliefs feels dangerous to most people, since we won't know what to do if that belief is taken away. Therefore, most people react to new ideas with resistance, not curiosity. You need to anticipate that.

At work, one of your major goals is to make yourself understood and get others to listen to your good ideas or what you want, right? And, most of all, to get others to agree.

In order to achieve this goal, you need to overcome certain basic obstacles to listening and learning. People are inherently conservative at first. They don't like newness and change. Here's why. They may be:

Resistant

Learning feels threatening to many people so they resist it. Folks try climbing the ladder at work only when they feel ready and strong enough. When someone else moves in and says, "It's time for a change. Take this challenge now," this can evoke an opposite response: "Change? I'm doing OK. I know this scenario, but not the new one being presented. Who knows if I *can* change, or what that new scene will look or feel like. Better play it safe. The devil I know is better than the devil I don't know."

Competitive

Have you noticed how competitive people are, especially at work? Competitiveness creates another kind of resistance to new ideas: "It's *your* idea, not mine!" You were smart enough, creative, even brave enough, to think of it—and they weren't. They're afraid that if they accept your idea, you've gotten ahead of them and it puts them in a weakened position.

Intimidated

No matter how high they go and how much they accomplish, many people feel anxious about their own competence. School was not a great confidence builder for many people, and those old feelings still affect them when they're confronted with the challenge of learning something new. When they listen to your presentation, their major concern becomes: "Can I do it, learn it, be good at it, as competent as I am right now?"

So, whenever you, the message giver, the proselytizer, the new-idea person, present something involving change, self-preservation causes them to yank on the reins and say "Whoa!"

Now, what can you do about all these fears and resistance? Here comes the remedy.

HANDLING RESISTANCE AND FEAR OF LEARNING

Folks don't know how to listen to new information since they can't imagine it or relate to it yet. And we also need to feel like we're on solid ground before we venture forth to the unknown. We need reassurance that our past information and experiences, as well as our own abilities, will be valuable and useful in a new situation.

The safest way to discuss new information is to begin with what people *already know*. To handle their anxiety, begin with where people in your audience are now. Then think of walking beside them as you launch your new idea. Start with the known and the familiar. Then add new variations or takeoffs, one at a time, to this solid base. This makes people feel much more secure, more grounded and competent. The next steps— the new ones—seem within their grasp. Establish first what is *now*, making everyone comfortable, before you introduce what *could be*.

SUMMING UP

Well, we've been on a long journey in this chapter.

I wanted to give you the absolute basics of what it takes to make anyone listen to you in any situation.

- Getting people to listen takes motivating your listeners.
- People's basic motivation is self-interest: what's in it for them.

- You must always start by letting people know why they should listen.

- People evaluate and react to you as a teller; this determines how, or if, they will listen.

- You need to be real, human, and informal to your audience. Use today's getting-to-know-you tone. We're used to TV's up-close-and-personal approach, not a formal and starchy style. Humor is good; it bonds audiences to you, but only if you're good at it. . . .

- Your techniques of telling are the third reason people will listen to you.

- Your techniques need to be many, varied, visual, and original.

- People process communication nonverbally and instinctively, not just through words.

- Credibility takes a unified message: words must match body language.

- Always use words that are in common use, succinct and accessible to all.

- Remember how we feel about learning anything new; ground us in what we know before you take off on new paths.

These basic principles set the stage and lay the foundation for what's to come.

Now that you're prepped with all this basic information, it's time to start building.

The next chapters will tell you how to prepare for, design, and discover a host of effective techniques for what you want to say and how to say it.

We'll talk about how to make your messages visual. We'll also discover the secrets of one-on-one encounters, presentations in front of an audience, and making meetings great.

Turn the page to gather some tools for strategizing any encounter. The Pre-Think Chart is waiting.

4

THE PRE-THINK CHART:

STRATEGIZING ONE-ON-ONE ENCOUNTERS

PRE-THINKING

Strategizing a one-on-one encounter has a serious built-in problem. No matter what *you* plan, you've got another person to deal with! How do you give him or her your script to act out so your plans get fulfilled?

Enter the Pre-Think Chart. This is a system for discovering what the goals, emotions, and expectations are on *both* sides so you're clear about what might happen and how you might accomplish your mission.

Pre-Thinking uses three basic questions and a predictable series of steps to help you develop your strategies.

To demonstrate my system and why it can help you get you what you want, let's take a look at a typical business encounter: at how these usually go and what's basically wrong with the improvised, "seat-of-the-pants" method of communicating that most of us use most of the time.

A TYPICAL WORK ENCOUNTER: WHAT CAN GO WRONG AND WHY

Note: Please read the characters as gender-neutral. We all know male *and* female bosses and staff members like the ones I show. I used two men just to avoid the "his or her" pronoun dance throughout the text.

SCENE:
An executive's office. A staff member is being called on the carpet.

CAST:
BILL: *a competent, ambitious, hardworking executive who wants his staff to work like clockwork.*

MIKE: *a staff member who's been getting his reports in late.*

ACTION:
BILL: *(irritated)* "Look, Mike, I've told you twice now that your reports are late. I won't have it happen again!"

MIKE: *(defensive)* "Let me explain why. It's—"

BILL: *(curt)* "No more excuses. You've got to turn this around. Can you do the job or can't you? I need and expect those reports on time. I don't want to hear any more talk. This is business."

MIKE: *(looking down)* "Okay. Sorry. You'll have them."

A fairly common encounter, yes? But read it again.

• Do you think Bill solved the problem?
• Does he now know any more about *why* the reports are late?
• And has this helped Mike change what's been happening?

Uh-uh.

What have we got so far?

- Bill is frustrated and angry.
- Mike will never say, "No, I can't."
- Mike's anxiety level will be raised.
- Mike's reports will probably be late again.

In the scene just described, Bill must now depend on what Mike *says* he'll do. What's really needed? Bill needs to find out *why* the reports are late in order to solve the problem. Relying on the old "I'm the boss and I want it" routine may engender a momentary feeling of power, but it doesn't change the situation.

And Mike? By promising he'll come through, he's *compounded* the felony. And he's doomed to fail since he hasn't been able to explain the underlying cause of his lateness—not enough lead time, not getting input, not being clear about what the boss really wants. Again, both sides are coming at the problem from only their own perspective, without understanding the other side's issues.

What If?

What if Bill and Mike could each recognize that this is a problem for both of them? What if they could predict what each one would probably do? They might choose a much more constructive path.

For example, what if Mike understood that the boss . . .

- Has real needs. Mike's late reports create problems and get the boss in trouble with his superiors.
- Doesn't know why Mike's reports are late or how he can help.
- Feels disrespected because Mike is ignoring the boss's directives.

And what if Bill understood that Mike:

- Wants to keep his job and is very scared about what will happen.
- Knows he's supposed to deliver reports on time and feels bad.
- Would agree to and say anything to get off the hook.
- Can't admit that he doesn't know how to fix the problem or ask the boss for help.

If they each thought through what *else* is at work here before the meeting, they could both act on these other truths.

Bill would realize that Mike is probably scared and also stumped. This could signal the need for creating a nonthreatening environment to help them both get at the problem.

And Mike could get the boss on his side by telling him the truth about where he's stuck. Adding that he feels bad about creating problems for the boss and needs his help would surely win more points than just hanging his head and promising.

To Strategize Any Encounter and Get What You Want

Understanding your colleagues—seeing things from their perspective—is the only thing that can ever produce realistic, effective solutions.

"I win, you lose" can never work. The other person's needs won't allow it! Realistic success is based on "I get some (not all) of mine; you get at least some of yours." A win-win solution satisfies both sides and makes for a lasting outcome.

But this means learning what's true for both of you—getting down to what's really going on and discovering what factors are at play. This makes it possible for each person to respond to both people's needs and feelings.

"Great, Sonya. How in the world do I go about doing this mind-reading act?"

Enter the Pre-Think Chart.

THE PRE-THINK CHART

THE BASIC IDEA

You must think ahead and get to know your audience in an organized, deliberate way before you can communicate anything successfully.

To go into any meeting prepared with the best approach, you always need to start with audience insights.

Pre-Thinking gives you a format for thinking things through. It makes you analyze any situation in an organized, predictable fashion before you say anything. Whether it's a one-on-one encounter, a presentation in front of an audience, or a group meeting, the Pre-Think Chart will give you a handle on what unspoken issues people are bringing to the occasion that can deeply affect the outcome.

What motivates your audience and what stops them cold?
What's important to both of you?
Where do your goals and theirs clash or connect?
How will your goals affect them?

Whatever communications challenge you face—an encounter with friend or foe, client or colleague, cold call, employer or employee—the Pre-Think Chart will:

- Give you a basic framework for collecting your thoughts in a predictable, orderly fashion
- Organize your insights so that you can figure out what and how you should communicate
- Help you understand what to expect and why
- Reveal how the other side's issues compare with your own
- Lead you to productive techniques and answers

Pre-Thinking works whether you're the originator of an encounter or the responder—or even if you're being called on the carpet! Doing the chart before the meeting shows you what the other's motivations might be.

You can learn to predict how things will probably go, thus avoiding certain pitfalls. You can predict what you need to do to create a willing audience for your plan, to answer criticism well, or to sell your product.

Why a Chart?

Making a chart forces you to sit still and purposefully think about motivation issues; it graphically shows them and makes you consider both sides:

- It takes your thoughts to a much more clear-headed level, away from the instinctive, emotional one of operating by reflex alone.

- It forces you to reduce ideas and feelings to simple, succinct statements of fact.

- It causes you to edit and evaluate, classify and prioritize ideas.

- It gives you a framework for your task—a shape and a discipline that relieves the anxiety of how to get started.

THE PROCESS

Get some paper, a pen, and a ruler. Then draw the Pre-Think Chart like this, with three sections:

YOU	THEY

My chart is just a demo made to fit this page, but you need to make your sections bigger since you'll be writing in them when you do your chart.

Notice that you'll be writing for *both* sides—YOU and THEY—your opposite number(s) in this encounter. Ultimately, your chart will have three sections: GOALS, EMOTIONS, EXPECTATIONS.

To show you how this chart works, we're going to draw on our previous example: Mike and his boss, Bill. In this scenario, YOU means Bill; THEY means Mike.

SECTION ONE: GOALS

YOU (BILL)	THEY (MIKE)
GOALS	GOALS

This is the section that lists your bottom-line goals for the encounter. You need to ask yourself, "What do I want to happen at this meeting?"

Here you'll list your practical, objective goals, in order of priority: What key issues do you want to solve that caused you to be in this encounter in the first place?

Let's see what basic goals you, the boss, might want to accomplish to solve the late-reports problem.

YOU (BILL)	THEY (MIKE)
GOALS	
1. I want those reports on time! 2. Be sure Mike gets the message and complies. 3. I don't want to deal with this again!	

See how the boss's goals are all about what *I* want and *I* need? But the chart visually emphasizes that there is *another* side, Mike. Mike must have his *own* goals and motivations, some of them very different from the boss's. And these goals will definitely affect whether the boss can achieve his goals and how the encounter turns out. *That's* the piece that was missing from the original scene.

So let's move to the other half of the chart and fill in Mike's side.

Filling Out the Other Side

Simply project yourself into Mike's position. Based on what you know of human nature and people's needs and goals at work, you can just climb into his shoes and ask yourself, "What would *I* want as I enter that office?" What would *anyone* called on the carpet probably be thinking and hoping for? Wouldn't his (your) goals read something like this?

	THEY (MIKE)
	GOALS
	1. Keep my job! 2. Avoid the boss's wrath. 3. Work out something about the reports.

This is the essence of the Pre-Think Chart: to project yourself into someone else's circumstance and understand what his or her problems, issues, and feelings would be in a given situation. This gives you a handle on how to predict the event, motivate others, handle the situation best, and get what you want.

Can We Understand the Other Side?

Yes, because we're all vulnerable, needy, extremely *human* beings and the basics of life are true for all of us. So we're eminently able to know and understand these elements in others. Let me show you how easily we can, and do, project ourselves into any human situation.

- You notice that someone's sick. Right off, your instinct takes you to empathize and understand, even ask if you can help. But at the least, you definitely notice and are concerned because you've also experienced that and can imagine how it feels.
- Someone's lost a job or a loved one. You know all about how they feel with no added information needed.
- Someone's going to apply for a job. You feel her anxiety and try to bolster her ego or send her off with some extra courage and a smile.

Of course there are differences between us. But the ability to recognize and understand our *similarities* is why we can always fill in the other side of the chart.

And that process can help you change and adapt your communicating style and behavior. Adjusting how you talk and what you say based *first* on what *others* need and want—this is the direct route to personal power and accomplishing what you want.

Where We Get Stuck

The problem is Me First. We're programmed for our own survival, from the beginning. To take care of number one, especially in the workplace. Passing the plate and saying "After you" makes us afraid our turn may never come, that someone will get ahead of us and get more. So most of us move too fast, too often, pushing for the front of the line and thinking only of our own needs. And so we lose our chance to make allies and get help from *others* in getting what we want.

How the Chart Changes Things

Just look at both sides of the chart. As you compare each side's goals horizontally, point by point, can you see that they hardly intersect at all?

YOU (BILL)	THEY (MIKE)
GOALS	GOALS
1. I want those reports on time! 2. Be sure Mike gets the message and complies. 3. I don't want to deal with this again!	1. Keep my job! 2. Avoid the boss's wrath. 3. Work out something about the reports.

The boss's first goal is to get the reports on time—but that's third on Mike's list. Mike's first goal is to keep his job! Often our goals have nothing to do with the other person's, and can even be in opposition, especially in a one-on-one situation.

Filling out Mike's half of the chart as Bill makes plans for the meeting, he'd think, "I never thought about that. Mike's probably pretty scared."

This can then lead Bill to handle the scene very differently than he did before. His thoughts might go as follows:

First: He sees that "being furious and powerful feeds right into Mike's biggest anxieties about losing his job and incurring my wrath. That would shut down Mike's thinking system and turn up the volume on his survival/defense mode. And it gets me nowhere."

Second: Pre-Thinking makes him/her realize that: "Mike, along with being scared, would probably also like to get the reports in on time and get praise rather than disapproval from me."

"Mike could use some outreach here to help us both solve what's been going on. I need to open a dialogue—to talk and question, not just to demand."

The boss's new approach could go something like this:

BILL: "Mike, I can see you've been having problems getting your reports in on time. I'm sure you don't like it any more than I do. Let's sit down and figure out what's wrong and how to fix it."

See how this approach—open and full of belief in Mike's goodwill and desire to do things right—opens the door for Mike to respond honestly? Rather than the earlier door-slamming technique of "I'm the boss and I want the reports now!" This troubleshooting approach makes Mike able to tell the boss:

MIKE: "Thanks so much for understanding. I can see what a problem this creates for you. But I can't get the reports in on time because I don't get the updates from the rest of the staff in time. And frankly, I'm not exactly clear about how much you want me to say and in exactly what format, once I do get them. Can you help me solve these issues?"

Bottom line: Pre-Thinking provides some very different, much more constructive approaches to a stalemate. It bases solutions on tapping into another's self-interest in order to accomplish yours, making it safe for the truth to come out.

SECTION TWO: EMOTIONS

YOU	THEY
GOALS	GOALS
EMOTIONS	EMOTIONS

Emotions: The Other Powerful, *Hidden* Drivers

Section One of the Pre-Think Chart—*objective* GOALS—deals with *objective* factors. EMOTIONS deals with *subjective* issues—much less accessible. It takes time and thought, even a little squirming, to get at our personal feelings, especially at work.

Emotions affect everything we do—at work, at home, with family and friends. Yet we're such a goal-oriented society, so bent on outward manifestations of success and external reassurance, that we don't often consciously look inside ourselves to find out how we really *feel* about things. What our most basic needs are. So we have trouble coming up with these hidden, inner truths.

Everyone Has Needs

Affirmation
  Affection
    Approval
      Acceptance
        Admiration
          Recognition
            Respect

Whether it's at home, at work, or in some other aspect of our lives, we all need and look for emotional gratification. Love is as basic as food: we all need love to survive. These words all represent forms of love.

But here's the rub: most of us experience conditional love as we grow up: "I'll love you *if* . . ." or "I do love you *but* . . ." This kind of love with strings attached lasts for a lifetime and permanently affects how we communicate. It teaches us to edit our behavior in order to win love and approval: "If I say or do X, *then* they will accept me." "If I say or do Y they'll reject me so I better say (or do) Z and hope . . ."

Emotions at Work

You probably recognize these emotions at play in family and personal relationships. But work doesn't readily spring to mind, does it? After all, we're grown-ups. Work isn't about feelings. It's about money, and making a living. About climbing aboard reality and being a player of some sort in the world.

True. Work is tough and hard and tremendously competitive as everyone jockeys for position and—self-focused—tries to find a niche. Success goes to the strong and unflappable. There's not much room in this scene for accessing feelings or hoping others will notice or care about them.

Yet affirmation, acceptance, and affection do happen at work in many forms, and they surely matter. Getting a raise, a promotion, winning kudos for a job well done, even a simple invite to lunch all gratify our primary emotional needs and motivate us to do more and do better. What we say and do springs as much from that hidden subjective place of needs and feelings as from our more objective goals.

Again, this is a generational issue. Boomers haven't seen concern about emotions role-modeled at work, thus finding it harder to address and make important, as Gen X and Gen Y would.

Hiding Our Feelings on the Job

At work, where we have so much ego invested, with the biggest need for return, we're *most* careful and *most* circumspect about our feelings. We're conditioned to behave and talk from outside our emotions.

We fall into what seems to be the accepted, expected way to behave. At work, what we see is mainly fact-filled, product-producing behavior. Feelings like fear, confusion, and insecurity don't surface too often as part of the mix. We therefore assume that suppressing or hiding our feelings means being more grown up and more "professional."

It would seem that letting people know how we feel would makes us too vulnerable. It would make people think we're weak or needy. So we're extremely careful about even *knowing* our basic needs and feelings. And the higher up we go, the more we have to lose, the worse we get at being open, direct, or three-dimensional. But it's costly.

Ignoring or denying our feelings can make us behave in enigmatic, often irrational ways. Not being in touch with *all* of what we want, we can't be direct about asking for it. We resort to subterfuge, indirection, and tangents, going way off base about an issue or solution. You've all seen people become inappropriately angry or hurtful, demanding or defensive, negative or critical in a discussion or meeting.

So not being in touch with how we feel or what else we want makes our colleagues confused and our message enigmatic. People get misdirected and turn us off.

Not a very effective way to communicate or get what you want, is it? And all because we don't get in touch with the second dimension of what motivates anyone to do anything—the *emotional* effect of any encounter.

Winning Strategies Can't Bypass Emotions

Emotions are here to stay. To build communications strategies at work and get what you want, you must accept these basic truths:

- The drive to fulfill emotional needs is central to how people work.
- This drive shapes what else we want from any encounter, beyond the practical goals.
- We're conditioned to make emotions the hidden, unacknowledged agenda.
- We must be totally in touch with *all* of what drives us to handle any issue realistically.

What Else Is at Play

Let's get back to our example of Mike and Bill to find out how this works. What feelings drive them as they enter the upcoming meeting? What are the hidden issues?

These are some of Bill's feelings:

- I delegated a job; it didn't happen. My authority is being challenged, which is actually threatening as well as infuriating.

- I'm afraid of not getting total compliance. Then what would happen?
- I need respect (even a little awe and fear). I want/expect/need to prevail!
- I hate confrontation. I want things to go smoothly.

And this is how Mike feels:

- I feel bad, ashamed, ineffective, guilty about late reports.
- I'm afraid of punishment and how I'll deal with the boss's anger.
- I've lost face, affection, esteem, and the trust of my boss.
- And I still don't know how to fix the problem! What if I tell the boss he hasn't allocated enough time or been clear about the format and exactly what he wants? It'll sound like criticism or an excuse.

Now all this presents quite another dimension to the meeting between Mike and his boss.

See how much more deeply you can now understand why the original scene played out as it did? Imagine Bill questioning his underlying emotions before the meeting and filling out his side of the chart. It might look something like this:

YOU (BILL)	THEY (MIKE)
GOALS	GOALS
EMOTIONS	
1. I feel furious: no respect or compliance. I'm the boss!!! 2. My authority is being challenged. 3. I hate losing in a confrontation.	

If he challenged himself to think about how Mike must be feeling, he could come up with something that looked like this.

YOU (BILL)	THEY (MIKE)
GOALS	GOALS
EMOTIONS	EMOTIONS
	1. I feel bad, ashamed, and inept. 2. I lost the boss's respect and my self-esteem. I need reassurance. 3. I'm afraid to tell the boss the truth. Maybe I can't ever do reports right.

Seeing this, imagine Mike also filling out the boss' section of the chart. How much *he'd* learn as he tried understanding the *boss'* feelings! Let's compare all the information on the Pre-Think Chart so far.

YOU (BILL)	THEY (MIKE)
GOALS	GOALS
1. I want those reports on time! 2. Be sure Mike gets the message and complies. 3. I don't want to deal with this again!	1. Keep my job! 2. Avoid the boss's wrath. 3. Work out something about the reports.
EMOTIONS	EMOTIONS
1. I feel furious: no respect or compliance. I'm the boss!!! 2. My authority is being challenged. 3. I hate losing in a confrontation.	1. I feel bad, ashamed, and inept. 2. I lost the boss's respect and my self-esteem. I need reassurance. 3. I'm afraid to tell the boss the truth. Maybe I can't ever do reports right.

Both Mike and the boss, seeing the encounter through two pairs of eyes, could make many different choices, ahead of time, about how they would communicate with each other.

Seeing this comparison, Mike has a route to "being compliant" for the boss. And the boss, projecting himself into Mike's feelings, suddenly recognizes that he needs to reassure Mike, to help him come clean and to straighten out the problem. Something like this:

> BILL: "I'm sure that not getting the reports done in time has gotten you pretty worried."

Putting a positive spin on it, and bolstering Mike's self-confidence, the boss continues:

> BILL: "I know you're a good guy and would rather get things done right. Something must be stuck. What's going on? Let's solve it together."

Factoring Mike's feelings into the equation, Bill has now put them on the path toward solving the problem.

And Mike, enlightened with how the boss must *feel* about all this, gets Bill's need for respect and affirmation of his power. And how asking for help would satisfy *both* their goals. Disarmed and relieved, Mike can open up about what's going wrong:

> MIKE: "That's true. I really hate bringing the reports in late. I tried solving it on my own, but the truth is, I've hit a wall and am stuck with several problems."

As Mike describes them, the boss can now move on three fronts:

1. Create a realistic timetable for input from others Mike needs to get the reports going.

2. Demonstrate what the format should look like and what he wants covered.

3. Develop a fail-safe system of check-ins along the way to see how the reports are developing. This is good for both since it

sets small deadlines for Mike and a place for the boss to troubleshoot issues as they come up.

Because of the environment the boss has created, Mike can
behave like an adult rather than acting guilty and defensive. The
door has been opened for a joint solution, and both people walk
away feeling satisfied.

Mike has also learned what to do with other problems when
they come up. He now knows that it's safe to tell the truth and
talk things through with the boss, because the boss ended the
meeting with this:

BILL: "Look, stuff happens. What works best is to give me a
heads-up on problems early so we can fix what's wrong and
move on. Much better than just continuing to screw up on a
project. Don't forget. *I'm* as interested in having things run
smoothly as *you* are."

See how the EMOTIONS piece of the Pre-Think Chart helps
you become aware of things like anger and fear and head them
off in any communications encounter? This allows the really constructive work of any meeting to take place.

Generational Differences

Although there are wide variations in response, Gen X and
Gen Y usually have an easier time accessing and expressing their
feelings than Boomers do. It may therefore be harder for Boomers
to recognize or understand feelings, as an important part of how
people work. Many learned to *act* like everything's OK, no matter
what. Acknowledging feelings, let alone learning how to handle
them, was discouraged in their growing up. So filling out the
EMOTIONS part of the chart may be a little harder for them.
And handling feelings in a meeting will, also.

Planning vs. Improvising; The Secret of Success

With two-thirds of the chart filled out so far, can you now see
why spur-of-the-moment communication, based on nothing but

sheer gut-level reactions, doesn't work effectively as a system for successful encounters and outcomes?

Remember my principle:

You must Pre-Think and get to know your audience in an organized, deliberate way before you try to communicate anything successfully.

Knowing the motivation, and predicting the GOALS and EMOTIONS on *both* sides before you enter any communicating session will always give you a great advantage. It eliminates the bumps, let alone the solid walls, that can arise when you sail forth from only your own pier without noticing that someone else's ship crosses your bow, making a problem, if not a crash, inevitable.

Bottom line: Understanding and taking care of your opposite number's goals and emotions, and truly, consciously, understanding your own, puts your planning (and your eventual actions) on a solid plane of awareness and informed choice. The amount of sensitivity and thought you put out to probe your own goals and feelings, and to imagine and understand your opposite number's, is in direct proportion to how quickly you'll get back what you want and need.

OK. On to the last section of the Pre-Think Chart.

SECTION THREE: EXPECTATIONS

This is all about what we *expect* will happen. Past experience has given us a certain ability to foresee and predict. To be able to imagine a future encounter and what could or probably would happen.

But why is it important or valuable to try to predict what will happen?

Analyzing Expectations Prepares and Demystifies

Just walking into an unknown event, especially a very important one, causes us anxiety. So we automatically try imagining how it will be, to feel more self-protected and prepared. On an inner screen, we project images of what it might look like, what we and the others will probably do, and how it might come out. But in this random effort to lessen our anxiety and feel more secure and ready, we only raise our anxiety, since we don't know how to translate any of this imagining into directives we can use for strategizing.

Productive Imagining Works

Learning how to deliberately, consciously predict, rather than just plain worry, has these major benefits:

- It analyzes the expectations of both sides and makes you judge whether your plan is still the best choice of action, given what the other side is geared up for and expects you to do.
- It alerts you to your *own* attitude and how that has colored what you might do. Do you expect failure? Success? Hostility? Conflict? Then this is the attitude you'll walk in with and the tone you can very well generate.
- It compels you to concentrate on what needs to be avoided. If all you do is fall into the pattern of what others expect, your message is old before you begin and more easily dismissable. They've already imagined it, as well as their answer to it.
- The best reason to analyze another's expectations is that it allows you to use the element of *surprise*.

Surprise: The Secret Weapon

One of the best attention-getters is to do the unexpected—to simply behave very differently from what someone anticipated or what the situation usually calls for. Surprise instantly cuts through already existing attitudes—resistance, fear, even hostility.

When you analyze the upcoming meeting, imagining what your opposite number probably expects and is gearing up for, you get a chance to approach the matter from another direction entirely. This gives you four distinct advantages.

- **It gets attention.** Surprise at an unfamiliar or unexpected tack results in total attention to what you're saying.
- **It disarms.** With no previously conditioned response at the ready, they're wide open.

- **It elicits a more honest reaction.** It engenders a much more genuine and unguarded reaction to what you're saying and doing.
- **It energizes the meeting.** Surprise also puts new life and energy into the meeting.

To be effective, your communication style and content should always have elements of surprise in it, to snap people out of their lethargy.

How? By becoming aware of what they expect will happen, and then doing something different—like delivering your message with this opening.

"I know you think I'm going to talk about X, but I'm not! I'm going to talk about Y, our biggest issue. In the process of listening, you'll probably discover, on your own, why X is the best solution."

The best way to build in these surprises is by Pre-Thinking. Discover what's expected, then snap your audience to attention with a new approach.

So, let's do it. Let's go back to Mike and Bill to see how this last section of our chart works.

Imagine that Bill hasn't filled out *any* of Mike's side of the chart yet—that he has only filled in his own side. He has no enlightenment yet from filling out Mike's side and making the comparisons.

YOU (BILL)	THEY (MIKE)
GOALS	
EMOTIONS	
EXPECTATIONS	
1. I'll be firm and irritated. 2. Mike will be defensive. 3. He'll make excuses and promises. 4. I'll give him another chance. 5. I'll get my reports on time.	

As you read Bill's list, look at all the dead-end streets! Bill will be "firm and irritated," while Mike will be "defensive," and "make excuses and promises." Can this possibly result in the final expectation: "I'll get my reports on time"?

And if he's going to "give him another chance," what's the use of the first three items? You—and Bill—can see that the planning and the reasoning are specious.

Furthermore, when the boss fills in the *other* side of the chart and discovers Mike's fears and genuine need for help, he would clearly start rethinking his plans and move in a very different direction.

So what should he do? How about surprising Mike with the following:

> BILL:"You probably came in expecting see smoke coming out of my ears! And I do have to admit I was pretty sore about all this lateness and the problems it was causing me. But there must be some way for us to solve all this, Mike."

This approach would disarm Mike and let them both get to the real business at hand.

See how writing out just your own EXPECTATIONS works? Conscious of what will probably happen, and reminded of what he *really* wants out of this encounter, the boss is motivated to find another path to fulfillment than the one that habit would have dictated.

EXPECTATIONS: THE OTHER SIDE

Now think about Mike. Imagine what you, or Mike, would expect to happen at this meeting.

Bill starts filling out Mike's side:

YOU (BILL)	THEY (MIKE)
GOALS	GOALS
EMOTIONS	EMOTIONS
EXPECTATIONS	EXPECTATIONS
	1. The boss will be mad. 2. He'll demand the reports on time. 3. He won't want any excuses. 4. He wants me to promise to get it right. 5. He might give me an ultimatum, even fire me!

When Bill looks at his own side, what he needs to do becomes very clear.

YOU (BILL)	THEY (MIKE)
EXPECTATIONS	EXPECTATIONS
1. I'll be firm and irritated. 2. Mike will be defensive. 3. He'll make excuses and promises. 4. I'll give him another chance. 5. I'll get my reports on time!	1. The boss will be mad. 2. He'll demand the reports on time. 3. He won't want any excuses. 4. He wants me to promise to get it right. 5. He might give me an ultimatum, even fire me!

Now let's go to the other side of the table—not the person with the power who called the meeting but the person who has to appear at same.

THE OTHER SIDE:
A GUIDE FOR THE SUMMONED

Clearly anyone summoned to a meeting not of their own making is the more nervous of the two parties. *That's* the person who most urgently needs to anchor him- or herself with some insights.

DON'T BE A VICTIM

No matter what the meeting's subject, the secret is to be proactive! You're *not* just a victim, with no choices and no power, even if you're in trouble. You, too, have choices and strategies you can devise to make the meeting come out your way.

If you fill out the whole chart, you can gain insights that will calm you down—"The boss is a person with needs, too! Whaddya think of that!" You can also find the many places where you can surprise the boss and come through as a real and purposeful participant, not just a bystander who's passively taking it.

Now, imagining the boss's GOALS, EMOTIONS, and EXPECTATIONS can be a little strange. It hard for the more dependent person, with less power, to imagine the realities of the boss's position.

But it just takes a little thinking and imagining. When you, as the summoned, or Mike, fill in the whole chart, you become so much more knowledgeable and responsive to the true issues at hand—and so much more able to find options on how to behave.

Here's my basic premise and the secret of effective personal communication.

Take care of the other person's needs first. If you are aware of, and can give the other person something of what he or she is most concerned about first, you'll surely get yours—more easily and with much less resistance.

OTHER THINGS YOU CAN DO

Rethink your whole position. Make the boss an ally in solving the problem!

In Mike's case, the chart shows that it's in *both* of their interests to get the reports in on time. So Mike takes the initiative and starts the conversation himself:

MIKE: "Before you begin, let me just say that I know my reports have been late and I've been really unhappy about that.

"Frankly, I need your help, since I'm sure it has created quite a problem for you. Guess I wanted to do it all myself and couldn't admit I was stymied.

"Here's what's gone wrong: the timing for getting the material I need from the rest of the staff. They try but it's just too short for me to hit the deadline. And one more thing: exactly how much information you want in the reports, and in what format, is still a little unclear to me. So I'm stuck. Can you help me find a solution?"

When Mike takes the bull by the horns *before* the expected bawling out, bingo! He gains points in three different areas:

- Surprises the boss by *not* giving an excuse or a promise (as the boss had expected).

- Shows the boss his good intentions and his true desire to fix the problem. And shows that he has courage!

- Puts himself in the active role, lessening the need for the boss to make critical comments and vent some spleen. It also shows another side of Mike: eager and able to make change.

See how you can move yourself out of the passive role? You simply need to become aware of all the dynamics and components in any given situation. And then choose to *participate,* rather than just standing by passively.

Because Mike knew what was coming, he could take the initiative and also handle his own fears.

Be Honest!

The most important element Mike used was *the truth!* Being open and honest—human—is the *most powerful weapon* you can bring to any confrontation. How can the boss revert to an "I'm the boss!" tactic when Mike has already moved him into a confronting-reality mode. This demands a constructive, well-meaning response from the boss. By saying out loud what both of them were thinking, Mike has brought them both into an authenticity that doesn't happen often in our daily lives.

The truth is guaranteed to startle whenever we hear it and to make us feel relieved. It puts us on solid ground and actually draws us closer.

For Mike, telling the boss the truth makes it safe for the boss to go there, too.

As for the boss? He is moved to respond with something like this:

> **BILL:** "Well, you've done the right thing by focusing on what the trouble is and how to fix it. So let's get right to it, no wasting time, because this has been giving me lots of grief."

Use a Touch of Humor

It's really surprising how rarely we allow that extra dimension—lightness and humor—to enter the workplace and our business dealings.

Work is serious to most everyone. Very serious. But too many people lose their sense of proportion as they concentrate on achieving a goal.

Lightening the atmosphere actually *strengthens your hand.* In any meeting or event, being able to use humor shows that you are in such control, and so much at ease, that you can afford to lighten up a sober moment or important situation. Not only do you give everyone a moment of respite and relief—you must be pretty comfortable with yourself to be able to do that.

Humor has the additional benefit of disarming everyone and cutting the tension. It lets people open their fists and let go of their entrenched positions.

Example: Suppose the boss started the meeting with this:

BILL: "Listen. I'd love to just indulge myself right now, pounding on the table, steam coming out of my ears, and yelling at you to get those reports in on time. But what good would that do? You'd be shaking and quaking and those late reports, which are causing me and the team so much grief, still wouldn't get solved. Right?"

Remember Bill's original goals? "I want those reports on time! Be sure Mike gets the message and complies! I don't want to deal with this again!"

See how quickly the boss has set up an environment in which to accomplish his goals? And to guarantee a willing listener?

Of course the challenge is much greater for Mike to open the meeting with a little humor. He's in trouble and needs to respond with sincerity and concern. That's the big caution about using humor. As powerful as it is, always be sure it's appropriate to the occasion and to your role in it.

SUMMARY FOR THE SUMMONED

You're not a victim! You need to become proactive:

• Face the problem.
• Listen!!!
• Think creatively about solutions.
• Be open to what the other person needs and suggests.
• Tell the truth about what's gone wrong.
• Embrace a constructive, positive outcome.

Most of all, keep your sense of self. Bring the best of you to the meeting. Leave the defensive person with the caved-in posture and the darting eyes at home. This is a time for some squared shoulders, some even, steady gaze and some good intentions.

And lots of insight and understanding that you've gained from doing the Pre-Think Chart!

THE COMPLETED CHART

We've done it! We've completed both sides in each category. And you've seen how looking at the elements makes people change their minds—*and their strategy*—about how to handle themselves and the other person in an expected meeting.

Developing an environment for honesty makes troubleshooting problems and finding solutions easier and more direct. As opposed to the scene on the opening page, which was a lose-lose situation for both parties.

Let's put it all together to get the full picture of how the Pre-Think Chart solved the original problem.

YOU (BILL)	THEY (MIKE)
GOALS	GOALS
1. I want those reports on time! 2. Be sure Mike gets the message and complies. 3. I don't want to deal with this again!	1. Keep my job! 2. Avoid the boss's wrath. 3. Work out something about the reports.
EMOTIONS	EMOTIONS
1. I feel furious: no respect or compliance. I'm the boss!!! 2. My authority is being challenged. 3. I hate losing in a confrontation.	1. I feel bad, ashamed, and inept. 2. I lost the boss's respect and my self-esteem. I need reassurance. 3. I'm afraid to tell the boss the truth. Maybe I can't ever do reports.
EXPECTATIONS	EXPECTATIONS
1. I'll be firm and irritated. 2. Mike will be defensive. 3. He'll make excuses and promises. 4. I'll give him another chance. 5. I'll get my reports on time.	1. The boss will be mad. 2. He'll demand the reports on time. 3. He won't want any excuses. 4. He wants me to promise to get it right. 5. He might give me an ultimatum, or even fire me!

PRE-THINKING RESULTS

Bill is now clear about his own goals, emotions, and expectations. And, most important, by doing Mike's chart and comparing it with his own, he now sees where the dichotomies lie and what needs to be changed so that he can achieve his goals.

Based on this new understanding, Bill changed strategies, creating an environment for Mike to tell the truth. When he heard about the time crunch, Bill was able to change that process. And he became much more explicit with Mike about the exact format and content he wanted. Because of the openness and nonthreatening nature of their exchange, issues were solved and, finally, the reports appeared on time.

Mike, who was focused only on himself as the victim, also started strategizing. He stopped being defensive and began to see the situation from the boss's point of view. Understanding so much more, he was able not only to listen, but also to act. To find openings to make himself heard, to tell the truth, and to help solve the problem. Having mended fences with the boss in the process, he now comes through as a proactive, realistic staff member, anxious and willing to change and deal with issues. And he gets all his needs met, too.

All these changes took place simply because both parties started looking at the issue from both points of view in a methodical and directed way.

Seeing the Other Side Is Very Humanizing

It's funny. Whenever you think about, actually write down and look at someone else's emotions and expectations, that person suddenly becomes much more human to you. Focusing on *them* and what *they* could be thinking about something you're so involved in introduces aspects you never thought about.

You can quickly sense vulnerabilities, anxieties, and other very human foibles that would never occur to you as you think about *your* goals and how *you're* going to conquer the opposition. Seeing *another's* needs—*their* agenda, and where *they're* coming from—opens a totally different, more human dimension. This is another benefit to the Pre-Thinking. It puts you in a very different frame of mind—equalizing power and getting rid of some preconceived attitudes about others.

MAKE YOUR OWN CHART

ANALYZE A PAST OR FUTURE ENCOUNTER OF YOUR OWN

Now try making your own Pre-Think Chart.
For a past encounter, analyze:

- What you and the other person needed
- What attitudes you brought to the meeting
- How you could have started it differently
- How you could have averted certain snags you ran into
- Why it didn't go as well as you wanted
- What did work and why

For an upcoming encounter, think about:

- How to achieve both sets of goals
- How to handle both your emotional needs
- Your opening and how to present your objective
- How to get more information and how to compromise
- Ending on a high note, with clear results

USER TIPS FOR YOUR PRE-THINK CHART

Always fill out your entire side—the "YOU" of your GOALS, EMOTIONS and EXPECTATIONS—before you start filling out the other side. It's relatively easy since you basically know what *you* want, need, and anticipate will happen.

Fill in the other side *only after* you have completed your side—not before. If you go back and forth between the two sides, you're likely to be more constrained, less open, and more inclined to self-edit before the whole truth is out.

Then start comparing the two sides. You will be surprised at how sharp the contrasts are and how clear the road to action becomes. You *will* actually be able to describe what the other party wants, needs, and feels. Just go across the line and focus!

Wait till you see how this all plays out and what you'll discover. So many things you never thought about, either for yourself or the other person. And this will help you develop insight and strategize what you can and will do and what to avoid.

Be open and honest with yourself. Give yourself a chance to discover your *true, unedited, nonjudgmental* reactions. And when you fill out the other side, really work on getting into their heads and feelings about the issue.

Now you can strategize based on solid information. No need to guess and improvise.

Completing Your Chart's Emotions Section

Focus on how you *really* feel about this encounter of yours, or how you felt when you analyzed a past one. Be introspective.

- What was, or is, at stake for you?
- Do you/did you feel threatened? Angry? Unappreciated? Falsely accused?
- What were you/are you afraid of or worried about?
- What do you/did you need from the person or group you're dealing with?

Uncovering and admitting your emotions gives you tremendous insight into finding out how you might (or did) behave as you tried to cover those feelings or deny them. And what else you might do to get those needs met.

Guidelines for Completing the EMOTIONS Section

After finding out how you really feel about the issues and where your worries, fears, and angers are:

- Put yourself in the other's shoes: how do THEY probably feel?
- What's at stake for them? Where are the losses, the conflicts?
- Ask yourself, "How will I reach out and include the other's emotional needs as I reach for my own goals?"
- Discover the productive and sensitive way to make your request or deliver your bad news, keeping *both* sets of emotions in mind.

Look What You Discover About Them

They'll seem much less formidable and enigmatic! Or, you may decide that the idea you're presenting is too difficult or threatening for them, causing them to turn it down.

You can now start thinking about how to modify your goal, or change your attitude and perspective—ways to adapt your ideas to also include what others need and want.

You now see how powerful EMOTIONS are, how nagging and insistent, how pervasive those feelings would be. How they can provide such powerful motivation for agreeing or resisting new ideas or anything that doesn't also fulfill their needs.

Learn from a Previous Encounter

If you've been dealing with an encounter that has already happened, you have the great advantage of hindsight. But don't engage in recriminations, please! No beating up on yourself for things you didn't see or do at the time . . . We all know about 20-20 hindsight.

Instead, use your hindsight to get really wise about what you thought would work and *why* it didn't. And think about what *did* work and why.

What was the opening like? When did the tone change? Can you now see what caused these changes to happen? Setting the tone for a discussion or a presentation is the key to how people will receive it and participate.

- Were you very pressured and insistent?
- Were you too product-oriented to make a personal contact first?
- Did you take the time to stop and ask for reactions to what you were saying before you steamrollered ahead?
- Did you create a dialogue? Were you as interested in the other person's ideas as in your own?
- Why and how did the other person's tone and attitude change?

Examining a past encounter can be a major step toward a greatly improved future encounter that could really pay off for you.

Analyzing a Future Encounter

If you're making a chart for an upcoming encounter, think about how you'll set the tone for your encounter. Who will you be? What role will you play in this event? Will you be:

- The oracle, delivering an incontrovertible position?
- Ready to hear someone else's thoughts?
- Defensive about your position?
- Combative or confrontational? Is that how you feel about the event?
- Excited about sharing a new idea, setting a spirited tone of eagerness and anticipation?
- Easy and relaxed, setting people on that path?
- Empowering, making people feel that their input is important to you and that you're genuinely interested in what they think?

Here's a convenient checklist to help you prepare your Pre-Think Chart.

THE PRE-THINK CHECKLIST

MAKE A CHART

Draw a chart as shown on page 80. Complete your side entirely; then complete the other side.

1. Discover and state your goals.

If you dig, you'll find out *all* you really want to have happen at the meeting. You can use that as an agenda to be sure these issues get dealt with.

2. Be honest about your emotional needs.

Without judging their merit, acknowledge your emotional needs and feelings. Have the courage to discover, recognize, and state them in writing. Recognize the effect they will have on your behavior at the meeting.

3. Discover what you expect will happen at the meeting.

Write down what you really expect will take place. Recognize the course of action those expectations might dictate for you.

4. Analyze the other side's goals.

What outcomes would that person or group probably want from the meeting? See their position clearly. What do they want for themselves and what do they want from you?

5. Uncover the other's needs and feelings.

Using your imagination and perception, write down your opposite number's probable feelings about the upcoming meeting. Use your knowledge of the person or group to add to your insights. Imagine if it's someone you don't know. Compare as you write their emotions opposite your own.

6. Imagine the other's expectations of the meeting.

Use your insights and previous experience to imagine their probable expectations of this encounter.

STRATEGIZE FROM YOUR CHART

1. Study and compare.

Where do the two sides mesh and where do they differ? By how much? What does that tell you about the adjustments you need to make?

2. Adapt your original plan.

Be flexible. Use your new knowledge to create a new strategy that takes everything into account. You now have great information to work from. Stay aware of the major differences between you and them and the obstacles that may exist.

3. Motivate with what you now know.

Find what you can do to show that you will try to satisfy the other person's needs and drives. Motivate them to want to accede to your needs because theirs have been met and your idea is good for them, too. Show how your needs and goals dovetail and serve each other.

4. Use surprise.

Don't do what they expect you to do! Your opening should set the tone with a very different beginning. Try a new approach to get their attention. Use that greatest of all elements of persuasion—the truth!

5. Use humor when you can.

Remember the power of humor: you can quickly clear the air with some lightness. Do it only when it is appropriate so that you don't sound frivolous.

6. Be sure everyone is on board.

When the meeting is over, make sure everyone heard the same thing. Before you leave, reiterate what happened, who agreed to what, and what happens next.

7. Always end on a high note.

End by saying something positive. Find something to say that makes everyone feel the meeting was worthwhile, that something was accomplished and you're glad you all got to know each other. Mention something to look forward to. Make sure everyone leaves with some sense of fulfillment.

OK. Now let's move on to discover some of the finer points of handling yourself and others at one-on-one meetings.

- What techniques make for successful achievement of your goals?
- How do you engage others in getting interested and staying with you?
- What gets agreement?
- How do you handle hostility or boredom?
- What do you say and how do you say it?
- How do you make your part visual and creative?

We're off!

5

CLOSE ENCOUNTERS:
ONE-ON-ONE

The Pre-Think Chart in Chapter 4 gave you tools for *strategizing* your encounter. Now it's time to develop some new personal skills for implementing your strategies.

A typical one-on-one meeting has four segments:

1. **Openers**

2. **Presenting the Substance**

3. **Handling Problems, Issues, and Negative Reactions**

4. **Closure**

Understanding these four phases will help you organize your thinking. It also gives you structure, so you'll know where you are in the meeting, where it's going, where it needs to go, and when it's time to move on. Following this kind of blueprint helps give you structure while you're talking and reacting, even though those inside jitters are in full flower.

Sections 1 and 2 will fill you in on some great ways to make smooth moves and convincing arguments. And Section 4— Closure—has some good tactics for the place most folks slip up on. But Section 3—Handling Problems, Issues, and Negative Reactions—is *particularly* important. That's where we'll handle some typical bumps on the road, giving you specific advice for difficult situations. You'll discover:

- How to handle anger, hostility, boredom, and inattention
- How to criticize effectively—and how to *take* criticism
- How to share the power as a peer or subordinate
- How to handle raises, promotions, and painful meetings

But let's begin at the beginning. The place where you make your first impression and launch the encounter.

OPENERS

At the beginning of this book, I took great pains to make personal contact with you before I launched into my "product"—the text. I found ways for you to get to know me and my style, in a mutual conversation, with no hard sell and no "getting right down to business" as our first contact.

The opening moments in any human encounter really matter!

In Chapter 3: "What Makes People Listen to Anything," you discovered that people want to decide how they *feel about you* before they're willing to listen to your message.

And in one-on-one, it's even *more* important because you're talking directly to only *one person.* The size and force of your presentation has to be scaled down to the intimacy dictated by the size of the room and how close you are physically to the other person.

Here's where that first impression comes in. What are people looking for in the first moments of any meeting? There's mutual curiosity about the *person* as well as the issue at hand, on both sides.

So openers not only introduce you to each other. They also set the tone for the rest of the meeting.

BEFORE THE MEETING

Decide on Your Approach

Of course you'll anticipate your "audience" with your newly acquired Pre-Think Chart skills, right? You'll analyze the other person's goals, needs, and expectations, and use them to organize your approach and your material.

The next step is deciding how to actually handle yourself: your approach, your attitude, and your demeanor. How do you want to come across in this meeting? Do you want to be

• Cool and efficient	• Authoritative
• Open and listening	• Interested and curious
• Warm and friendly	• Skeptical
• Supportive	• Enthusiastic
• Available	• Reasonable

Choose whatever approach best fits the situation and your material. Feel comfortable enough in it so you can maintain that approach throughout. Once you establish yourself in the opening moments, you've got to remain consistent. No Jekyll and Hyde here, since one of your major goals is to establish credibility.

Balance the Power Between You

If You're the Visitor

Coming into a meeting as a "seller" or a petitioner can be intimidating. You may feel less secure, without as much power as the office resident. To communicate well, you need to feel some balance in the power between you.

Of course the boss, client, or customer has the ultimate power—the power to say no. But people communicate best when they feel some power of their own. So you should enter the meeting with an awareness that you will *contribute*. Don't just expect to receive or react to a verdict. You can and do make a difference in the outcome. Develop enough sense of your own power that you'll be heard. Feel you can prevail over at least some of the things discussed at the meeting.

Sensing your own power comes from:

• Being committed to your idea

- Being well-grounded in your material or product
- Proactively energizing the idea
- Explaining why your idea or product is valid and beneficial
- Knowing that you can see the solutions

These concepts give you the boost you need to feel powerful and competent in a meeting.

Most of all, as the less powerful one, always remind yourself that you were fine before this meeting and you will survive, no matter how it turns out. Never walk into a meeting feeling that your entire sense of well-being hangs on the outcome!

If You're a Subordinate

How much power you can hope to exercise in this encounter depends not only on the subject matter and circumstances of the meeting but on the person who's sitting across from you. Some executives need to feel in total control when dealing with their staff. Know your boss. Think through his or her major motivations and work style. You have to acknowledge your *boss'* power before *you* can get some.

As long as you feed the other's primary need, you, too, can share in the power by questioning processes or suggesting additions. Show where and how something can be upgraded and improved. Just don't come on too strong or become inflexible.

If You're the Decision Maker

Realize how much power you can afford to share. You surely know that subordinates worry about your power and so do visitors with something to sell. Calling or allowing a meeting puts you in a powerful position indeed. It takes a little perspective and some inner security to know that because you do have power, you are in a position to share. You're not losing your power—you're just loaning some of it to the other person to make a meeting as fruitful as possible. Consider these moves:

For an outsider who has come to sell you something, create

an open environment in which you can consider the total package. Tune in totally and avoid instant judgment. Participate. Be interested and attentive.

For an insider, like a staff member, create maximum room in your subordinate's mind for listening and contributing, to insure an honest exchange. If you wish to clarify something or find something out, you need to let your subordinate know that he or she has some power, too. For example:

"Susan, we're going to talk about some issues that may be controversial. And having you feel free to talk about them is really important to me. So, for this meeting to be productive and solve what I need to get solved, let's do this. Talk freely about these issues. Interrupt me with questions. Take an opposing stance, if you feel that way. I know this might feel strange, but it's really important, so I'm asking you to help me in this way."

Be sure that you *really mean it*. No reprisals! Otherwise, the first time Susan speaks up and you start getting vague or fight back or don't really listen, she'll know never to do that again!

When Being Asked for a Raise or Promotion

It's always tough to find the proper power stance. Knowing you *do* have all the power—the ability to say yes or no—should make it easier for you to at least create an open environment in which to hear the plea. You can also gain some great insights from listening.

Tune In to the Other's Needs

Whether it's a colleague, a client, or a potential customer, listen so well that you find your openings, based on the *other person's* expressed needs or doubts. Don't push too hard. Be smart enough to cede the turf to your customer or client. Give before you get. There's plenty of room for both of you. Just keep *your* goals firmly in mind and find ways to hook into whatever the other person's goals are.

OK. Let's go to the meeting.

OPENING TECHNIQUES: FIRST MOVES

How You Greet

If You're the Visitor

- *Smile!*

Sometimes, in your anxiety or rapt concentration, you forget to smile. A concentrated, intense face can often look forbidding, nervous, even angry—off-putting. So, no matter what knots you feel inside, relax your face and greet with a smile.

- *The Handshake*

If you're the meeting originator, it is surely a welcoming gesture. In a meeting where you're clearly a junior participant, wait till the senior member offers a hand.

- *"Jack," "Jill," or "Ms. Hill"*

American informality in the workplace generally dictates first names. To decide this issue, consider the general tone of the meeting and the culture of your workplace. What's appropriate? How well do you know this person? What's the meeting about? The relative age and seniority of the players can make a difference in making this choice.

In general, people outside the United States do *not* like our first-name habit. They consider it a little too intrusive and presumptuous. Formal titles are the safest route for them until you hear "Jack" or "Jill, please."

If You're the Host

Consider the first moments of any meeting to be a little like welcoming someone to your home. Sounds corny? Not really. Recognize how comfortable you are in those surroundings and how—even for a few moments—your visitor feels a little like a fish out of water.

Since we all come into any encounter, especially a planned one, with some anxiety and tension, the host can quickly put the visitor at ease. So, unless you mean to be intimidating, make your visitor comfortable with the typical "here's where to put your coat" and "would you like some coffee" thing as step one.

This makes us feel cared for. It helps to interrupt the jitters that most people carry into such a setting and gets the conversation going.

Note to Visitors: By all means say yes to coffee offers! Even if you don't plan to drink much, the chatting that surrounds the process is a great ice breaker.

Small Talk

Hardly "small"! The next few moments are an untapped gold mine—*if* you know what they're for and how to use them.

Small talk:

- Covers the slightly awkward moments of settling down and settling in, whether you know each other or not
- Helps you get accustomed to each other's style, mood, energy level, voice and speech patterns
- Starts the ball rolling, if you know each other; makes the first personal connection, if you don't
- Establishes a relaxed, non-product-oriented, personal contact first
- Becomes a source of personal data collecting—if you really tune in—that you can refer to and use later during the meeting as a link
- Lets the other person begin to know and relate to you

Most of all, small talk makes a much smoother transition into your subject, rather than immediately "getting right down to business."

Visitors

Until your meeting began, your host was involved in something else. Your job, therefore, is to find a way to help her actively step on the brakes and change gears. To focus her attention on this meeting. In order to do that, you need to create a little time in which to help that other person slow down, stop, and restart with you. Here's how.

You're now in someone's personal space. See what you can learn. People's offices are essentially an extremely revealing personal statement. People display their most precious or meaningful objects, to impress and be admired. So tune in and discover:

- Personal passions and hobbies (fishing, photography, collections)
- Family photos, particular books, antiques
- Awards and diplomas (is *that* where she's from!)
- Autographs or other mementos that reveal political leanings and connections
- Controversial subjects (so he's an NRA member!)

So, notice. Then, comment. People love to be asked about or admired for their interests, even the view or the spaciousness of their office.

Small-Talk Sampler

Bonding Possibilities

"I see you're a skier (sailor, fisherman, golfer, etc), too. Where do you usually ski? That's a great place. Have you ever tried . . .)"

Contact! You've opened a conversation vein, discovered something you have in common, and gotten the opportunity to tell the other person something about yourself.

Personal (to Someone You Know)

"Gee, the family's really growing up! (Most people have a family picture around.) "Is that a graduation picture?"

Contact again! You can spend a few moments listening to his

attitude about the passage of time, or something more about the family. Everyone has something to say about that.

Or "You know, we're expecting a child next month. I can sure use some advice from a veteran." Again opening a third dimension before you zero in on your message.

Personal (to Someone You Don't Know)

"This is a great office. What a view! Must be kind of relaxing to look out that window. Helps you get a little different perspective on the world, doesn't it?"

Contact on another level! She is all geared up for a hard-nosed business encounter and here's someone who has a little more dimension than just that!

Informational (and Flattering)

Ask a question; "Isn't that Johnny Damon in that picture with you? Wow, how did that happen?" or "I see you're a Red Sox fan, like me!" Or ask about anything else you see in the room—a Kermit the Frog puppet ("There must be a story about this"), a fire helmet, antique books or maps. All of these will generate small, but oh so useful, warm-up talk. And they'll get your host to talk, too, giving you a chance to get to know his or her style, attitude, and energy level.

Business Small Talk

You can always fall back on discussing some general aspect of business, current issues, breaking news, keeping everything cool and factual, if you're not comfortable with the more personal approaches above. Use your own style and match your choice to something you care about that also reflects you. But do remember the principle of small talk. It works!

A note of caution: Don't take too long! It's just a little appetizer. Always be sensitive to how small talk is being received and when it's time to move on to the next step. Pick up impatience signals.

Host

Making small talk with a visitor depends on your goals for the meeting and how you want it to go. Generally speaking, taking the initiative in establishing some mutual conversation or making some personal contact puts everyone at ease, since there's usually a little tension at the start of any encounter. And it also gives you a chance to take a measure of the person you'll deal with—a great prologue to the work at hand.

Small Talk to Someone You Don't Know

Conversation can range from the weather to what kind of traffic jam was out there, or "I've just been looking at the news about XYZ. Did you hear about it?" all the way to the solicitous "Would you like some coffee?"

What you say should help the visitor to chime in and add to the conversation. Lots of folks need a little help getting started. The welcome you put out can establish the tone of the meeting and help the visitor relax and settle into the business at hand in a shorter time span, with less need to overimpress or oversell.

Small Talk to Someone You Know

Even here, putting that person at ease is important. Any personal contact before jumping into the business of the meeting is important and fruitful. It sets a comfortable tone for the meeting.

Where to Sit

This is kind of a ticklish issue, yet a very important one, since it can affect the balance of power in the room.

Visitor

Don't sit right down! Take a quick look around first. What are the options? Is there more than one area in which to sit? Stand still or walk around for a moment, ostensibly admiring the view, until you can decide where you'd like to sit. Here are some things to think about.

Sitting Directly Across the Desk

This is the weakest position. The office owner has all the marbles on his side. All the items on the desk say: "This is *my* power place—*my* computer, *my* day book, *my* saying-no place. I'm at home here and you're an outsider, a petitioner, asking for something." And that desk is also a big, visible, *physical* barrier between the two of you.

Sitting to the Side of the Desk

Sitting at the corner nearest the host is the second best position. As your host sits behind the desk, this lets you both see each other more equally, with only a corner of the powerful desk image between you. The host must turn toward you. The barrier is greatly diminished. And you can show and tell without awkwardly reaching across a desk or looking at your materials upside down.

Sitting in a Neutral Corner, Like a Round Table

This is best of all. If the office has another seating area—a couch or two chairs and a coffee table or a round worktable and chairs in a corner, *that's* where you'd like to be. Here you start out almost equal, away from the workday reminder of the desk and its entrenched power.

How to Get There

Have a reason for wanting to go anywhere but across the desk: "I have something to show you and it would be easier if we were next to each other rather than across from each other, so could we sit here?" Good reason. Not pushy or controlling. Especially if the host has indicated you should sit across the desk.

Host

Knowing the above, you can select where *you* want the visitor to sit, based on what the meeting is about, what tone you wish to set—aloof, cool, removed, powerful, negative, or the opposite—and what you want the outcome to be.

Body Language

As you now know from Chapter 3, body language is the clearest truth teller. It tunes you in to the attitude of the other person, be it your host or your visitor. Here's what to look for.

How He or She Sits

- Leaning forward in the seat—tension, heightened attention.
- Lounging back—not necessarily relaxed. Sometimes this is an attempt to *look* relaxed. Need other clues to verify this.
- Changing positions—looking for a comfortable place to settle into; too much movement means some discomfort; hard to settle down. *Warning:* if it happens during the meeting, he or she may be getting impatient!

Hands

- Clasped: possibly tense, but notice how tightly they're clasped. Do you see fingers opening and closing? Another sign of tension.
- Open and relaxed: a good indicator that this person is feeling comfortable, in a listening mode, and in control.
- Fiddling with objects: unsure; needs tangible touching to feel comforted and anchored. Also signifies a person with highly charged energy. Better move right along or get them engaged in your subject.
- Clutching chair arms: looking for grounding and support. Can be another sign of tension.

Eye Contact

How and *if* we make eye contact is perhaps the most eloquent source of information about someone's mood and attitude, especially the other person in any close encounter.

- Steady gaze: calm interior, sense of security or inner strength.
- Shifting glances: obviously unable to hold his ground to confront you head on. Much more nervous and concerned about the meeting.
- Looking over your head or looking down: a solo monologue, not taking the other person into account. This can mean arrogance and self-centeredness, no concern for the visitor or the subject of the meeting, or a mind that is already made up.

Impatience, Hostility, Boredom

Throughout the encounter, stay tuned for signs of mood changes and drifting attention.

- Faster breathing, accelerated movement, fingers drumming: annoyance, impatience
- A marked change of position, sighing, or a sharp breath intake: annoyance, "Let's get this over with," "I've had enough."
- A major move, like looking up at the ceiling, bringing the hands down on the table: sharp disagreement, even hostility. Stop and find out about this at once! (We'll discuss this in Section 3: "Handling Special Issues.")

PRESENTING THE SUBSTANCE

HOW TO BEGIN

There are three important points you need to cover right at the beginning.

Time

To get attention right away, find out exactly how long your meeting can be. Although you have the appointment, lots of things happen between the plan and the reality. Last-minute things have a way of intruding, so double-check: "I know how things happen. Do you still have half an hour for this meeting?"

Otherwise you may sail forth on your planned 15-minute sales pitch and demonstration, expecting to follow that with some discussion and troubleshooting. About 4 minutes into it the other person tells you that, regretfully, she has to leave in a few minutes. That attention span? Zilch. Good selling and discussion time? Nada.

But if you know your time's cut down, right at the start, you can edit your plan at once: "Well, in that case, let me just give you a short overview." Then schedule another appointment.

Even if there is no immediate problem, the other person's telling you how much time he *expects* the meeting to take allows you to immediately parcel out the time so you can cover everything and still leave time for discussion.

Your Goals

Busy people want to know where you're both going; what the subject is and what they should focus on. Cut to the chase. But remember to always make your goal clearly relevant to the other person's self-interest.

Your Agenda

Describe your agenda in simple, clear bullets, letting your listener know the parameters of the discussion and what your focus is. Only give the highlights, not a detailed exposition.

MOTIVATE YOUR LISTENER!

Make them *want* to listen to you because you speak to their self-interests!

When you present an idea, product, or issue, you need to know what the other person's primary concern is. Is it:

- Saving money?
- Becoming more profitable?
- Greater efficiency?
- Improving quality?
- Public relations?
- Product recognition?
- Gaining new influence in the workforce or marketplace?
- Developing a new product or system?
- Career development?
- Company growth?
- Innovation?

All of these create a core motivation to at least *listen* to your presentation, let alone find *agreement*. Naming any of these is the opening wedge to get your listener's attention.

ASK BEFORE YOU TELL

Asking what the other person needs, wants, objects to, or has a problem with *before* you volunteer all your solutions or your product leads you in exactly the right direction for your pitch. You become a nonthreatening, positive collaborator.

To get someone involved right at the start, and insure you're on the right wavelength, *don't* start with the big sell! Take a breath. You'll get your chance. A flat-out one-way pitch automatically raises sales resistance and does nothing to make your pitch unique.

Instead, grab your listener by first asking a few questions:

- Present a basic idea and then, stop. Ask, "How does that sound to you?" or "Is this something you've considered?"
- Ask, "What has been *your* experience with Y?" or "What do you see as the biggest problem you have with X?" As you listen to the answer, you will get directly to the heart of this person's business need, something you think you can solve.

This approach is so much more effective than the usual sales pitch. And the answers to your questions can lead you directly to what could motivate the customer. You'll know at once where to alter and adapt your approach.

Develop a Dialogue

Raise an issue: "Have you noticed the news about this trend, or some changes in the marketplace?" Quote a few statistics and ideas you've read and then ask, "Is this what you're seeing in your business?"

Listen, then hook your idea or product into the discussion, showing that what you want to present represents the latest thinking in the market. This establishes your expertise in the field generally, as well as your knowledge of the specific subject.

Now, you're totally connected to and more knowledgeable about this specific person you're talking to. *Now* you're ready to start telling and explaining.

Telling and Explaining

This is such a vast subject that I have devoted the next three chapters to explaining how to visualize, organize, and present your message. So we'll just touch on the basics now.

Here are some specific ideas about how to make your explanation or statement clear and compelling. Then we'll find some effective ways to improvise responses to whatever comes up.

Be Clear and Organized

You can't just talk on and on.

We, your listeners, need a highly structured, visual way to see where you are and where you're going, as you present verbally. Having given us your agenda first, we now need you to remind us, section by section, where we are. And we need some discussion after each one.

Just talking in paragraphs doesn't work. Outline form does. Headings and bullets. People really can't stay tuned if you don't present your material in a logical, orderly fashion.

Begin with an Overview

What is your product or idea, and what can it do? We all need orientation to the basic concept *before* we can understand the next step and tune in to the details.

Think chronologically to decide what your listener needs to hear first, second, and third. What should follow what? What do we need to know, understand and agree with *first,* before you go on to the next section?

Present Facts in Bullet Form

Organize your data into one-liners, lists, and numbered items. These short forms make people really hear you and pay attention. They help people visualize and remember your facts and explanations.

Make Your Ideas Visual

Adding the visual not only grabs attention but adds clarity. We have a hard time picturing something we haven't seen before. Also, we need to see the *before* (the present status) in clear, objective terms, in order to evaluate the *after* (your proposal for change) and its benefits.

You'll get lots more ideas about this in Chapter 6, but here are some specific suggestions for the small one-on-one meeting.

Improvise Visual Images

Not only should you bring visual demonstrations and pictorial support. You can also improvise on the spot by creating a little action!

Example: If you want to explain your new system for routing a product, don't just talk!

- Draw a diagram on a yellow pad. This is easy to do, but it's also flat and two-dimensional. Better still:
- Use a few tangible objects on the desk: cups, paper-

weights, paper clips, pens. Ask permission to move them, first! Have each piece represent an aspect of your plan. Move them around to show the before and after.

This has the advantage of being three-dimensional and dynamic—and much more creative. Your listener can also move them to show his or her preference or question. You can then come back with still another possibility and keep adapting.

This system is not only explicit; it gets you more animated and interesting. Most of all, it invites the other person's participation—a guarantee for getting attention and involvement in your subject. All in all, it's a more original way to tell your story and gain comprehension.

Show Examples

You can also provide:

- Pictures of finished products or systems operating
- Demos of the product
- A comparative demo or visual showing their system before and after using your product

Concrete examples are key to helping anyone understand something they haven't seen or used yet.

Establish Credibility

A major problem with presenting something you are selling is suspicion and sales resistance. Of course they expect *you* to say it's great. But what if you could give objective proof from an uninvolved party?

"I don't expect you to just take my word for it. Look what . . . says about this new trend in the *Wall Street Journal*. Or "In a speech before the Harvard Business School, the CEO of XYZ said this and kind of shocked everybody," or "Here's a new survey CNBC just reported about this very idea."

Bring proof from some credible source; *that* will impress far beyond what you say. Show and talk about other places where you've made this work and quotes from satisfied customers.

Bring Take-Aways

To avoid too much talk and too many details, create a good-looking take-away packet that covers your résumé and track record. Include letters of commendation and press clippings, as well as specific details like start-up and ongoing costs, support systems, and more pictures of your product. People like to think and discuss later and need something tangible to do that with. (Take-aways are discussed in more detail in Chapter 6.)

DIALOGUE, NOT MONOLOGUE = SUCCESS

Audience participation is essential in today's proactive, get-your-own-information society. Monologues, particularly in the close quarters of a one-on-one meeting, are truly unrealistic. Also, if you're trying to communicate anything, you need to know if the message is getting through. Feedback is essential to know if you've hit a roadblock, and what *else* you should be bringing up now.

Create a Dialogue

When you introduce your idea, say right away, "What I'd like to do is tell you my major concept and then hear what *you* think."

Dialogue and the exchange of ideas doesn't just happen. You have to make it happen—especially since most people still expect to wait until they're asked to speak.

If you're selling or introducing a new idea without testing how it's going as you go along, you may not achieve your goal because you zigged when you should have zagged and never knew it. To avoid this pitfall, you need *audience involvement* and *mutual participation*.

And pace yourself. Notice when you've been talking too long. Stop and ask, and *really* pay attention to the answer.

Listen!

You know, we all have a funny habit. Although we *intend* to listen, we hate silence—"dead air," as it's called on television. So we start by listening, but as soon as we get the gist of what we *think* the other person means and where he's going, we start formulating an answer *while he's still talking*! And we miss half of what's being said and the opportunity to digest it and think it through before we zip back with our ready answer.

In our zeal to be right there with a smooth, articulate answer, we end up not answering on point. We also miss great little clues that could help reinforce our ideas.

So to encourage you to *wait till the end*, let me suggest you try these:

- Make eye contact and lean forward when someone speaks.
- Check to be sure you understand what was just said.
- Repeat the end of his answer or pick out key words within the statement to use as your opening words.
- Saying "what you just said" makes your answer so very relevant. It's also flattering to the other person—proof that you're listening very hard.
- Say, "I hear what you're saying. Interesting. Let me take a moment to think about that and answer you exactly."

Notice *how* they hear you. Are they also paying attention? What do they seem to disagree with or are nonplussed by? Get on that at once.

Really Consider the Other's Ideas

Be open! Give credibility to *each* idea. We have a tendency to close down just because it's not our idea. And since you've been thinking about your subject for a long time, some questions sound so elementary. "Hasn't he been listening?" "Is *that* all she cares about?"

So, suspend judgment. Your real goal here is to deal with exactly those things that others bring up. They help you to keep your listener, and your ideas, on track. And if he or she isn't getting it, maybe you're not explaining it too well. Here's your warning signal. Noticing gives you another shot at it.

Notice and Comment on Questions

"I see that this issue is very important to you. Thanks for telling me. Let's just focus on that." Become very conscious of the underlying theme and direction of the other person's questions. Not only should you comment to keep the discussion flowing, but by doing so you encourage more straightforward responses. You also find out the hidden agendas of the other person, which will be useful later.

Keep the Dialogue Going

As you present each section of your plan, stop and ask for a reaction. Troubleshoot the problems after each item presented rather than waiting for a Q & A period at the end. There's no point going on if you've already hit a snag. Solving as you go along can only happen if you keep the dialogue going. *Never* walk into a meeting expecting to hold forth till you're done. Unless you make the discussion *participatory*, you'll lose your audience.

Know When to Finish

Keep alert about when you've said enough. You presented; you showed; you discussed, you did some clarifying and troubleshooting. Time to move on.

HANDLING PROBLEMS, ISSUES, AND NEGATIVE REACTIONS

Problems such as negativity, hostility, criticism, boredom, inattention, and sales resistance can and do develop, no matter how good a communicator you are. But one-on-one meetings aren't only about selling. Here are some issues that the person who called the meeting can encounter.

HOW TO CRITICIZE

A tough thing to do but sometimes very necessary. Here's something we all tend to forget:

The main purpose of criticism is to *fix* something.

It's meant to be <u>con</u>structive, not <u>de</u>structive,

and

to end with a positive result, not a negative one.

Why is criticizing difficult to do and why don't we like to do it? Major reason: "I hate to hurt someone's feelings," right?

And inevitably feelings and ego *do* get hurt when you tell people know you're displeased with their work. But you *do* have to tell them in order to fix the problem.

What We Do Wrong Most Often

We usually start the criticism with blame: "Look what you *did*! What were you *thinking*?" SPLAT goes the self-confidence and the image we'd like to present to the world.

Blaming and being judgmental fixes nothing. It has exactly the opposite effect. Blame destroys our self-confidence and makes us even less able to fix a mistake.

- Blaming only indulges the berator. It never "teaches a lesson." It just provokes anger.
- We already feel bad, dumb, inept. No need to rub it in. Harping on it only makes us more defensive and resistant.
- Berating paralyzes people: "Why try to fix something? I'm a klutz and I can't do it right!"

Most of all, being judgmental derails constructive problem solving.

Since you've just deflated my ego and exposed me as a goof, where will I get the confidence to move forward? To believe I *could* tackle the problem and do it better?

Creative Criticism

Folks need reassurance that they *can* fix a problem. It does take a little will power and understanding for you to let the steam out of your jets and not dwell just on the accusations, as tempting as that might be.

If you have to criticize someone's work or actions, here are some ways to fix things in a constructive manner and get the results you really want.

Before You Begin

Just put yourself in mind of any of these scenes:

- You're 10 years old. Your father walks in: "Is *that* what you call taking out the trash?"
- You're in school, age 8. Your teacher asks: "Is *this* how you did your homework?"
- A highway patrolman looks you in the eye and says: "Just *how* fast do you think you were going?"
- You're at your first job interview. The personnel director says: "I don't see much in this résumé about why you should get this job."
- Your boss leans across the desk: "What am I supposed to make of this?"

Let yourself experience these feelings for a minute. This will set you up with quite another attitude.

Focus on the Facts, Not the Person

We often get carried away by our self-righteousness, attacking the person, not the problem: "Look at this job! Only a very sloppy person who doesn't pay attention to what's going on would let that go through!"

Instead try something like this: "Well, this job sure went wrong. What happened? How did it get through without anyone catching it?"

This puts the focus on the problem—and how to prevent a recurrence.

Adopt a No-Fault Policy

By stating clearly what went wrong, it's possible to discuss the problem from a practical point of view. Like a detective, go back to where the mistake occurred. This puts you on the road to fixing it—and making sure it doesn't happen again.

Ask Before You Accuse

People become defensive when they're accused of something that's not entirely their fault. Then the session becomes all about justice. There's no listening or fixing involved. So start off with easy, casual, nonaccusatory questions, in order to get at the facts. When you know the *whole* story, you can start fixing the problem and address your comments to the right person about the right issue.

Accentuate the Positive

Before you tell someone what was wrong, spend a little time on what went *right*.

"Harry, that writing job you did was short and to the point. It made sense and was well-written. Now let's look at a few things that could make it even better." Don't start with "This doesn't work. It needs fixing."

If you praise *before* you criticize, folks are much more likely to listen, dropping their guard. They'll hear that at least you're not totally displeased and they're not totally deficient. And this will give them some incentive to fix things.

Be Specific

What's wrong with this approach? "Wendy, that report? On time, yes, but generally dull and unconvincing. Do it over and make it shorter and more interesting."

What does Wendy do with this kind of criticism? What's "interesting"? How should she make it more "convincing"? And how much "shorter"?

To her, everything she wrote seemed important. What, exactly, should she now leave out? By the way, that opening "on time" phrase is truly damning with faint praise.

General, nonspecific criticism is not useful. It doesn't lead anyone to know *how* to fix something; it just makes people feel bad and incompetent. Unless you can explain specifically what's wrong when you criticize, you haven't started fixing anything.

To help someone fix something, know *exactly* what you object to and how you think it should be fixed. Specify what needs improvement: which phrases don't convince, what could be cut, what good alternatives you suggest. This sends Wendy off on her mission with new vigor, clarity, and purpose.

And remember to save face for someone by giving some objective reasons for the disapproval. Like this:

"Wendy, it's good but a little too long to keep people's attention, I'm afraid. Maybe right here you could take out all this background section and cut to the chase much sooner. Include some customer letters. That'll keep their attention and be much more convincing. What do you think?"

Of course this approach requires that you spend a few moments actually marking up and editing the places you don't like before Wendy comes in.

Ask the Other Person for the Solution

Try this: "Look, Jim, since this doesn't work, what do you think we can do to fix it? Got any ideas?"

Although you may think you know just what to do, if you really want to get it fixed, engage the other person in the solution. He or she will work twice as hard to do it, and you may find better answers from the one person who knows the most about the issue.

If You're the One Being Criticized

Ugh! I know how we all hate to be criticized, and found wanting in some way. Me, too. But it happens, especially in the workplace, where the product you turn out is always open to judgment. Here are a few ways to handle criticism and recapture your self-esteem in the process.

Listen First

Don't jump directly to your own defense. That will just set up a competition about who's right, and if it's someone you work for, you will lose. So learn to hold your tongue and listen first. Let the critic get done with the whole spiel. Concentrate on two things:

- What is being said;
- How it's being said.

Find out just how bad the other person thinks this is. This will give you a heads-up about proper reactions.

Don't Get Too Defensive

"Well, there are lots of reasons" or "It's not *that* wrong" is a weak and often hostile position to take. Weak because you're not coming to grips with the boss's problem. Hostile because you're saying he is wrong to be criticizing you.

Recognize that if you're being criticized, *something* has indeed gone wrong. Take it seriously. Your responsibility is now to find out what that is and how to fix it. That makes you get task-oriented instead of defensive.

Get Clear About What You Need to Fix

We react very quickly to negative feedback and often don't hear, while we're agonizing about what's being said. It's important to get clear about *exactly* what went wrong and why your boss is unhappy.

Ask for a Progress Check

To be sure you understand *exactly* what they didn't like about your previous solution and what's needed to fix the problem, ask questions and build in a fail-safe system:

"How about if I do it this way? Would that solve it? Let me go back and do XYZ as you requested. But then I'd like to check back with you and see if the new way is what you mean, OK?"

This shows great willingness to fix things on your part. You also protect yourself by checking back to be sure this is *precisely* what is called for, before you go on and do it wrong again.

"Thanks for Telling Me"

Here's a really cool idea. Rather than leaving with a downcast expression, try this: "Thanks for being so straight with me. Of course it's upsetting. Who wants to be found ineffective? But you've given me a chance to fix what went wrong. I like doing good work and this helped me understand more of what you want, for next time." Ending on a positive note not only shows you are strong and taking it in, it also makes the boss feel better, since no one really likes to criticize.

HANDLING ANGER AND HOSTILITY

The most difficult, and the most intimidating, kind of negative reaction may be hostility and anger.

We all experience anger and hostility, both our own and others', and none of us like it, right? It helps to understand the reason, in order to deal with it better. People get angry at work because they:

- Feel inept, misunderstood or betrayed
- See inefficiency
- Are not being heard or listened to
- Are being self-protective
- Feel resentment, jealousy, fear, or threat.

- Even being very committed to and passionate about a position or idea that no one gets or is turned down.

Here come some constructive solutions.

What We Do Wrong Most Often

The major clue to handling anger and hostility is:

When You See It, Deal with It. Say It's There!

But usually, we don't. . . . We try to ignore anger, hoping it'll go away. Since anger directed at us makes us uncomfortable, our first line of defense is to pretend it isn't there because we're unsure of how to confront or dilute it, let alone get rid of it.

In a business setting, people with more power allow themselves to express anger or hostility much more readily than their subordinates. But are you then just supposed to sit and "take it"? Better to find some way to *deal* with the anger so you're back on a more equal footing and on to a constructive outcome.

Maybe the best way to tell you how to do this is to tell you a personal story.

I was the host of my own daily TV talk show in Boston for many years. Nothing makes you learn faster about human communication and what *doesn't* work. Interviewing, talking with, and handling people on live TV before a million viewers is a major learning experience in human relations!

Here's how I learned about handling anger and hostility. I was slated to interview a famous movie star whom I'd had on the show before. I was very comfortable with him because I'd gotten this man, so identified with tough-guy roles, to be mellow, sing his songs, even recite his own poetry! He was filming a big feature on location near Boston, and we'd promoted this interview very heavily on the air in advance. Although he'd initially agreed to an interview during his lunch break, he kept putting us off until the day before it was to be aired. When we finally got the appointment, my sizable crew and I trekked off, in mid-December, to a cold, bleak forest glade where they were shooting the film.

Our movie hero appeared, and stalled us with a rather sarcastic greeting: "Oh, I see. You want us to stop shooting our silly little film and start shooting your *interview* now!"

Here's where the lesson begins.

What's the truth here? He's furious and being uncooperative. But what did I do? Faced with this amount of hostility from a powerful movie star whose interview I needed, I got scared and chose to make nice! To try to smooth things out. I smiled sweetly and said, "No, no, please. We'll just wait till you're done." I was clearly denying the anger both to myself and to him.

Result? We waited all that freezing December afternoon, overtime clicking away for the crew. Our hero was ready for us— at 5:00 P.M. Of course, 5:00 P.M. in Boston in December means it's *dark!*

Since the original appointment was in the daylight, and our equipment was parked far away at the edge of the woods, my crew now had to go scrambling back to the van to get lights. And here's Mr. Movie Star, furious and complaining loudly about their ineptness as they tripped and fell over roots in the dark. We finally sat down to begin our—uh—talking/sharing/listening experience together. Right!

Again, ignoring the seething messages I was getting, I sallied forth into my interview. Now here's the Big Lesson I learned— one I have never forgotten and that I teach as a major strategy all the time.

Still denying the truth to myself, and to him, I started on what I wanted to be a great interview with—a snarling tiger! The more questions I asked, the testier he got. I continued on my Little Bo-Peep path, pretending all was well, convinced that it was somehow *my* fault. I kept looking for great questions and *he* kept being more openly abusive and ridiculing. All of this was, of course, being captured in living color on tape, to be shown the next morning to an eager audience, as advertised. Finally, my producer gave the "wrap it up" sign and, still smiling sweetly, I said "Thank you" and called it a night.

Then I ran to the van and broke into tears. "What a failure!" I didn't blame Mr. Movie Star, I blamed *myself* for being so inept. "If my questions were better, I could have turned him around!"

And I learned right then and there how unrealistic, harmful, and useless it is *not* to deal with anger as soon as you see it happening.

But don't let me leave you here. Here comes the happy ending and the moral to my story.

Riding back to Boston all I could think of was: "What could I do with this disaster of an interview? What can I show my audience in a few hours?" I decided that here was a great object lesson for everyone, because we all generally try to ignore anger and keep sailing, as I had. So I decided to show it to them, telling them about my terrible failure. And periodically I'd stop the tape to show what I coulda/woulda/shoulda done at each turn, letting everyone learn something from my fiasco.

Like what? I *should* have stopped and said, "Y'know, you seem to be very angry. What's going on?" and then let him respond to that. Not judgmentally. Not accusingly. Just honestly *commenting on what was happening.* Curious about what was making him angry. Putting the ball in *his* court, we could *both* have been on the solid ground of the truth. Then, I could have let him vent about whatever was making him so angry. I could have dealt with what was *really* happening instead of what I thought, and hoped, *should* have been happening.

So, I said all this to my audience as I showed segments of my disaster interview. I talked about how often we all do this with anger. How we don't deal with what's really going on. Either we blame ourselves for not being able to fix it or we act like it wasn't there. Above all, we hope it will just *go away* or get better on its own!

Not yet a happy ending? Wait.

Time marched on. I'd learned my lesson. I handled many hot topics and hot-under-the-collar people using my new technique. I would say what I saw happening right away, with no judgment, only curiosity. Then I was able to defuse and deal with the situation effectively. And it worked!

And then my turn with Mr. Movie Star came around. He was

back in town to promote his new movie, and his people asked to book him on my show.

It was wonderful. I did everything I taught my audience and myself to do, based on my bitter lesson. We started by talking about the last time we'd seen each other. I mentioned how annoyed and reluctant he was to talk. He said, "Well, you guys weren't prepared!" "No," I replied, "that's not what happened. We had to wait because . . ." All said with a smile.

Again he became angry, saying "Aaah, you TV interviewers ask too many personal questions." I said, "Sure, but that's the business, isn't it? You want to be on my show to promote your movie and I want you here so people will listen." And then I said, "Hey, look, we're doing it again, You're getting mad!" And you know what he did? He laughed and said, "Yuh got me!" and off we went to an absolutely splendid interview.

So, the number one message is this:

You can't sweep anger under the rug! It'll trip you up every time and never solve the reason for the anger in the first place, which might actually represent another, far different, problem.

Just remember:

The major clue to handling anger and hostility is:

When You See It, Deal with It. Say It's There!

Techniques for Handling Hostility

It's really hard to fight human nature and stay calm and rational when someone is negative, hostile, or downright insulting. But if you're going to turn it around, you must stay calm and rational.

Take a Breath

I don't expect you to be a saint. You just need to take a beat or two:

- Recover from the shock of the hostile reaction.
- Recognize what's going on.

- Drop your put-your-dukes-up-and-fight reflex.
- Squelch the *"My* fault! What did *I* do wrong?" reaction.
- Get curious about what's happening.

Actually you're in a pretty good position to do all this! It's the other person who's out of control, not you! You're still calm and engaged in selling your idea. So take a breath. Slow down a peg or two and start thinking.

Name What You See

The biggest mistake people make when trying to handle hostility is to pretend that it's not happening. Going blithely on makes you seem either too weak to handle it or too dumb to notice. Most of all, if people's anger is not recognized and dealt with, they stay mad! And often get madder!

Allow the Anger

When people get angry, especially in a business setting, they're in a very exposed position. They're in danger of losing face because they're clearly out of control.

Not only is this something we don't like to show at all, especially in a professional setting, we need help to get out of it. That's why the best thing you can do for the other person is to recognize their anger and then *allow it!* Be nonjudgmental. Just state what you see, like this:

"I see you're reacting pretty strongly to this," or "This material seems to raise some real feelings in you," or "Something we're talking about seems to have ticked you off," or "You seem pretty committed to another point of view." All of it with pleasantness: no attitude, no flavoring, no judgment—just a flat statement about what you see. This needs attention, right now, before you go on.

What happens after you acknowledge their anger?

From all my years of experience, trust me—*this* is what really happens: The other person slowly calms down and explains. You've given him or her the way out because you asked. You'll hear, as the heat diminishes, something like:

"Yes I am! Do you realize . . . ?" or "Look at today's market. Do you think we can do this?" or "We tried this two years ago and it failed!"

What people need most when they get angry and lose control is a way out. They realize they're out of control but they need to be heard—to calm down and just plain talk.

Uncover the Problem

You've now opened the door and can hear the real issue. Once they've vented whatever they're feeling, you can tune in to what's *underneath* this reaction and where the real problem or obstacle lies.

And you've helped save face for the other person and given them a way out of their hostility. *Listen!* Let them talk. Hear what's really going on. What made them so angry? What's the first thing they talk about? Ask about it and let them go on, so you learn more about how your material has threatened or challenged or angered them.

What's in It for You?

If someone is reacting with hostility, *they cannot hear you!* You're not making your point, your sale, your defense. So what's the use of continuing to pretend that everything's fine? Waste of time.

Getting to the underlying truth lets you deal right then with the basis for the negative reaction. This leads to solving the problem or learning what else the other person needs to arrive at a positive outcome. *Now* you can go on, in a much more positive environment, to fix the real obstacle. And the other person can finally listen to your message with a much more open mind.

GETTING AT THE TRUTH

Human behavior and reactions are often so predictable. Getting at the truth, face-to-face, is always challenging. Think how people react when you say, "Listen, tell me the truth." Who likes to be put on the spot?

If you're someone in power, here's how any junior person would automatically filter your question:

- Why does he want to know this?
- What will she do with the answer? Who else will she tell?
- How much of the truth shall I tell? How much does he need to know?
- How does this affect me? Who else will this hurt?

If you're trying to make a sale, your client may just hedge. People generally don't like to say anything negative, especially face-to-face. They'd rather smile vaguely, and then let the whole project die from attrition. Later they may dismiss you very briefly over the phone later or send an email to turn you off.

Though some people *can* be very direct and let you know yes or no right away, hearing "It's very interesting" or "Well, I hadn't thought about this before" doesn't really give you what you want.

So how do you get people to really be straight with you?

If You're the One in Charge

If you need to troubleshoot an issue or a system that's not working, know that everyone is self-protective and not into tattling. So here are some ways to get at the truth in a nonthreatening, productive manner.

Describe the Expected Response

Before you start trying to get some information, clear the air and surprise the other person this way: "I need to know the straight story about X. So I was thinking, before you came in, about how I would feel if someone asked me to talk about that. I guess I'd be pretty careful with my answers, so I imagine that's how you'd feel, right?" This opens the conversation on a healthier note, showing you know how people really are. You can then deal with their fears, resistance, or concerns about "tattling."

Say What You Want to Know and Why

Your *intention* has everything to do with whether someone will answer you openly. If the reason sounds useful and valuable for the group or the company, or would provide some benefit to colleagues, you've begun to provide motivation. If your issue deals with fellow workers, there is loyalty to consider. Staff generally bonds together, not necessarily with the management.

"Y'know, heading up the team on this project, I have a problem. I'm not out on the floor to watch the day-to-day operation of it. Since we've hit a few snags, I need your help in trying to fix them. It would make day-to-day operations easier and less pressured."

This is a pretty good reason, with a clear, objective purpose and a goal that seems beneficial to the group. It could encourage most folks to get into such a discussion. And your asking for help makes people feel quite powerful.

Say What You'll Do with the Answers

People want to know what you'll do with the information. Tell them. And always assure them of the *privacy* of these answers—but only if you can guarantee that the message goes no further. Trust is a hard thing to come by, and losing it is lethal.

Help by Leading

"There are probably a few things you can tell me about this issue. You worked on that project, so let's start there."

Leading people toward some organized discussion is more reassuring than a completely open-ended request for information. Leaving them to flounder in a sea of choices looks dangerous. Also, when you start them in a direction, you can ask follow-up questions to pinpoint information more specifically or move off to another direction.

If You're Not Getting What You Need . . .

Say so. "This is very helpful so far, but I'm not too clear yet about point Y. Maybe we could start from a different place?"

Telling the person the problem with the discussion so far and what's missing keeps the dialogue open and honest. Beware of cross-examining the person or you'll turn off the water supply! Just explain what *else* you need.

Be Appreciative

Be aware that you've asked someone to do something hard. They've shared personal thoughts about which they're still a little worried. Thank them profusely, in advance, for helping you out: "I know this was a tough thing to ask you to do and I really appreciate you're being so candid. It was *very* helpful. And let's both agree to keep this matter just between us, OK? You've given me some good ideas about how to solve the issue."

If You're the Outsider

You've planned and prepared and here you are selling your heart out. Don't you want to know how you're doing? What the other person thinks so far? Where you need to refocus to make the final sale?

Stop and Ask

Just asking, "What do you think of it so far?" gets you the "nice" response, the one they think you want to hear, the non-committal, easy pass: "Oh, I think it's very interesting," or "Hmm, you've brought up something to think about."

What did you learn? Do they like it? Hate it? Think it's ridiculous or too expensive or too hard to do? Who knows? You haven't found out anything because the question is too vague. And you haven't given them a reason to get into much more than that.

What about this: "Well, here I am, talking away, explaining this thing I believe in so thoroughly. But let me stop right here to find out how it strikes *you* so far. Tell me: Does this idea (product, service) hit some of your core issues? And if not, what part do you see as useful and what is not?"

Check the Body Language

What do you *see* as you hear the answer? Does the body language match the words? If the client says "This is interesting" but won't make eye contact with you or shifts position or looks away, you'd better follow up. Someone who is really interested has eyebrows raised, head cocked. And if their brow is furrowed and drawn together, what does this tell you?

Listen and Follow Up

"Is this something you see in your business now, like that *Journal* article we discussed?" Stay with the specifics till you find out what is *not* working for your client. Find out what seems irrelevant or useful, what is not yet understood, and what *does* seem to fit in and work for them.

Explain and Check Again

Hearing the stumbling blocks, adapt your material to fulfill this newly expressed need or doubt. You're so steeped in your material that changing course or backing and filling isn't hard. What's hard is swallowing the fact that things are not going as well as you hoped. Set that aside and focus on answering what's missing for your potential client.

Be careful not to let your annoyance with the other person show—no testiness or exasperation in the voice, or slowing down your speech. Think: "How can I explain that better or differently, with more relevance?" Put your frustration into capturing your target better. Always ask along the way, "Is this what you meant?"

"Thanks for Letting Me Know"

Always be sure to thank people for being honest, even if the truth hurts. It does take effort, even courage, for them to be straight with you. But, since you asked for it, notice and be grateful when you get it, even if you hate what you hear. Try another sales approach, but continue selling in a pleasant manner.

Even if things don't go well, keep the relationship going as you adapt your stuff to what you now know. Maybe you can come back another day with more adaptations to what's needed. Tell your clients how helpful this was, and how much more you now understand about their particular needs. And don't forget to smile!

HANDLING BOREDOM AND INATTENTION

If people lose interest or feel irrelevance about any aspect of your presentation, they've stopped listening to you or your logical presentation. For some reason, you've lost them. Stop, notice, and take care of the situation immediately. Ignoring it puts you on the road to an unsuccessful outcome. And you won't ever know where you missed the boat.

How Can You Tell?

Body Language

Tune in to what you *see* at all times, when you're communicating. People are trained to be polite, and they're also generally good poker players in business. But you have powers, too. The power to observe. So just tune in and notice what *else* is going on.

You're talking. They're listening. But what else?

- Have you noticed some movement and change of position?
- Some fiddling with objects on the desk?
- What about eye contact? When did she start to look away?
- Clearing the throat?
- Rocking in the chair a little?
- Jiggling a leg?
- An intake of breath?

These are all signs that your audience's attention is wandering. Body language is the real truth teller.

When Someone Seems Bored

Notice!

The biggest mistake you can make is to go on and on, ignoring the fact that you've lost your listener. People get more and more annoyed when someone bores them and just *continues!* Boring people is a primary transgression, so see it, get it, and *stop talking!*

Say It!

Say (with a smile or a laugh), "Well, I seem to be going on and on and I think I've lost my audience a little!" That's a real shocker—most of us would rather die than admit that we're boring, let alone admitting it to the one we've just "bored." So, break through the fog you were creating. Furthermore, you've already begun to make a friend. Acknowledging it means you're going to save the listener from more of the same!

Ask Where You Lost Them

"Let's see, we were doing OK till I got to talking about X, right? Was *that* the place where I lost you?" That's right. Dare! If you can find out what *doesn't* interest them or what seems irrelevant, you're ahead of the game.

- You won't keep talking about that.
- You can find out why that was boring or irrelevant.
- You can start another subject, or fix the focus of the one you're on, and get your audience back.

Don't Feel Bad!

Think about how much better you can now feel. Look what you've accomplished:

- Your subject matter changes to something much more productive.
- You'll surely have a much more positive outcome than if

you went blithely along without stopping and they couldn't wait to get rid of you!

Continue Checking In

Now that you're on your way once more, be sure you don't start boring them again. Periodically check in: "Now how about this aspect. In what way does this apply to your company or situation?"

Or ask your clients to *tell* you when they feel this doesn't apply to them. Once you've shown them that you're a realist who wants to stay on target, you'll surely earn points—and the truth.

CLOSURE

Closing effectively would seem to be simple. Wrong! This is a real weak spot, one that is mishandled most of the time. Results, actions, and final solutions often don't get nailed down, and people walk away with vague, even incorrect, notions.

Maybe it's because it's such a relief to just be done with the meeting. Or you may not really *want* to know exactly what you accomplished. Or you're not clear about what each of you is supposed to do next.

In any case, it's an area that sure needs some work.

There are four clear steps to closing a meeting:

1. Recap and clarify: What happened.

2. Troubleshoot areas still not resolved.

3. Agree on next steps.

4. Follow up: confirm in writing.

RECAP AND CLARIFY

"Let's wind this up by going over what we talked about, just to be sure we're both on the same page." This sounds so simple, but I can't tell you how often people forget to do this.

And it's so important!

We really don't all hear the same thing. We tune in to what we *want* to hear and tune out what we *don't want* to hear. Don't assume your points all landed just because you said them. Both parties come to the meeting with their own agendas, needs, and self-protective coating. Focusing on different things, each assumes that his or her version is the correct version of what was said and done. That's why closure matters so much.

If It's Your Meeting

Do your closure very methodically. Start from the beginning of your original agenda and go down the list. Check off each item you came in with.

- What did you both decide?
- What were the disagreements?
- Were they resolved? How?

If It's Another's Meeting

Take the initiative and do the summary, if the host has forgotten, just to clarify and better understand what you accomplished.

TROUBLESHOOT AREAS STILL NOT RESOLVED

If It's Your Meeting

Here's your chance to come to some *final* conclusions. In the meeting, you may both have dropped areas that weren't quite finished. The great advantage of doing this recap is to discover what's still undone and to finish it.

Finish Unfinished Business

You can now both focus on just this one issue, since so much other business is now taken care of. Also, because you've already accomplished a great deal, there's a mood of compromise—a willingness to get the whole project moving forward.

If Things Haven't Gone Well

Focus on finding things you can agree on! Salvage what you can. Resolve at least some points, even if the major ones elude you. This is the time to demonstrate some flexibility, to focus on possibilities for the future. You want to end up with both sides feeling you can do some business together rather than leaving with a climate of frustration.

If It's Another's Meeting

Be sure you speak up during this phase of the closure. Don't just agree. Sometimes this is a better place to make, even win, a final point. When other parts have been resolved and something unsolved still remains, bring it up again. There's been some distance created from the first time you talked about it. If the discussion was heated then, things have cooled down and it can be reconsidered.

Here's a way to reopen a discussion: "You know, that still makes me uncomfortable. Maybe we could look at it this way" or "I'm still not altogether clear about our intentions about this from now on." Then try to resolve it in some final way. Do not belabor it. If it's stuck, it's stuck. Better to live and fight another day.

Warning! "Maybe" Is a Lethal Word

Never leave anything at "maybe" as an answer. It isn't. It's a trap!

As Carole Hyatt describes it in *The Woman's New Selling Game* (McGraw-Hill, 1997), "A *Maybe* is to put you off or get rid of you. Unless you reshape it to a definite *Yes* or *No*, it is a worthless answer you can't do a thing with. . . . The best thing to do with *Maybe* is refuse to live with it any longer than you have to."

Now sometimes "maybe" is only temporary, waiting for an

upcoming result or another's approval. In that case, you must set up a timetable for arriving at a real decision. But be definite. Hyatt suggests saying:

"Maybe we can work something out in a few months. . . . That gives us both time to think through my proposal. Let's make an appointment to meet then and [come to a conclusion]."

See, this means the ball is still in play. Recognizing the danger of a "maybe's" limbo-land, you move to change the maybe to a yes.

If you're selling something, Hyatt suggests getting specific: "What other options are you considering? Do you have someone else in mind to fill your need?" or "Perhaps I can help you in making the decision." Refocus the discussion to the place where you might still fit.

No matter what, take an *active* role to help the undecided. Never just accept "maybe" as an answer. But know when it's time to back off. Measure how important total agreement is, what can wait for another day, and what parts of the issue you can settle for.

AGREE ON NEXT STEPS

Again, proceed methodically. Tackle who does what, now and next. What will each of you do now? What's the timetable? This needs to be written down as you both talk about it. Making notes helps get it clear. Don't rely on purely verbal conclusions. It should go something like this:

YOU:

- "I'll do X and you'll do Y, OK?"
- "I'll have it done by Thursday."
- "You'll send me the items we still need to see."
- "We'll let the group know about this by the 4th, right?"

OTHER PERSON:

- "You still have to get agreement from Z before we go ahead. When do you think you could do that?"

YOU:

- I'll try to get that done by the end of the week."

OTHER PERSON:

- "Would Friday morning be realistic for me to call you, so we'll know if we've got a go?"

Notice how specific I'm being and how I'm trying to get the other party to pinpoint dates and times? That's what it takes. Otherwise you're both *assuming,* not *confirming,* what the next steps should be.

Again, be sure you both discuss and agree on who will be doing what and when you'll do them.

Note: This process holds true equally for both peers and clients.

FOLLOW UP: CONFIRM IN WRITING

If this is your meeting or you're the more involved party, the next step is go back, sit down, write up, and email what just happened ASAP.

- What you both agreed happened at the meeting
- What you both agreed should be done next
- Who will do what
- Dates and times: Long-range calendar and short-range to-do list
- When you'll follow up with each other

Be sure you ask for a reply so that you know you're on the same page. Doing all the above will save you *so* much time in extra emails, phone calls, and meetings.

END ON A HIGH NOTE!

Whichever role you played, the final exit lines and the mood at the end of the meeting is very important.

If You Weren't the Host

Always leave the host with some positive thoughts about you, as you go toward the door. Wind up and exit with some vigor, no matter how the meeting went. This can reflect on how the other person remembers the meeting.

Didn't Get What You Came For?

"Okay, Bill. I heard you very clearly. X and Y aren't what you want or need right now. But I also heard that Z interested you and that it might be a good tool in the near future. Since I know so much more about your business now, let me come back to you in about six months with some much more customized ideas for you. I'll be in touch."

Or "Thanks so much for the meeting. I really enjoyed getting to know you. I especially liked your style of doing business and being so up-front with me. I think we can do something else together. You've given me lots to think about. Let me be in touch when I see something particularly suited to you."

You left the door open to return with another idea.

Didn't Get the Raise or Promotion?

Ugh, that hurts. But do you mean to quit? If not, you've got to gather together your ego, your dignity and, most of all, show that you're still a valuable member of the company. How? Obviously tailor this to your own style and situation, but the basic principle has to be that you didn't die from this! It wasn't a be-all and end-all thing for you.

Deal with the *reason* for the denial. Your boss has other issues to deal with—budget, hierarchy, timing, business conditions, his superiors! Show that you heard and understood.

"I see this is the wrong time to ask for a raise. Would coming back in six months be a better time to open the subject again? And, in the meantime, is there anything else I should be doing to move up on your list?" Or:

"Well, you now know *why* I need the raise as well as the fact that I think I deserve it for work accomplished. But I clearly hear you saying what else you need from me to rise to the next level. Meanwhile, thanks for the meeting and the information. And, without sounding too predictable, but because I never get a chance to tell you this, let me tell you how much I like working here. I have much faith in the future and my role in it. And leave with a smile and a brisk step. . . .

Meeting Was Critical of You?

Were you being called on the carpet? All the more reason to end on a high note! You need to recover and impart a sense of energy about tomorrow and optimism about what happens next—what needs to be done and how you'll fix it. Say what you learned and what you'll fix. Leave with a show of strength. Make it clear that she can trust you.

"Let me end by thanking you for the meeting. You gave me a heads-up and a chance to fix what was going wrong. It shows that you have faith in me, that I'd want to know what's not working so I could fix it. I won't let you down. Let me please check with you in a week just to see if you feel the problem is being solved, as you wanted it to be."

See how much better this makes the boss feel about the whole exchange (which she didn't particularly relish, either)?

Always walk out head high, not whipped. *After* you leave is the time to let go of all the other feelings! But not until you've pulled off the visible exit with dignity, leaving a positive echo.

The Project Isn't Working?

"Okay, Linda. I heard it all. What we tried didn't work. But it's okay. There are still so many good ideas in it I feel there are many things I (or we) can do to change what's happened. Let's get started."

Always the positive. Always find something good, something that *did* work, or a good reason to go at it again, and emphasize that as you go.

If You Called the Meeting

"High note" endings to a meeting by the convener should reverberate as you show someone out. The other person should feel good, purposeful, competent, energized, and motivated. Unless of course you never want them to darken your door again!

A Tough Meeting?

This is the time to heal and soothe. Walk with the other party to the door. This is the time for a figurative, or even a literal pat on the back.

"Carl, if anyone can do this job, you can. I look forward to our check-in meeting to see how it's going. Meanwhile, I'm here if you have any questions."

Always end by saying something positive about some part of the meeting. Let your last words be encouraging, or at least pleasant. Use a compliment if it's in order. Remember this: you're the one who can help save face for the other person. It really goes a long way if you do.

A Productive Meeting?

Let your opposite number know how much you appreciated what you both solved. Talk about what you look forward to, what the list of next steps means.

"I think we got a lot done. I heard you and you heard me. That's pretty good! I look forward to our next talk together. I know we can make something happen."

Being gracious and graceful in the workplace, being an accessible, available person really pays off.

CHECKLIST FOR ONE-ON-ONE ENCOUNTERS

BEFORE THE MEETING

- Pre-think and know your audience!
- What's your approach: what role will you play?

- Balance the power between you
- Remember to listen; use what you hear; stay open

OPENERS

- Warm-up and small talk
- Help change gears; make a personal dent
- Office as turf; notice and comment
- Decide where to sit
- Amenities; the "gift" of coffee
- Body language; the key weathervane

PRESENTING THE SUBSTANCE

How to Begin

- Three points: how much time?; tell goals; give agenda
- Motivate your listener
- Start by asking before you tell

Telling and Explaining

- Clear and organized: the only route to getting and keeping attention
- Begin with an overview
- Present facts in bullet form
- Make your message visual; prepare/ improvise/show examples
- Proofs of credibility
- Bring take-aways

Dialogue, Not Monologue

- Create the dialogue
- Listen!

- Really consider another's ideas
- Notice and comment on the questions asked
- Keep the dialogue going
- Know when to finish

HANDLING PROBLEMS, ISSUES, AND NEGATIVE REACTIONS

- Creative criticism
- Handling anger and hostility
- Getting at the truth
- Handling boredom, inattention, or lack of understanding

CLOSURE

- Recap and clarify
- Agree on next steps; beware of "maybe"
- Follow up: confirm in writing who, what, when, where
- End on a high note!

So that's it. Now we need to move on to showing you how to make your messages visual, an essential component for twenty-first-century communications.

And then we'll go on to find out all about Presentations: how to design and develop really great speeches and how to deliver them.

6

SEEING IS BELIEVING:
MAKING YOUR
MESSAGE VISUAL

WHY VISUAL?

Today's audiences are superimpatient. Their information comes visually, not aurally. So you really *must* include visual support and interest as part of your message. Here are three ways to make your message visual.

1. Show *and* tell, to be clear and memorable.

2. Show, *then* tell, to capture interest and give context.

3. Show but *don't* tell. Visuals can be enough by themselves.

Most of us are accustomed to verbal communication, but now I'm asking you to move into a realm of tools and concepts that aren't nearly the natural, verbal ones you've always used to communicate. And you're thinking: "I'm no artist. What PowerPoint choices should I make that are really effective and persuasive in color, design, impact, and style?"

I understand. Let's start by thinking about it this way.

TAKE A NEW APPROACH

Move past using only the cool, didactic, data-oriented *left* brain, which puts ideas into words. Activate the imaginative, pictorial *right* brain which form ideas visually. Shown, not said.

Think: How does the outside world talk to you now? Whether it's political campaigns, computer pop-ups, shopping web or emails, the message is carried visually.

Just think about the ads you see on buses, subways, airports, magazines, and television. How much of any ad is words and how much is pictures, color, and graphic design? You not only notice; you get the message fast, and even appreciate how cleverly that message was conveyed.

Just look at this ad for Oxford Health Plans:

Look at how powerful it is! How much it says to you through the *picture*. And the words only serve to point up a concept and to identify the source.

Here's another one you've seen many times on TV from the Partnership for a Drug-Free America campaign:

Again, the eloquence of using an image all of us have experienced has such an impact. You can practically hear the egg— read, *your brain*—sizzling and getting destroyed from drug use.

In truth, we're now a visually sophisticated society. We're conditioned to *seeing* information, not just hearing it. This chapter will help you get on board.

HOW VISUALS AFFECT YOUR AUDIENCE

To master this concept, you need to know how visuals affect people and help persuade and inform them.

Making your messages visual makes them:

Precise and accurate: Visualizing your data and ideas puts audiences on exactly *your* wavelength or subject instead of imagining their own variations. For accuracy, numbers, lists, facts, and data must be *shown.*

Clear, succinct, and edited: Making messages visual imposes a discipline to *edit* before you tell: to distill your ideas into bare essentials. Fitting ideas onto a screen or chart shortens talking and gets audiences straight to your point.

Participatory: Monologue becomes dialogue. Just listening makes speakers active but audiences passive. Visuals free the audience's dependency on only the speaker for information. They're recast into a proactive, interactive role.

Attention-getting: Visuals capture and keep the audience's attention with image, color, and design. They create change and add movement to an otherwise static situation. *Going* to your computer, *writing* on your board, *walking* to the screen, *changing* slides, *pointing* to your ideas, all sharpen interest.

Credible: Seeing is believing. Documenting that what you say is true with statistics, quotes, letters, and demos provides objective proof of what you're saying and overcomes skepticism.

Reinforcing: Getting your audience to read on their own encourages and supports independent thought. Repeating visuals instantly reminds people of your original points and helps them to remember. Repetition reinforces learning. It also helps those who didn't get it the first time to catch up.

Memorable*: Visuals are remembered; streaming words are not. People can hardly ever quote exactly what someone said, unless it's a quip or some saying like "If the glove won't fit, you must acquit." But they certainly remember what they've seen.

Add emotion and impact: Visual images deeply affect feelings, in very different ways than words. Who will ever forget the images of 9/11? Or the Katrina disaster? Responding viscerally, unguided by anyone else's interpretation or explanation, is the true power and potential of visual communication.

Simplify complex facts and ideas: Concepts become clear when you diagram cause and effect, relationships of ideas, and how to get from one point to another. They allow you to stop at any point, go over some wrinkle, answer questions, and never lose your audience. Each part of your idea is visible, showing where you are and how you got there.

Provide contrasts and comparisons: This is the fastest way to teach and persuade anyone about anything. Convincing anyone how much better, quicker, cheaper it would be to use your idea than what they've got, gets done at once with simultaneous visuals, not sequential talking. Seeing two ideas, points of view, facts, *together,* side by side, convinces your audience without you having to argue at all!

To present an idea about why to change something at work, agreement comes fastest by comparing it with what the competition does.

Example: Your company has launched a website that doesn't seem to be generating nearly the business you expected. Your competitors seem to be going great guns with theirs. To explain what needs to change, you display both websites, analyze both, and then describe what needs work by showing this comparison:

---

* Try it yourself. Draw or diagram something and show it while you're explaining your idea to someone. Then explain the same idea to someone else, but only verbally. After two or three hours, ask the first person to draw exactly what you showed them. Ask the second person to repeat exactly what you said.

XYZ'S WEBSITE	OUR WEBSITE
1. Engages consumer in 5 seconds	1. No clear message on homepage
2. Prime searchability	2. Listed #6 in web search
3. Smart links to sources in market	3. Only links within our website

People see the differences and advantages between the two positions for themselves and get your point instantly and independently. You can then tell what concrete plans you have for changing the situation, using your chart to organize your plan.

Now, let's try to do that kind of persuasion orally, with no comparative charts:

"Y'know, the XYZ company is getting ahead of us. They have a very user-friendly website, and their customers have a better idea of what to do when they enter it. When people do a web search, XYZ comes up under many different key search words. Their website gets linked to other market sources."

Hoping they'll remember what you just said, you then start describing your company:

"Now in our company, we don't seem to have a clear action message on our homepage. And we're seeing that web searches turn up XYZ's name, but not ours. Also, we seem to be missing out on the opportunity to link to other markets. This means that they're getting way ahead of us in sales. We need to do something."

Which do you think works better and faster, with more impact and less pressure from you? The visual way is self-explanatory, with immediate impact. The strictly verbal way makes persuasion depend only on your word and your advocacy. Contrast and comparison can only work their powerful advocacy if you *show*, not just tell.

Now that you're convinced of the benefits of "speaking visually," it's time to learn how to do it.

MAKING MESSAGES VISUAL

WHAT TO SHOW, WHAT TO TELL

- What kinds of information need visual support?
- What needs to be only verbal?
- What needs some of both?

The answer? It all depends on the subject matter, your goals, and what effect you're looking for.

Which Subjects Need Visual Support

The left side of the brain—the organizing, data-collecting, fact-oriented, list-making side—needs visual backup. It needs concrete images and incontrovertible, hard-nosed information that stands still for study, reinforcement, and clarification.

Subjects that need visual support include:

- Numbers, facts, quotes, lists, trends—information that people do not and cannot collect and remember without seeing it
- New data or images, known only to you
- Data known to all but never before presented in this context or with this interpretation
- A message that needs documentation or support from objective data or other sources in order to be credible
- Chronological data, like time lines, that need to grow and accumulate.
- Material that needs to be repeated and remembered from one segment of your talk to another
- Contrasts and comparisons

You'll find explicit ways to do this later on, under "How to Design Visual Messages," page 169.

Which Subjects Need Only Telling

Just telling is the way to go when there's no mathematically right or wrong answer. To get a personal message across and give your audience pictures to see in their own minds, your words, gestures, and vocal nuances are best. When you're looking for personalized, emotional responses, not just acquisition of facts and data, you alone must generate the visuals, through your words.

Material that lends itself best to just telling is anything that needs a more emotional, less documentary approach.

Subjects that need only telling:

- Material that is narrative and dramatic
- Personal information, like your own story or others' experiences
- Presenting yourself so others get to know you at work, applying for a job, and surely asking for a raise or running for office
- Building morale; inspiring and motivating people; gaining loyalty
- Engaging people's imaginations
- Persuasion through common experience, not just facts

To make personal contact with your listeners and to present yourself as the source of information—as a person of character, integrity, and understanding—you must talk straight to them. Your message is still visual, only you provide the images.

You'll find explicit ways to do all this soon, under "Making Your Message Visual, Verbally" on page 179.

Which Subjects Need Both

Sometimes you need to mix both verbal and visual materials.

You may need to use visual data to present logic and facts, to demonstrate the new system, product, or idea you propose.

But then, to get real agreement—closing the deal, making the sale, getting the commitment to try something new—you must change gears and appeal to the more personal, emotional level of thinking.

That's the time to set the charts aside.

To slowly close the Magic Marker, or close the laptop and put down the mouse.

To walk forward a couple of steps closer to your audience, and sit down on the side of the table.

Or stop, lean forward in your chair, and make direct eye contact with the others in the room.

And then just talk, person to person. Intently. Intensely. Intimately.

ALWAYS PERSONALIZE YOUR MESSAGE

Successful communicating at work means making yourself visible, showing *your* unique approach to your work and how *you* come to conclusions. Emerge as the originator, not just the message giver. Always find a way to become known personally, beyond your material. What people should remember is *who*, not just what.

Inside Your Company:

- Tell them what it took for you to come up with this plan: the research, the doubts, the stops and starts till you got it right.
- Level with the group about knowing what it will take for them to do this.
- Go back to your visuals and show them your awareness of them: what supports are being built in to help them deal with this new idea.
- If you're the leader, tell them why you're committed to making this work.
- Finish eye-to-eye, personally, letting them know that making it work is finally up to them.

As an Outsider, Trying to Sell a New Product or Service:

- Talk *personally* about how aware you are of what else it will take to make this work.

- Explain what you'll do to help and support.
- Give examples of how you got this to work at other companies.
- Finish by telling them that your take-aways will help answer lots of questions, but that you're there for more questions right now. Personally.

All this can only be done by metaphorically "getting closer": relaxing your body into a conversational posture, making eye contact, lowering and softening your voice. Talk straight, person to person. No slides. No visuals.

VISUAL TAKE-AWAYS

In the heat of your personal presentation, only some of your information gets in on the first round. We all need time to think things over before we commit ourselves to anything.

Therefore, leave material behind so they can read and think about what you said when you're gone. Take-aways also give them support for the proselytizing they'll have to do with their superiors.

It's important to create a packet of materials that graphically and succinctly presents your case when you're not there to sell it yourself.

As you're presenting your basic ideas, be sure to tell them all along that you have materials to leave behind. Materials that will support and detail what you're telling them, with references for follow-up.

This is very gratifying to your audience, since they can relax and concentrate more on the ideas you're presenting while you're there, knowing they don't have to remember every detail. Make sure your material is *pictorial, colorful, and tightly edited!*

Note: Do *not* give out this material while you're speaking! You'll lose your audience as they read ahead and pay no attention to you. It's only for later, *after* you've spoken and left.

Take-Away Ideas

- A *succinct* summary of your product/service/idea goals for this meeting

- Copies of what you told them or showed them, for reinforcement
- Basic points you want them to remember
- Documentation for what you said
- Extra information you did *not* introduce during your presentation: background material, articles, previous reports
- Testimonials and examples of what you (or others) have already done
- Quotes from speeches given by others, inside or outside the company
- Memos from the CEO or senior executive, if it's an inhouse presentation
- Letters and positive feedback from customers
- Additional information about you, if you're selling yourself, or if this is a new group that doesn't know you. A subtle "I'm terrific" packet will do: bio, experience, past accomplishments and awards, client list, all tightly edited

Of course, you don't leave them a 5-pound package! The above is just a menu for you to pick from. *Be selective!* Just remember what your stickiest points are and what data you have—and they need—that best supports your position.

HOW TO DESIGN VISUAL MESSAGES

GETTING STARTED

To make visual decisions, you've got to first edit your subject matter down to your *most basic and essential points*. Only then can you choose what to make visual and how to show it. Ask yourself:

- What are three basic truths I want to transmit?
- What information does my audience need to come to a decision?
- What else do they need to make my message persuasive and compelling?

Only after this kind of soul-searching and thinking can you think about which visual form will serve your message best.

EXHIBITS CAN BE SIMPLE

Don't assume that you need to make your visuals complex and formal. Bigger isn't always better and expensive isn't always more.

- Who's your audience?
- What have they seen too much of?
- What else can you do, to be original, proactive, and involving?

There are many times when the best visual medium is simple and informal—just you, talking and writing spontaneously in front of them. Always consider first how complex your message is, how much data you need to impart, and what impression you wish to make. Don't think about what can make the biggest splash.

Form follows function . . .

CHOOSING THE MEDIUM

We have been, and continue to be, exposed to so many forms of media that we develop preconditioned reflex reactions to them. What effect do you want to create for your audience? Who are you to them and how will your choice of media show that?

Do you want to come across as:

- *Personal, informal and improvisational?* Then spur-of-the-moment graphics, handmade at the moment, is the way to go.
- *Professional, classy, and top-of-the-line?* Then you need graphics prepared in advance, slick, handsome, well designed, and sophisticated.

Are you looking for:

- *An emotional response?* Pictures and video can do that for you.
- *Capturing attention and surprising your audience?* Make it a live demonstration. Or use a live guest with testimonials. Or do interactive, experiential activities with the audience.

Choose the Medium That Fits Your Message

Think through the wide range of visual devices.

- Which are you most comfortable with?
- How good are you at doing it alone or designing it?
- How much help might you need?
- How much can you spend?
- How much time do you have?

A FEW BASIC DESIGN PRINCIPLES

Good Design Makes a Difference

Audiences are now enormously experienced, graphically. Therefore, just opening your PowerPoint and writing black words on a white screen or popping a graph isn't going to do it today. There are real design concepts to learn in order to clarify, enhance, and deliver the impact you wish. The quality and design of your graphics really count.

Picture and Icons, Not Just Words!

Don't let graphics simply repeat what you *say*. We'll hear that. Use pictures or icons to make your point whenever possible. They are much more interesting and attention-grabbing than printed words. They're more memorable and bear much repetition. They also add emotion and punch to your ideas. *Illustrate* your material; don't settle for just re-saying it graphically.

Danger! Control Your Information

The biggest mistake I see in all my consulting work is *overloading* visual aids with too much information at once! If you show it all, not only will we read it all; we'll read it 20 times faster than you can say it.

Result? You lose control of your audience and the information they're supposed to be getting from you. While you're explaining the upper left-hand corner, your audience members are already down at the bottom, making their own judgments of what you mean and totally missing your explanation of the material.

Remedy: the build-slide system. Control your information. Animate it so you show only one piece at a time. Accumulate all the information *only at the end.*

- Show bullet 1, then talk.
- Add bullet 2 and talk.
- And so on till all the bullets are visible.

The accumulated information your audience gets will be only what *you* meant with each bullet, *not* what the audience decided as it read ahead when you showed all the bullets at once.

Making Graphic Design Clear and Compelling

- Always start with something that shows us your theme. Then we need to see your agenda so we know how your material is organized.
- Don't waste your headings! Each heading should pertain to and describe what that particular slide or chart is about, *not* just the general subject.
- Make major points on separate slides, as a summation, for greatest impact.
- Make information self-explanatory, to develop audience independence.

Be Original! Don't Use the Same Colors and Format for All Slides

I know PowerPoint gives you many ready-to-use formats. But everyone uses the same ones. So be original. Create your own formats. People need variety not only to renew interest but because a routine, repetitious format becomes predictable and uninteresting and belies your new subject matter. Using the PowerPoint formats as a base, try for something original and stimulating.

Don't use the same format and colors for each subject of your speech! It isn't logical. The various aspects of your speech engage different issues and are meant to evoke different levels of response in the audience.

When you move from one subject to another, change your background and colors, within the framework of your format. This visually alerts the audience to the shift in topic and raises interest again. Color-coding your subjects is like turning the page and develops a new focus for each section of your speech.

MAKING AUDIENCES LOOK: EFFECTIVE PRESENTATION OF GRAPHICS

You can have the best visuals but if you don't know how to present them to your audience for maximum effect, you're losing their use and juice.

Use your visuals as an extension of yourself, to explain and underscore your points. And to feel comfortable and secure, master whatever medium you're using.

Visuals Trump Talking

We're always drawn to action over listening. If you show anything graphic, your audience immediately has a more active role. They become independent of your words. Always remember: When you show something, you and your visuals now share the stage and your audience's attention. So be sure your visuals *support* you and don't compete with you.

Lead into Your Visuals Before You Show Them

Whet their appetites. Tell your audience where you're going and why *before* you present a graphic: "Here's a chart that will surprise you as you see the trend." Once you reveal a visual, you've lost your chance to build curiosity. They're already looking, not listening! To build interest, tell them *why* they need to see the next idea and what it will explain for them *before* you show it.

Let Your Visuals Speak

Visuals are eloquent. They can and do speak *on their own.* So let your graphic do its work. Introduce it so your audience knows what to look for and why. But then stop. Reveal it and wait, while they look. Only then should you continue to make your point based on this new graphic. Let it have an impact first.

Create a Glossary

If your message has technical/financial/contractual/regulatory terms in it that may be unfamiliar to your audience, create a glos-

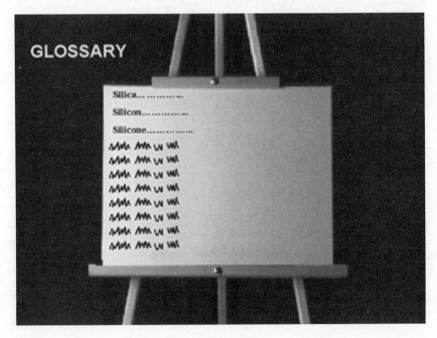

sary for easy reference. Using a chart on an easel, write a one-liner definition or explanation on it the first time you use any technical or unfamiliar term.

Or prepare a chart in advance and reveal each term as you say it. This gives your audience their own private reference guide, always visible. They keep listening and you don't need to keep explaining.

Use Phrasing, Nuance, and Vocal Shading to Enhance Visuals

If you're building up to a surprising new piece of information or a dramatic example, use your voice to let us know that something's coming. Change the rhythm and pace with which you present your slides. *Let us know* that the next one has something unexpected or that this is the final answer. You can help build anticipation by *how you talk* and how *slowly* or *rapidly* you present your visuals.

Stay Active with Your Visuals

Be interactive with your slides. Lead your audience through your slides, telling them what to look *at*, what to look *for*, what to *compare*. Go to the screen; look at what you're showing. Point to the special things you want your audience to notice. It keeps you visible, active, and involved with what you're showing them. *Caution*: Those laser pointers can really wobble as you point, broadcasting how nervous and shaky you feel, even if it's only that you're all charged up. Practice by leaning your elbow against your body to steady your hand. It's often better to just walk to the screen and point.

Tell Them What to Look For

Direct your audience's seeing: "Notice that fourth bullet, especially. That's the newest research in the field." "See how the figures from last year, the blue ones, compare with the green ones that we projected for this year."

You'd be amazed at how much power you have over your audience. *You're in charge.* You have the mike or the floor and they will do what you tell them! Try it, it's true!

Don't Let Them Read Along with Hard-Copy Handouts!

If you give your listeners material to read *while you talk*, you'll lose your audience!

- They can read much faster than you can talk.
- They'll be ahead of you and all over the place, turning pages, looking for what interests them, while you're still explaining page 1.
- You lose your role as the primary message giver and enlightener.

Having worked on developing rapport with your audience, why would you want to release center stage so everyone can get the information by themselves? They need to look at graphics *with* you while you show them, to get your message. Handouts are for later, *after* they leave, *after* you've explained and finished telling them, *not* during your presentation. Promise them handouts with all the data you're showing, at the end, for their personal use.

I know. People may want your graphics so they can write notes on them. Well, there's only just so much control you can have over your audience—especially the press. Try supplying pads, pencils, and pens for note-taking. Make your headings or slide numbers very visible on your slides and mention them so that when you do give them the handouts, they'll be able to match their notes to the corresponding slides they saw. If you *must* capitulate to handouts, do deliberate departures and speak *between* slides, to make them look at you from time to time.

EFFECTIVE USE OF COLOR

Color is everywhere. But it's not just arbitrarily decorative and nice to look at. Color is loaded with its own information and ability to evoke responses in us. Thus color can affect and change the messages we get from hard information. It is an invaluable and powerful source of visual communication.

But lots of business people don't realize that. They don't factor the effect of color into their design as they plan their visual aids. Color "colors" how otherwise cold, factual information is seen and responded to. It creates:

warmth and drama   **moods**

sharp contrasts   **interest**   **variety**

pleasure   **excitement**

positive or negative responses

What Black-and-White Graphics Do

Black words on a white background drain the ability of any message to affect us emotionally. Yet sheer habit has conditioned folks, as well as companies, to go on using black print on white slides rather than using colored backgrounds and words.

Black words on white paper are so commonplace (think books and newspapers) that they send no message at all. In dress and decor, black and white can be dramatic, but as words on a background, they transmit: "This is a fact." "Here's a list of numbers." "This is the subject." Nothing about whether that's good or bad, cautionary or surprising. Or that this is a serious or a dramatic or wonderful subject for us to consider. By the way, unless they're in unusual designs, black words on white graphics spell "out of date." When was the last time you saw a black-and-white movie? Or TV?

How Color Affects Us*

Since we make decisions viscerally and emotionally, even before they're made cerebrally, this is where color comes in.

---

* The following material is garnered from psychological research reported on the Internet and from the Luscher Color Test as well as research with various graphic designers.

Color sets a mood. It can cause your audiences to be more or less receptive or alert. It has been found that nurseries decorated in brilliant poster-color graphics that were changed frequently created much more alert babies while dull rooms with little or no color diversity created lethargy in infants. That's how intrinsic color is to our natures and our emotional responses.

Color affects us emotionally through the common associations we make from nature and from our own life experiences. Color in graphics has unique effects on your audience.

We all have our own color favorites: we express them in our choice of colors for cars, homes, and clothing. Yet, due to cultural conditioning, our responses to individual colors and combinations can be predicted and generalized. I'll just touch on a few basic concepts to show you how colors work to evoke emotional responses to your message.

Primary colors are red, blue, and yellow. In graphic terms, what evokes the strongest, most direct, and positive reactions are red, blue, yellow and green.

Red and blue are the most affirmative, bold, and appealing.

Red is a "hot" color. It's exciting and gets attention. It means energy, warmth, life, lushness, and passion. It's emotional and intense. But be aware of our culture's connotations: it also means *warning* and *danger* (stop signs, fire engines, hospital precaution symbols). It reminds us of blood. When used with numbers, it says loss and debit. Since it is such an "alarm" color and so dominant, it must be used cautiously and in small doses, for accent, not background.

Blue is calm and infinite. Think sky and water. It's also cool, a cerebral color, evoking peace and tranquillity, not attention-getting emotion. It can evoke solitude, wisdom, trust, and dedication. Blue is one of the most popular colors to Americans of both genders. Strong blue expresses stability and loyalty ("true blue"). People retain more information when it's written in blue ink.

It creates the opposite reaction from red. Relaxing the nervous system, blue can cause people to be more contemplative. Darker shades can feel cold and depressing. Think about your material: would it be served best by cool, calm blue? What other colors might you want for more emotional reactions and livelier, more provocative presentations?

Green is the strongest color in nature: like trees, grass, spring. It has many symbolic meanings: life, youth, renewal, hope, vigor. It's positive and much more emotionally evocative than blue, representing health, growth, a positive outlook.

Green is the easiest, most restful color on the eye. It makes things easier to read. It's also a calming, comforting color; hence "green rooms" where performers wait before going on stage or on TV. It's also used in hospitals, especially in doctors' uniforms.

Bottom line: Psychologists report that color impression can account for 60 percent of the acceptance or rejection of a product or service. And remember, since we do business globally, be especially aware of this not only here but in cultures other than our own. Be sure your graphics, both in color and design, suit the cultures they're intended for and really help get your message across.

MAKING YOUR MESSAGE VISUAL, VERBALLY

USING WORDS TO MAKE IMAGES

Verbal Images Bond You with Your Audience

You establish a common bond when you take people back to some universal experience, like childhood, family, school, fear, failing at something, the awkwardness of growing up, loving or hating something, and so on. Stressing the common humanity you all share *connects* you, no matter what the reality of your individual positions is. Going beyond the workplace into universal human experiences and laughing or reminiscing about them together is a great equalizer. It not only bonds the speaker with the audience; it speaks volumes about you, too.

Paint Recognizable Word Pictures

What you paint with your words needs to be something that is immediately clear and available to all. So know your audience well.

Understand what they would know from their own life or their work. Recognize their generational and gender differences, and how that could predict what your audience has experienced and knows about. What about their ethnic backgrounds? How would that change what you select to conjure up before them? What you're describing must be something *everyone* can relate to.

Share Some Sensory Experience

Go to the senses. Engage the right brain by calling forth a yummy taste or great smell, something tactile or visual, or a memorable, even annoying, sound.

Suppose you want to talk about folks expecting *instant gratification,* which may not happen with your report or suggested plan. Imagine how you can transport them with this:

Describe walking into that pizza joint on the corner and experiencing the smells of that tomato sauce and cheese as it melts in the oven. But then, remind them how you have to wait in line; how once you get the pizza home it's kinda cold; maybe you can't wait and sneak a bite right away; how that first bite tastes. (Did I just do it for you? Are you on your way to the phone right now to order some?)

See how it works? How you can get transported by your own senses with just my words? And this is all without actually experiencing me, live, delivering the words with the proper intonation, in hushed tone, with slow phrasing! Or even seeing my face, all lit up and smiling, as I build up those tastes and smells!

See how just words alone can create such a sensual experience in your own mind?

You can use this technique of appealing to the senses whenever you want to bring alive a process at work that everyone can imagine. How about this:

Suppose you need to launch a new project. Start talking about finally seeing the spring, with trees budding in that great shade of light apple green:

"Isn't it a relief to finally see daffodils and tulips coming up instead of the ice and slush of that long, gray winter? How it kind of gives you a lift, seeing all that new life and growth?" And then use those new-growth-and-energy pictures as a novel way to transition into feeling just right about launching this new project you're introducing.

Taking your audience out of the familiar presentation format into another type of experience is a *major* attention-getter. It not only surprises and involves your audience. It brands you with a special trademark, as a unique, memorable, and original kind of speaker.

Use Familiar Sayings, Analogies, and Quotations

Wrap up your ideas or make your point by using a line from another type of venue: a slogan, a motto, a folk saying, a little Shakespeare or Yeats, or even the Bible. Either it's familiar to everyone and rings a bell, or it explains your concept with a punch line, or it shows that *you* have another dimension than just a presenter of facts. And they make people picture ideas.

Using quotations gives weight plus wisdom to your message. Clever, pithy, thought-provoking messages from famous, sometimes surprising, people provokes a thoughtful "Hmm" in your listeners.

- "In the business world, the rearview mirror is always clearer than the windshield." —Warren Buffett
- "They always say time changes things, but you actually have to change them yourself" —Andy Warhol
- "Success isn't permanent, and failure isn't fatal." —Mike Ditka

Chapter 8, "How to Deliver Great Presentations," has more quotations and analogies on pages 239–240. Check them out for more ideas about using colorful speech to make your verbal messages more visual and more vivid.

Now let's move on to Chapter 7 to find out about designing smashing presentations.

7

HOW TO CREATE GREAT PRESENTATIONS

THE CHALLENGE

Do you know what the number one reason for personal panic and fear for the American public is?

Giving a speech!

Amazing, but true. Yes, there are some people who are born to speak, and even relish it! But for the vast majority of us, public speaking is terrifying. True for you?

Well, that's a problem that needs solving, because there's a basic truth we all must face, especially in this technological wonderworld:

If you're going to move ahead—to get noticed, to sell yourself or your ideas, skills, or product—there is *no substitute* for appearing in person and speaking.

Whether you're talking to an individual, a small group, or a large audience, no matter what level you're at, to get anywhere in your work or career, you've got to learn to stand up, take the floor, and *make others hear you.*

The next two chapters will lay down some basic principles and uncover some new secrets that will make you a great presenter, or, if you already are one, move you up a couple of notches.

You'll find out how to:

- Understand any audience and what they need from you
- Capture the attention of your sales-resistant workplace listeners and accomplish your goals
- Feel effective, comfortable, and even excited, about presenting
- Make audiences remember you as original, well-organized, entertaining, clear and compelling—a speaker they'd like to hear from again

Whew! Tall order? Well, I can't make you into a movie star, but I *do* promise to give you lots of information you haven't heard before in quite this way. And to include practical, how-to-say-and-do-it examples.

Let's start with *creating* a great speech. Then, in the next chapter, we'll talk about how to *deliver* one.

PLANNING YOUR PRESENTATION

GETTING STARTED

There you sit, scheduled to make a presentation. "Where to begin? What's my opening? What should I talk about, what leave out? What's the best way to tell it?"

Start with a basic question:

What is my message?
What am I actually trying to get across?

Find Your Theme

Planning begins with a theme around which you wrap your message. To find it, you need to get tough with yourself. Sort and edit till you arrive at a one-liner that states the absolute essence of what you mean to tell them.

Next, decide what explains and supports your theme best.

Boil that down to no more than two or three basic concepts: people can't absorb any more data at a single sitting.

Now put these ideas into three topic sentences. These form the bare-bones outline of your speech. That's the start.

An Easy Editing Process

Editing is easier when you think through to your end product: What do you want to *accomplish*? Here's a shortcut to finding that out.

Imagine yourself standing outside the meeting hall after your presentation, asking your audience members what they got out of your speech;

- "What did you learn?"
- "What do you now understand that you didn't before?"
- "What action will you now take, because you heard this presentation?"

Write down what you'd like the answers to be. These answers become the guide on which to build your speech. They will help you keep your material and your planning right on track.

Now you've figured out the three things you want your audience to know. But here's the next wrinkle: How do you make your audience *listen?*

So the next focus is—your listeners.

KNOW YOUR AUDIENCE!

No matter what you're hoping to say, you'll need to move your listeners from an inert, self-involved state to one of active interest in your subject.

This takes a major effort. You must capture and energize your audience to rise to your level of interest and involvement, and then get them to *agree* with you or even be willing to spend money or effort on your idea—two things no one gives away without a struggle.

Designing your presentation must always start with a sharp awareness of your audience. What do you need to know to tailor your speech to this *specific group* with its unique needs, goals, and interests? To motivate them to listen and help them understand?

What Makes Any Audience Listen

Remember the three magic components we discussed in Chapter 3 that motivate listeners, anytime, anywhere?

- **WHAT'S IN IT FOR ME?** Why should I listen?
- **WHO'S TELLING?** How the teller relates to the audience.
- **HOW DO YOU TELL IT?** The techniques and style of getting your message across. How you capture and intrigue them and support your information.

Since self-interest is the number one motivator, you have to get to know your audience well enough to figure out *what they care about.*

What you need is Dr. Hamlin's remedy—the *Know-Your-Audience Checklist*—to be used before you start. Like the Pre-Think Chart we discussed in Chapter 4, the Know-Your-Audience Checklist will give you specific information to help you target your speech to fit each specific audience.

THE KNOW-YOUR-AUDIENCE QUESTIONS: DON'T SPEECHIFY WITHOUT THEM!

Here's what you want to know:

1. Who's in your audience?
2. Why are they coming?
3. What do they already know about your subject?
4. What are their basic goals and needs?
5. What's a current problem that could affect them?

6. What do you have to offer them?

7. What could happen because of your speech?

What follows will show you what the answers can tell you and how to use that information. But first, I hear you asking: "How do I get the answers?"
Your potential listeners come in two flavors.

- An inside audience: Like your colleagues at work, with whom you share common experiences, problems, and goals. Get the demographics from your colleagues, staff, or potential participants or think it through yourself.

- An outside audience you don't know: Get information from the meeting planners. Then, based on what you learned, think the answers through.

Now let's discuss the questions. As you read them, keep thinking about how these answers could help you motivate your audience and build interest into your approach and the content of your speech.

QUESTION 1. WHO'S IN YOUR AUDIENCE?

Create a group portrait—a kind of demographic profile—of your potential listeners. Here's what you want to find out about who's coming to your presentation.

Generation and Gender

Both of these are important because you'll want to use examples, analogies, metaphors, common beliefs, and reference points that are most meaningful to this specific audience. Your audience is most often mixed, generationally and ethnically, but do find out if there is a predominance of one group over another.

This helps you think through your use of sports analogies, family issues, current expressions, technical lingo, and references to pop icons, and to decide which ones are appropriate. To capture the attention of a predominantly young female audience, for example, think of which of the above would be most apt, instantly recognizable, and useful?

I know these are only generalizations. But these broad-stroke pictures can start you zooming in on your audience.

Ethnic Differences

Think about the differing belief systems and moral positions of different ethnic groups. Coming in with a fairly radical new plan, for example, blissfully unaware of the conservative family and business traditions in a certain sector, is a one-way ticket to being turned down.

Socioeconomic Level

You can know a lot about your audience by merely thinking about their salary level, their position, and probable financial status, and therefore their priorities and experiences. Think how you'd approach the same subject if you were addressing an audience of suburban-dwelling executives with two kids or a group of affluent, single, hip, downtown loft-dwellers or an audience of just-starting-out apartment dwellers with two roommates each.

QUESTION 2. WHY ARE THEY COMING?

This will tell you what mood to expect and how much intrinsic curiosity or concentration there is, going in. Are they coming because

- They were told to attend by the boss?
- They're really interested and curious about the subject?
- You do what they do and they want to see how?
- It's the weekly staff meeting?
- It's the P.C. thing to do, to see and be seen?
- They need help with something and hope you'll give it?

It's really important to be prepared for the attitude your audience brings with them, and to plan to deal with that right at the beginning of your speech. I'll show you more about how to do that in the next chapter.

QUESTION 3. HOW MUCH DO THEY ALREADY KNOW ABOUT YOUR SUBJECT?

Informational and Professional Level

At what level do you begin talking to be most effective? How much lingo, or how many acronyms should you use? Are you:

- Sharing new data? What do you need to fill in first, before they'll understand?
- Introducing new methods? What methods do they know about and use now?
- Questioning an existing belief? Are they ready to absorb and adopt it?
- Talking to newcomers? Do they understand the whole business, its goals and pitfalls?
- Coming to solve a problem? Would they recognize it as such?

Knowing the professional level of your audience matters: Are they hands-on people, peers, management, staff, customers, or laypersons? How much do they already know, how deeply do they know it, and how do they use it? This tells you at what level to pitch your talk. You could really predict how a beginner, a midcareer person, a colleague, a customer, or a boss would probably feel about your subject and how it would affect them and how they could use it.

Educational Level

Your choice of words and metaphors and how deep you go is also determined by your audience's educational level. Talking over people's heads is bad enough, but being overly simplistic is the most patronizing and self-destructive thing you can do. It's guaranteed to turn people off and make them hostile. It also helps you judge how long you can talk and how detailed you can get.

For less-educated audiences, edit yourself until your material is very clear and relevant but never talk down to them. *Make* it simple; don't make them *feel* simple.

For highly trained techies, you can be technical and detailed. They like that. But don't overstay your welcome. They like you to get to the point, prove it, and then get out of there. Don't linger. Demos are great for them.

For educated generalists, a more practical, less theoretical approach is in order, with more time spent on *why* they should listen, what's in it for them, and how to implement your ideas.

QUESTION 4. WHAT ARE THEIR BASIC GOALS AND NEEDS?

What are your audience's goals and needs?

In their lives: Keeping their job, feeling more secure, getting ahead, making more money, getting some balance in their lives.

In their work: People *always* need to feel competent and able. Learning how to do something better, making the job easier, seeing how transferable their skills are, gaining some leadership and communication ideas, learning more about their industry, about global business—all of these would matter.

In listening to you: They're thinking: "How do you do what I do, only better?" "Know anything about what our business future looks like?" "What problems are we facing?" They need to feel that you genuinely want to give them something *useful,* on point about them, their needs, and their goals.

QUESTION 5. WHAT CURRENT PROBLEMS COULD AFFECT THEM?

Think about their work. What could their current problems be?

- Mergers and acquisitions: Will I keep my job?
- Outsourcing of jobs: How will that affect me?
- Global competition: Is it cutting into our markets?
- Company losses, company reorganization: Will I still have a job?
- Changes in their customer base: Will our product be obsolete?
- Technical improvements: Who's built a better mousetrap?

A cornerstone of your speech is getting immediate attention. Talking problems and possible solutions is an express line to that.

QUESTION 6. WHAT DO YOU HAVE TO OFFER THEM?

In strategizing any presentation, you already know all about what *you* want to accomplish. But in order to motivate your audience to pay attention, you must constantly ask yourself, "Why should *they listen?*"

Ask yourself if your material can give them:

- New perspectives about their jobs
- News about their clients and the industry
- Information about what's happening in your or their shop or globally
- A look at the future
- Reassurance about what they can count on or how well positioned they are for what's coming
- New skills and techniques to make their jobs better or easier
- Help on being more efficient and more effective

Also, do share some of your *personal* experience to make your content more credible and you more valuable as a speaker.

QUESTION 7. WHAT COULD HAPPEN BECAUSE OF YOUR SPEECH?

What could be the consequences of your speech? How will what you say affect—even trouble—your listeners?

- Are you the big boss?
- Are you someone they report to?
- Are you a colleague, giving a report that can affect their work?
- Are you an outside expert, a consultant, a critic?

Any of the above can set in motion all kinds of thoughts that could affect how they hear you. Your audience will either resist or attend accordingly.

If you recognize this in advance you can look for ways to disarm and reassure your audience first. The best way is to address their fears right up front, showing that you understand. Then mitigate their fears with some explanation of how you plan to handle that issue.

If you're the big boss, reassure them that this isn't just an order to be carried out at once; that you want their input and suggestions about it. Don't forget to handle the fear-of-you factor at the top, lightly, with a little humor and recognition.

If you're someone they report to, don't just tell them about a change. Tell them first about the support system you've set up to help get this new project under way.

If you're a colleague, tell them right off what you suppose they're feeling, since you are one of them. This not only closes the competitive chasm opened by your being singled out to give the report. It shows them that your report will take them into consideration.

If you're an outside expert, consultant, or critic, admit first that you know you're an outsider. This will disarm them and help to dilute their possible resistance to you as a hired gun. Explain that you share a common goal in wanting to solve a problem—that your proposed solution can only work with their help and involvement. Become their colleague, not their competitor or critic.

Here are the seven questions with succinct explanations to jog your memory. Use this checklist whenever you start planning a presentation. These questions will help you know how to motivate your listeners.

KNOW-YOUR-AUDIENCE SPEEDY CHECKLIST

1. **Who's coming?** Generation, gender, ethnic, and socio-economic groups

2. **Why are they coming?** Told to attend, interested, want to learn, know about you, politically correct, seeking help

3. **How much do they already know about your subject?** Information, educational, professional level; work experience

4. **What are their basic goals?** In their lives, their work, and listening to you

5. **What's a current problem?** A head-on key to motivating audiences

6. **What do you have to offer them?** Reassurance, new techniques, outside information, perspective

7. **What could happen because of your speech?** Consequences to them

Now you're tuned in to your audience's self-interest, the prime motivation for people listening.

Who's doing the telling is the second motivation.

WHO'S TELLING?

What is your role with your audience? Just because they're in their seats and you're on stage or in the front of the room talking, even with a very pertinent speech, doesn't yet mean they'll listen or even want to try. You need to think through your personal approach to the audience.

Once you understand who's in your audience, think: What role does your message cast you in? What role will you play with this specific group?

Teacher	Hard-seller
Guide	Supporter/fixer
Enlightener	Sermonizer
Analyst	Inspirer
Critic	Subordinate
Realist	Expert

Think through what attitude would be most conducive to getting people on your side. And be aware that your subject matter can unwittingly cast you in a negative role. Always remember that, no matter what role, what relationship to your audience you decide on, you must remain true to your own style. The *type of relationship* can change, but not the intrinsic you.

Let's discuss a few possible roles and their impact.

Enlightener and Guide

Suppose you need to teach and explain something. Recognize the effect of pulling people out of their comfortable niche. You could come through as a patronizing know-it-all, with curt explanations. Instead, find as nonthreatening and understanding an approach as possible.

A protective enlightener/guide attitude shrinks the distance between what *you* know and what they *don't*—and may not even *want*—to know. If you acknowledge how change makes people feel, and the need for support in making change, you will make your audience able to hear you.

Inspirer

An instant turnoff is telling people what they "should do." Instead, become an *inspirer*. Develop a willing audience by leading them to a place where they'll understand *why* to do something. Without knowing why they should care about it, they have no reason to move into action.

"Before I even ask you for more effort, let me tell you that I know I may have a hard job. It's not easy to ask you for more than you're presently giving. But here's what's happened and why I ask it." Adding that bit of understanding—*giving before you get*—positions you to move forward with your request.

Inspiration also comes from giving your audience some of your own passion, to overcome their initial resistance.

Hard-Nosed (Though Optimistic) Realist

Suppose you've got the job of giving bad news. Times are tough, problems have developed, what your audience expected to happen isn't going to. Being the bearer of bad tidings will surely cost you.

Start mitigating the impact by being optimistic:

"Listen, just like anybody, I hate being the bearer of bad news. However, that's hardly *all* I'm going to tell you. There is light at the end of the tunnel." That's you being the optimist.

Then start being the realist:

"Let's first get the bad news out on the table. Then we'll talk about what we can do about it." Tell them what went wrong, factually, clearly, simply. Don't minimize. Tell the truth about the situation and how it will affect them.

Now switch to the next gear—the constructive, active one:

"OK, that's where we are now. But let's move on to what we're going to *do*. We don't just lay back and take it. We *fight!*"

Describe your action plan, moving into the "us" gear. Talk with optimism about how strong you see the team. Lighten the atmosphere, reminding them of past successes and solutions that worked because you all pitched in. Stay true to being a hard-nosed realist by not promising the moon. But go to your action-based optimist to engage them, as you get specific about the job ahead.

"Together" is the key word. And notice that you've now moved into another role: *Inspirer!*

Subordinate?

Now that's a role no presenter should *ever* fall into! Yet, so many newly arrived or junior people on a staff do. When senior people are present, many folks unwittingly sound soft, slightly apologetic, and not very convinced or convincing. They murmur things like, "I don't know as much about the subject" or sound tentative in what they do know.

Well, here's some strong advice. If you present your material from a bench-warmer position, you lose the whole purpose of your presentation: to present your information *and* yourself! Be who you are: a young person on the rise—interested, hardworking, willing to learn more, wanting to share what you know so far about this specific subject. If it wasn't necessary or valuable for the group to know, the boss wouldn't have asked you to report.

And remember, *no one knows* how scared, nervous, and unsure you are. It doesn't show unless you let it overtake you. *Act the part* until you finally believe it. *Take your space* as an information-giver. Make eye contact, take a breath, and begin!

When you stand in front of a group, you take on the role of leader. Visually, you're at the head of the pack for that moment. Know it. Choose *how* you will lead. Find a role that gets your message across but also makes them want to follow you.

Well, we covered the first three steps in planning your presentation:

- What's your message?
- Who's your audience?
- Who's doing the telling?

Now, let's move on to designing and organizing the presentation itself. This becomes How You Tell It.

HOW TO TELL IT:
THE TECHNIQUES OF TELLING

Organization is the key to understanding talk.

ORGANIZING YOUR MESSAGE

The biggest problem people face in listening to someone's message is trying to follow the order in which it's given. Unfortunately, the *lack* of order is the norm, most often. And that's guaranteed to lose your audience.

The Basics

To understand and follow *anything*, especially new material told verbally, the brain demands

- **Logic**
- **Order**
- **Chronology**

The brain cannot absorb new information when . . .

- No basic subject matter or theme has been established
- It has no frame of reference for the material
- It is unable to find a familiar frequency on which to tune in
- It lacks enough information to move forward
- It hears unconnected material that is out of sequence or context

We, as listeners, are passive recipients of what you choose to tell and how you choose to tell it. So we need our presenters to *anticipate* what we need in order to understand and follow. Or else we get lost.

Now, in normal conversation, when we're confused, we say "Whoa. Whaddya mean?" or "Slow down. I don't get it."

But when you're speaking and I'm in an audience, there's no such opportunity! I can't ask till it's too late—and by that time it doesn't matter, since I've long since tuned out.

HOW TO CREATE ORDER IN YOUR MESSAGE

Remember the outline form that we learned in school? That's the heart of it and that's where we'll begin.

Start with Your Basic Theme

Crystallize your theme into one sentence. Make this the first thing your audience hears, as the orientation to your message.

This requires discipline! Separating the wheat from the chaff to give us the heart of your message takes some effort. This can help:

Imagine that you're a headline writer. What would the *New York Times* coverage of your speech choose to highlight as the key—the major, surprising, innovative, important-to-know essence of your message? When you zero in on this, you've discovered the theme of your presentation—and even its title!

Create Your Outline

Next, put your message into buckets, into broad headings—the A, B, and C of your outline form.

I'm going to use a somewhat different approach, one used by the most successful and efficient purveyor of ideas and messages in history—television. Here's how TV writers and producers go about organizing new information so they won't lose their audience. Just watch any television news story to see how this works.

LS/Med/CU

Now *this* heading surely got your attention!

"What in the world are those letters? What are you *talking* about, Sonya?" (See how the brain doesn't like to get confused?)

These are TV script terms. They stand for *Long Shot (LS), Medium Shot (Med), and Close-Up (CU)*. That means what you, the viewer, will see and hear first, second and third, as any story or hard information unfolds. Based on a solid psychological understanding of how the brain absorbs new ideas, these are the progressive steps used by the storyteller to draw you into the message. This process will give you an easy, visual, and memorable way to understand how to break down your material into a well-organized outline.

The best way to teach you this system of organizing material is to let you experience it *visually* (the number one way we learn things now). Imagine that I am telling you a story on TV about something that takes place in a room full of people.

As you "see" the story unfold, notice how the LS/Med/CU system draws you in, grounds you, and inexorably moves you to the next step.

LS/Long Shot

The Long Shot is what is seen and heard first. It's something that makes people stop their own thoughts and start paying attention to yours.

My Long Shot (sometimes called an Establishing Shot or a

Wide Shot) would show you a roomful of people sitting at tables and facing a lecturer up front. That shot takes the brain *less than 2 seconds* to establish. It says: "Oh! This story will deal with something in this room—people, tables, a classroom. Gotcha. What's next? Give me a few more details."

Starting at the true beginning, The Long Shot shows the broad picture, the basic theme, the whole before the parts. It should tell the basic parameters of what anyone's about to learn. It's your outline letter A.

Med/Medium Shot

The Medium Shot now comes into play. Having gotten the basic idea across to the audience and caught their attention, I zoom my camera in for a somewhat closer look—a Medium Shot—that gives more information.

We now see only about one-third of the people, closer, in more detail. We see only a few tables, with things like yellow pads, pens, and glasses of water on them. This move draws us further into the story.

We've been oriented by the Long Shot's giving us parameters and context, so the Medium Shot makes sense as it loses the generality and zooms in tighter on more specifics. We see how we got from there to here, so we get more focused and curious about what will happen next. Giving the information incrementally, moving logically from one big basic concept to several smaller ones, you've got our attention.

Keep imagining all this as a business message: how you need to start with a general overview, A, before you move into tighter, more specific buckets, B.

CU/Close-Up

The Close-Up is about the details, the nitty-gritty of the story. LS and Med have prepared the audience to now concentrate on the fine points of the story, as the camera zooms in tightly and the screen fills with what was written on the yellow pad on just one table.

Because I brought my audience along, orienting them every step of the way, I can now tighten the focus and make them begin to examine and be interested in the *details* of my story. They're intrigued to look at this written message on the pad now because they know exactly how they got there. And they're ready to see and hear even more details of my story.

See how this continues to translate into a method for telling your story or giving your message? The Close-Up, your C, is for the details. But the details would make no sense without the progression from Long Shot to Medium Shot to finally hitting the details of the Close-Up.

Whenever you get up to speak, always keep this progression in mind: go *from the general to the particular* through a series of steps. No leaps. We can't and won't follow you.

WHAT SPEAKERS DO MOST OFTEN THAT CONFUSES US

What if I just showed you a CU of a yellow pad as the start of my story? Your brain pipes up with "What's this about? What's it for? Do I care?" It's too illogical for the brain to process.

In the world of verbal presentations, one of the biggest mistakes people make is to jump into the complex details of an idea much too quickly, *before* they've given the audience a chance to get interested.

We respond sharply and stop listening when something is not presented chronologically or out of context. We reject

- Out-of-sync explanations: Med/CU/LS
- Starting with B. and no lead-in;
- Unrelated ideas suddenly brought in and not connected to any A, B, or C bucket

We become annoyed or threatened by not understanding and being made to feel stupid. We eventually become resentful, bored, even angry that you're wasting our time.

Result? We tune you out and there goes your message.

Bottom line: Learn to *lead* the brain, not confound it, with your message. Enable your audience to follow you, logically, step by step.

BUILDING A SPEECH OUTLINE THAT MAKES SENSE

Your Opening

This is first-impression time with your audience. They're a clean slate, curious and interested, ready for you to fill them in. Start by relating to them. (See the next chapter for how-to's about great openings.) Then give them your theme and why they need to know your message. Finally, present your agenda—your A, B, and C—what you're going to tell them and how you're going to tell it. Now go to your LS/Med/CU.

A. *(Your Long Shot)*

Establish the general nature of your talk with a few bullets to make it clear—the general parameters: the historical background of what you're going to say; some major reasons for you to say this now.

B. *(Your Medium Shot)*

Present the basic components of your idea; the buckets from which you'll explain it; the show-and-tell bullets to break down each bucket. Keep relating each one to them and why they need to know this.

C. *(Your Close-Ups)*

Now you can explain the details of your plan: how it works; examples; what it needs to make it happen; what will change; what's the process, detailing each point you've made and how it will work for them.

Do a Self-Test

To really nail the above progression, view your last presentation or explanation through the LS/Med/CU lens.

What would you have had to tell us first? What would come second and third? How did you lead us from the general idea to the finer details of how it really works and what would work for us?

THREE APPROACHES TO ORGANIZING MATERIAL

Though I've carefully explained the easiest, most basic system by which people understand, I always like to serve a varied meal, with choices. So let me add two other options that might be more dramatic but might also work for you.

Your approach must always come from your topic: form *follows* function. Think through which approach would accomplish the most for you and what effect you want to create. Here are three routes you can travel.

Starting with the Whole

This is classic LS/Med/CU: Peeling back the layers makes us more curious about what's coming and what we'll find. The effect? Picture opening a package. First, you see the address and read the card. Then, you remove the wrapping, open the box, unfold the tissue. Doesn't your interest rise, the closer you get to the core?

Giving your message this way is like giving a gift to the audience. You want them to feel the enjoyment of deepening discovery and understanding, and the satisfaction of having finally received it.

Starting with the End Product, a Detail, or a Part

Think back to the TV story I just told you as my LS/Med/CU example, where the final Close-Up is the yellow pad with writing on it. In the movies, *opening* with a Close-Up of that yellow pad and what was written on it could be a great starting device. It would get you really curious just because it's illogical. You'd wonder what's going on and what will happen next.

The suspense would build as the camera pulled back, revealing a hand, lying limply along the edge of the table, the pen fallen beside it. Pulling back and down still farther (we're moving *backward* into a Medium Shot!) you'd discover a high-heeled shiny boot extended on a marble floor. Continuing the pullback and widening the shot, you'd see a body slumped over the desk. *That's* when you'd finally get your Long Shot of the whole room. the roaring fireplace, the . . .

Well, that's the movies. But in a speech?

This "illogical" process of going from Close-Up backward to Long Shot also works. It makes for impact and originality. By focusing on your CU end product first, you create a little attention-getting surprise. Then you start your audience working backward toward your LS theme, curious to find out what will be revealed and how that would finally relate to them.

This surely is another way to organize material. But when to use it depends on the effect you want to create *and* your subject matter. Close-Up first makes the focus on the final product much hotter and us more curious because the beginning is so puzzling. You do need to get to the point fairly quickly and to keep teasing with where you're taking us, why your audience needs to know all this, and how it can use the end product.

Caution: This approach is quite playful: "Just stick with me and we'll see where we're going." "Still confused? What about this." Know yourself. Can you do that? Would you be comfortable building a little drama and suspense for your audience? If it's not you, don't. . . .

Cut Right Through to the Heart of the Matter

Getting right to the core issue in one shot—the "pronouncement" approach—is also a workable system, understandable and attention-getting. It, too, can startle us and grab our attention. It tells us the bottom line right at the beginning.

Knowing that we've just gotten the major juice right up front, we're intrigued to stay tuned and get more information. This cut-to-the-chase approach, putting the major points on the table right away, is quite powerful. When to use it?

- For shock value, to get a jaded audience's immediate attention
- When you want to make a major, definitive statement about a dramatic issue
- To start us on what can be a tough journey by giving us the basic reason for it first

Choose this approach judiciously. It better be big and important. Don't yell when a lower voice would do.

Here's one more approach to organizing your material:

DON'T JUST TELL ME—SHOW ME

"Here she goes again! Nag, nag, nag!"

You're right. Here's why: You may *try* taking your speech into the perilous territory of talk-talk, assuming, and hoping, that your audience will stay tuned. But take it from me—a seasoned veteran in the fight for audience attention and understanding—you won't make it.

So—always:

- Use the *visual* to explain the *cerebral*.
- Show your points individually; continue adding visually for impact.
- Graphically support facts, figures, lists, numbers, diagrams.
- Show comparisons, connections between ideas, lists of what's needed to succeed.
- Prove your points objectively with backup data.
- Stimulate to create a proactive audience—get them to see, not just to listen.

You've analyzed, planned, and made lots of notes. Now it's time to create some written text; to put down what you're going to say and how you'll get from point to point. But don't just move into your usual data-writing mode. Read on for some perspective and techniques that may surprise you.

BEST WAYS TO LAY OUT YOUR PRESENTATION ON A PAGE

WHY NOTES MATTER

The way you put your message on a page makes a *tremendous* difference in how you present it.

"Wait a minute," you're saying. "How my notes are written affects my delivery? C'mon."

Yup. Here's why. Your notes are your road map, the blueprint for your speech. How you write them is how they'll guide you, alert you, and help you deliver all you planned to say—or not!

Your notes should be a catalyst. For greatest meaning and impact, they should clarify your message for you *in advance*, to help you know *how* to say what you mean, instead of just repeating what's on your page. So how you lay out your notes requires thought and some special techniques.

You say you don't use notes? You like to write out your whole speech so you say exactly what you mean to say?

Well, here's what happens to you, *and* to your audience, when you deliver written speeches instead of using outline notes.

WRITTEN SPEECHES VS. ORAL PRESENTATIONS

Most people want to write down their whole speech so they say it straight, without faltering or looking for a word. This handles their anxiety, giving them something solid and predictable that they've practiced.

Wrong!

Presenting an already written speech is *very* different from, and has nothing to do with, an *oral presentation* from written notes. Speaking directly to your audience requires that you be spontaneous, in the moment. Rereading a practiced, written speech is simply reciting something you gave juice to when you first wrote it.

Oral communication must always feel like—and really be—a *live dialogue* between you and your audience. It's personal and immediate. You're talking to them, right then and there, in this unique moment.

Written speeches don't do that.

The Written vs. the Spoken Word

Just think about the basic intention of writing.

Words on a page are written for an audience you imagine *now* but who will process them *later*. Written words—books, articles, news—are meant to be sent; meant to be *read* by others, not *said* to them by you. Written words alone must give your message. And they require independence and time: a solo reader who'll process the words alone and take his or her own time to read, reread, and understand what was said. The reader is in total control, since the words just stay there on the page.

Now this requires that written words be so explicit and evocative that they alone can serve to make someone understand the heart and soul of what you mean. Since you're not there when they're read, your written words become your voice, the *substitute* for you, talking.

But that's not how your audience will *receive* a written speech! You're not sending it to them for later reading. You're saying it *at the same time they hear it!*

And when you edit it, you're judging your words without the most important ingredient—your live presentation! Oral communication does not rely on words alone. You bring a whole new coterie of communication skills to an oral presentation!

Your physical presence and body language, pace of delivery, facial expression, tone of voice, inflection, phrasing, pauses, energy level, emotional nuances—all of these are now, truly, your voice. Unlike written communication, dependent only on words, oral communication depends only partly on words and mostly on the speaker.

Therefore how you critique and edit your speech is deeply flawed. You *read* it, you don't *hear* it being said. It's apples-and-oranges time.

The Effects of Written Speeches on the Audience

Marching up, written speech in hand, and plunking it down on the lectern to read to your audience brings forth an inaudible, but palpable, groan. You know. You've looked at such a sheaf of papers yourself and worried about how long it could take, right?

The written speech engenders conditioned negative reflexes, born of all the boring, pedantic, sermonizing speeches you've ever heard.

- They'll expect it's going to be abstract, distant, and impersonal, not unique. Most written speeches have *no* personal touches or identifying marks of the speaker, no departures, colloquialisms, even momentary pauses or rephrasings.
- People get turned off because your natural, conversational style becomes more formal, remote, and stilted when you read.
- If it's an audience you know, they'll see the contrast between how you usually talk and behave and this very different image.

The Effects of Written Speeches on the Speaker

Energy Level

Your stimulus comes from your paper, *not* your audience. The best of your energy was left behind in your office or workspace where you actively imagined communicating with your audience.

Standing before your audience, saying it *again*, for the tenth time (because, of course, you practiced your head off!), you give your audience a pale copy of your enthusiasm for your subject.

Eye Contact

You can't make eye contact with your audience. Your eyes are driven down to *read*, left to right, not to look up and connect with them. You can't judge if they're getting your message or getting bored. You're too busy reading. . . .

Security

"But I *need* to write it out! I feel more secure that way!" I understand. But the fact is, reading creates a *bigger* worry. You become very dependent on the paper.

What if you lose your place? You may even end up reading something you've already just said! Since your active, creative mind is mainly turned off when you're rote-reading, ad-lib departures are forbidden. They create a real problem when you try to get back to the printed page.

Oral Speeches from Notes

Energy Level

Working from your notes *and* the audience, not your pre-digested printed word, makes you present your material as *new*. Notes give you only the *essence* of your message and the direction you're going, which keeps you working to explain and persuade, with energy and commitment.

Eye Contact

Abbreviated short-form notes make you free to look down, check your next bulleted concept, and then talk directly to your audience. Your notes become a springboard, as you pop a look-down and then pop up to look at the people. You can now think about increasing the pace or explaining some more as you see their response. Eye contact is a catalyst, a continual reminder of why you're saying all this and who you want to get your message. Most of all, from the audience's point of view, you are there, with them.

Security

When you improvise from an outline, it *adds* security because your brain is alive right then, thinking of what you're saying and where you're going. Back-tracking, rerouting, changing your mind, or explaining something else are all easy! Your brain is immersed in what you're saying, ready to move, with notes to guide you.

You can't make a mistake because the audience has never heard your speech before! You're not reciting the Pledge of Allegiance where everyone can spot mistakes. You can speak freely, change your mind, miss something, and still recover, taking us along. We'll never know! It's your speech, being made up at the time you tell it.

Bottom line: Don't write out your speech, word for word!

For Addicted Need-My-Whole-Speech Writers

I know, I know. I hear you saying "Yeah—natural, extemporaneous. And what about fumbling and rambling and not very articulate? And *scared!*"

Well, that comes from not being clear about where you're going, and what you *really* want and need to say. It comes from not being at one with the *organization* of your speech, the order in which you'll tell your ideas.

That's why the outline and the pre-thinking that goes into it are your solution. Not the security blanket of a rigid written speech.

Freedom is what you need, freedom to let your good mind, the one who thought up the ideas in the first place, tell others what it knows. Seeing each set of ideas you wish to talk about, and the key words that signify the essence of each section, is really all you need. Yes, *you do know what you know.* You just imagine and then convince yourself that you'll fail, so you'll need that written security blanket.

Let go! Come through and be yourself! Let me show you how to write your notes out so they'll truly help support and lead you.

WRITING USABLE SPEECH NOTES
AND OUTLINES

To feel both supported and free, to be able to both think *and* talk, you must create notes that

- Are immediately understandable
- Are written in such a way that the order of where you're

going, as well as where you are *right now,* is instantly clear
to you

- Feed you information with short words that represent
  actions or facts or are catalysts for ideas
- Signal the organization of your speech: the headings, the
  bullets that explain, the change of subject
- Show you *in advance* the coming key pronouncements
  and thought-provoking phrases
- Tell you, visually, how you wish to deliver each concept
  and segment: where to slow down, when to shift gears to
  another emotional level

Of course, we all know how to write notes. But here's a little
snag. Notes we're used to taking in class or at meetings are all
written in a kind of shorthand, meant to be read and deciphered
later. But when you're *speaking,* you need your notes to be clear
at once, so you can read and translate them instantly into talking
points. They must be able to launch you—*"boing"*—toward your
audience and your explanations.

Here's a new set of concepts about how to make your notes
support you *visually.*

THE BASIC PROCESS

To Write or to Type

I always write my notes out by hand. The act of making the
letters myself makes them more personal and familiar than the
impersonal look of typed words. It's so effective for me that,
because I've written the notes, looked at and thought about
them, I hardly need to look at them at all when I speak. They
become so imprinted in my memory that I can "see" them in my
mind's eye because of how I laid them out.

What works for you? Do you remember better with writing or
typing? Try it out. Which is more natural and comfortable? As
you read what follows, imagine these ideas using *your* preferred
mode for writing.

How to Abbreviate Your Notes and Keep Eye Contact

The biggest mistake people make when writing notes is that they *write too much*! Start with a good old outline form—your A, B, and C headings. Put in two- or three-word descriptions to tell you what you'll be talking about. These are only catalysts to *remind* you about a talking point or section, *not* to spell it all out.

To give you a graphic description, here are two examples— what people *usually* do and what *I'm* suggesting you do.

Imagine this is a section of a speech about bringing in a new way of doing things. After reminding the listeners how we always did the process—**A. The Old Way;** and why it's outmoded or impractical now, **B. Why Change?**—the speaker goes to **C. What's the New Plan?**

Using just section C, let's see Versions 1 and 2 to compare processes.

Version 1: Here's the way lots of people would write their notes.

C. *What Is the New Plan?*

- What major differences will there be in how we do our work now?
- How will it be in the future with this new plan?
- What will be added or removed from the way we work now?
- What kind of budget do we have; what will it provide for?
- What kinds of training and support systems will we create for this?

Version 2: Much more useful *catalytic* notes:

C. *New Plan*

- Major diff. w/ old
- Future changes
- New additions/subtractions

- Budget; costs, coverage
- Training/support program

Compare the two:

See what all that wordiness in Version 1 makes you do? You have to read the *whole sentence* to see what you should talk about! But where are the key words that get you going? You're too busy reading to check on what's next and build a transition. You don't need all those words!

Now check out Version 2. See how the catalyst-words, using no prepositions or useless words, *instantly* tell you what you need to talk about. They easily show you where you're going. The short phrases set you off talking with assurance and security.

You're so much more comfortable and effective as a speaker when each word is a trigger; you see the word and know what to talk about. Your bullets signify something you *already know* (it *is* your report!).

For performance enhancement and continual eye contact, use the vertical process: look down, get the idea, look up to your audience and keep talking. Don't use the horizontal read-a-sentence method. . . .

Create Symbols for Style and Delivery Cues in Your Notes

Your outline should also support you and help remind you *in advance* how to deliver your message. It should tell you when to move your pacing up or down or pause to give your audience a chance to absorb a provocative or challenging idea. Even to alert you to change your style from serious to more informal or personal.

To demonstrate all this, I'll make an outline of the *whole* speech I briefly described above, about bringing in a new way of doing things. I'll add the **A. The Old Way** and **B. Why Change?** to the **C. What's the New Plan?** that I just showed you. This will illustrate what I mean about making your notes tighter as well as being catalysts for delivery styles. Notice that, although you don't know the subject at all, you can easily follow the content just from this abbreviated notes style.

A. THE OLD WAY *(describe)*

- Used XYZ products
- Comfortable; familiar
- Training module worked

B. WHY CHANGE??? *(alert them!)*

- Delivery system—s l o w *(time line on easel)*
- Industry standards *(read* Fortune *quote)*
- Cheaper Systems *(compare costs, on slide)*
- Customer complaints! *(slides with letters; video clips)*

(Pause, make eye contact)

WE ARE WAY BEHIND!!!

C. WHAT'S NEEDED NOW?

A C T I O N ! (strong!)

(lighter, conversational approach)

I understand:

- Change is hard
- Used to old ways; Jim's morning rounds
- Concern re training; time? New skills?
- *(upbeat!)* How we'll do it. We'll support you!

See how all these visual images and notes direct you to different kinds of delivery?

To present well, you need to know *how* to say what's coming next, not just to say things and *then* realize that was an important thing you wanted people to think about. You need to know where your summation comes, or that in the next section you need to shift gears and change the mood from a cool, logical description of facts to a more personal approach, with a story.

OK, now you're launched. Next step? The delivery itself.

• What are the best personal performance techniques for presenting and explaining what you want to say?

• How do you make yourself believable, persuasive, interesting, and memorable?

• How and where do you build in the fireworks? The surprises? The personal touches? The humor?

Thought you'd never ask . . .

On to Chapter 8 to complete the process of making you a dynamite speaker/presenter/explainer/persuader!

HOW TO DELIVER GREAT PRESENTATIONS

This chapter is for everyone who works, especially those who have Stage Fright.

Whether you're selling, explaining something to three people in your shop, giving a report at a meeting of your colleagues, alerting the boss to a problem, or delivering a major address to a large audience, the process of making a presentation is the same. It involves:

- Standing up and taking the floor
- Explaining something you know, want, need, and care about
- Understanding what it takes to hold anyone's attention
- Using words to make others listen to and understand you
- Making your presentation unique to you, creative, personal, and memorable
- Learning to feel good doing it

So we're off to accomplish all this. *And* to solving your stage fright, should that attack you.

THE TECHNIQUES

Any speech should be divided into three basic sections:

OPENINGS

CONTENT

CLOSINGS

OPENINGS

Since the job is to get your audience interested right from the git-go, the opening is crucial. It has to answer three questions:

1. Who Are You? What persona do they see? Relate to your audience and make a positive first impression. Absolutely crucial.

2. Why Should They Listen? What's in it for them if they *do* pay attention? How does your speech affect them and their lives?

3. What Will They Hear? What's the agenda? What will you cover that they'd want to know or stick around to find out?

WHO ARE YOU?

First Impressions

The first thing the audience wants to know when they meet you is—the first thing *you* want to know when *you* meet a stranger. "Who is this? How do I feel about him or her so far?" From the moment we meet someone, we're unconsciously evaluating and deciding whether to go further or not. And *that* depends on how interested we've gotten and how much common ground we've found. If we're not captured by *something* in those first moments, it's "Excuse me, I see a friend . . ."

True, these are snap judgments. But how do we make them? Where do these first impressions come from?

Think about what we do when we're introduced to someone at a cocktail party, at work, or at the corner Starbucks.

- First, we smile: We make eye contact, appraise physical appearance, get our first gut reaction. (What do *you* notice first? What turns you on or off at the start?)
- Next, we shake hands. A shortcut to experiencing each other *sensually.* Not just a formality, it's also an outreach, an effort to connect a little. All *nonverbal* signals so far . . .
- Then, we talk. Pleasantries, non sequiturs, nothing substantive. What "talks" to us is tone of voice, pronunciation, dialect, choice of words, sense of humor. We notice shyness in hesitant speech, energy in an easy delivery—information derived through *sensory impressions.*
- What do we say? A little wisecrack, a cool expression, a shorthand phrase—anything that shows our charm and personality. Putting out *something* to relate, connect, or impress.

And that's only in the first 15 or 20 seconds!

Group First Impressions

How does this relate to you standing in front of an audience, giving a presentation?

All this is also happening at the beginning of your speech!

Your *audience* is taking your measure—deciding who you are, and how willing they are to go further, and answering that big question that motivates listening: Who's Telling?

As they watch you relate to them, they're deciding if they want to listen to you.

But here's the rub: you don't get a one-on-one intro and some personal exchange with each member of the audience. *You* have to do all the work. For them, it's a one-way test. And does it matter!

Why? Because this impression of you affects how they meet and greet your mind and your message! It's a tough, tricky exercise—making a great first impression on an audience. . . .

How We Make First Impressions

First impressions are:

- 55% *nonverbal communication* (body language, gesture, posture)
- 38% tone of voice
- 7% words

What? Here you've spent all your time worrying about your message and what you're going to say—and your audience is noticing some very different things? Here's why:

Body Language

- **Body language is spontaneous** and unconscious and it tells *the truth*. Words, which are deliberate and edited, may not. There's your 55% vs. 7%.

- **Because body language is unconscious,** it's genuine. You have *no idea* what you're doing, and therefore telling, us. (Freeze right now and discover what you're doing: What's your sitting posture? Where are your hands? neck? feet? What's your facial expression? What mood would they convey? And did you know you were doing any of that? See what I mean—it's unconscious—but eloquent and truly you.)

- **What you're *saying* and what we see you *doing*** had better match if we are to believe it!

Tone of Voice

Thirty-eight percent of any first impression comes from tone of voice? Think about how quickly you knew you were in trouble when Mom or Dad just called your name! Doesn't someone's tone of voice tell you who's nervous or evasive and who feels on really solid ground when they start to talk?

Who Are You to Them?

You also need to think about what role your message thrusts you into and how you should relate to your discerning audience. Your body language and tone of voice will surely get that message across to your audience, anyway, so you better know beforehand.

Circumstance and subject matter can force you into some kind of role with your audience. Depending on whether you address them as a teacher or guide, critic or fixer, hard-seller or apologetic subordinate, you totally change how they'll receive you and your message.

But right here I have to stop and acknowledge a major issue:

Stage Fright!

Everything I've been telling you so far about how to deliver a presentation could already be getting drowned out by *anxiety*. Folks with stage fright feel it just *contemplating* standing in front of an audience and giving a speech!

So let me take care of that before we go any further. I want *everyone* on board, feeling comfortable and able to absorb the upcoming ideas without any interference.

All you non-sufferers: Skip to "Good Getting-to-Know-You Openings," page 224.

All you stage-frightened: Stay right here with me. We're going to lick this sucker!

STAGE FRIGHT

What's It About, Really?

Stage fright is based on a *myth:* Somewhere in the world there's a speaker who could deliver your speech with a perfect "10." You become obsessed with measuring yourself against that *mythical* speaker and that perfect "10," thinking about how far below that "10" you'll fall. This gives birth to an enormous case of anxiety! Performers call it "flop sweat." Lay people say "I *hate* speaking in public!" And they build a great big roadblock to letting themselves give the best speech they can.

All the "stage-frightened" can think about is: "How will I look?" "What if I lose my place?" "My boss (colleagues, clients) will think it's dumb (ill-conceived, confusing, dry), and that I am, too." Aaargh!

Add to that "My mother (father, teacher) always said I mumbled," "I just don't like making a show of myself," and you have the full complement of stage fright.

And what's it all about? Me Me Me—the speaker—instead of You You You—the people being spoken to!

Where Does It Come From?

- **Early imprinting:** what your family criticized in you plus your siblings' skills

- **Adolescence:** the real killer to self-confidence; the origin of our "unacceptable" message as we measure our potential against our peers. And find ourselves wanting . . .

- **Perfectionism:** our unrealistic demands on ourselves and our mistaken notions about others' competence and talent

Plus a few more adult insecurities about how smart, competent, or people-skilled you think you are (or aren't).

Given these ever-present voices in our heads, it's little wonder that so many people get freaked out with being on display in public. Or that they imagine their audience is full of critics who'll surely see every flaw they've been suffering with.

The Steps to a Cure

I know. Confronting your anxiety and overcoming it is really tough. But here are some steps that can help you solve this problem. Try them:

1. *Accept it.*

Admit your stage fright to yourself. And stop beating up on yourself with "Now stop it! Don't be nervous! You're a grown-up!"

The more you fight it, the more energy you give it, the more it'll dominate your thoughts!

Instead, say to yourself, "Wow, am I nervous! But that's OK! Most everyone gets that way. I'll just be nervous and now focus on my task."

2. *There is no 10!*

Remind yourself that there *cannot* be a perfect "10" in a speech. Perfection means there is a hard and fast formula that can be duplicated and would *always* give a "10" result. Impossible!

The time of day, the weather, your hunger or fatigue, noise outside, what just happened at work—all these would have to be *exactly the same each time*. To achieve an authentic, scientifically predictable "10," all circumstances would have to be repeatable each time, not only for *you* but also for all *audience members*. Impossible!

3. *There are many great ways to give the same speech.*

Using many *different* approaches and many styles, in front of many *different* audiences, the same subject matter could garner a "10" in *any* of them. This means that yours is just *one* way of giving a great speech. Successful speech making is not about pass-fail! It's all about how *effective* you can be in getting your message across. *That* must become your new obsession—*what's the best way for you to present your message?*

4. *Focus on your mission.*

Get totally involved in the best way to get your message across! Your mission is your message, *not* the grade your performance will get or what others will think of you. **Giving your audience a rewarding experience is what makes a speech great** . . . Speech making is all about your audience—*not you!* Picture your audience. Then commit to: "What will get them to listen?" "How can I help them understand?" "What can prove my point?" Start concentrating on "What am I trying to do for, and with, *them*? What do I want *them* to know and why?" You're the messenger, not the message!

Bottom line: look at the right goal. The more involved and excited about your task you are, the more you'll forget to be afraid. And the more successful you'll be in capturing your audience. And because you'll be yourself, focusing outwardly—on them—guess where the stage fright goes? Bye-bye.

5. *Don't forget: preparation is another antidote.*

Just winging it or writing notes the night before is guaranteed to give you the shakes at performance time. *Especially* if you're a stage-fright kind of person, getting solidly prepared can make all the difference.

We've just come from Chapter 6, where we discussed in detail how to prepare your speech. Thinking through your audience, your message, and your notes really helps with stage fright, too. The more confident you get with what you want to say and how you're going to show-and-tell it, the less your anxiety has a chance to grow.

6. *SHOW TIME! Getting yourself started talking.*

You get up and walk toward center stage and suddenly—there you are! You now need to get up to speed *all at once!* To charge up those adrenal glands, get your mind organized and going, and, most of all, kick that self-confidence up a few notches. Try this to help get you started.

While you're sitting and waiting to be introduced or called on, psych yourself up:

- "I know I'm nervous, but that's OK. They don't know, so I can fake it. Just stand up and look cool. No one can see inside you."
- "I did my work and I *do* know what I'm talking about. Just need to get rolling and it'll be all right."
- "Now, what do I want to accomplish with this speech? What are the three major facts and issues I want them to know?"
- "Who am I to them? Their guide, analyst, leader, colleague, voice of reason?"

- "They're people like me; they need/want/would like this material. Just stand up and give it—now!"

The amazing thing is, it works! This inner talk helps you focus on the task ahead, and banishes a lot of that free-floating anxiety.

7. *Energize yourself.*
Here are some other things you can do.

- Sit still and do energy-breathing exercises. Take some deep, relaxing breaths (no heaving and sighing). You've seen pitchers on the mound do it with one big breath. As you breathe out, let all the muscles go. Do it several times.
- Another way: take five or six short breaths in and then let the breath out slowly, relaxing the body as you do.
- Hold on to your clasped hands and squeeze tight, or squeeze the chair arm or press your feet down really hard. No one can see you do this and it does thrust you into a higher level of energy all at once.

Experiment with these. Get physically pumped for the task ahead, integrating all your strengths into doing the one job. See which one suits you.

My Big Send-off to You

Now that you've finally understood what lights the stage-fright fire, you're really on the road. The above techniques may not put it all out, but learning to live with some nervousness and to give your speech anyway is the cure. And you know what? Nervousness isn't all bad! A moderate, nonparalyzing amount really improves people's performance!

OK, we're all caught up. Everyone's on board. Let's discover some great ways to open a speech. What can you do to win your audience over right at the start? To make that great first impression and help them get to know you?

GOOD GETTING-TO-KNOW-YOU OPENINGS

Relating to your audience means:

- Finding a common meeting ground
- Connecting personally before launching into your subject
- Emphasizing what you have in common before you go into your differences in knowledge and position

Now what could you actually say to start making this happen?

First Words

How do you feel about saying, right after the introduction, "Thank you very much. That reminds me of a story. . . ."

Why do you think people do that? Because they think they need a gimmick to start reaching their audience.

And the story they tell? Either it's funny, and that's the last funny thing we'll hear from the speaker for the rest of the speech, or the story is off the wall and has nothing to do with the substance of the speech. In either case, it does nothing for *you*.

So now you know what you *won't* do at the start.

Some Possible Approaches

Think about what you have in common with your audience. *That's* where the real contact and relating takes place first.

The best approach is a personal, informal one, bridging the space that separates you from your audience physically and symbolically. How about:

"You know, preparing for this speech, I sat imagining all of you, and how many such audiences *I've* sat in, wondering, 'Will this be something of value or will it be the usual boring stuff, wasting my time and delaying my lunch?' So I know I have a real challenge—

to be useful and practical for you, energetic and not too *dull.*"
What does this accomplish?

- It makes you *one of us,* not someone apart. "Hmmm. Sounds like a pretty real person."
- It has warmth and humor and gets a genuine laugh. "This could be fun, not boring."
- It shows awareness of us. "Made with me in mind! Could be something I can use."
- It suggests you're pretty secure. People don't make fun of themselves in public unless they know that what they're about to do is pretty good and substantive.

If you need to talk about change, a new product, or something they need to learn, try starting with this:

"I have to tell you a little personal story. My daughter just entered middle school yesterday. The first kid. What a twinge! Seeing how fast time passes and how incredibly things change. Happen to any of you? Well, time sure has changed our business, hasn't it? Remember when we all started using *X*? Come with me into the future while I show you the newest form of *X—plus Y!* We'll all be using it before you know it!"

This is a more personal, less hard-sell approach that first addresses people's *attitude* toward change before it shows you how and what.

"Up Close and Personal" Style

Television has taught us that communicating now is more conversational and relaxed. Clothing styles in the workplace are more informal now, and so are presentations. A distant, formal approach is passé. Sure, you may wear a necktie to a speech, but that shouldn't prevent you from relating personally to your audience—*especially* in your openings.

Just remember: you're trying to get the audience to warm up to you before you begin your message. This is at the heart of opening your speech well and capturing your audience.

Getting Personal May Be Hard for Some

Being informal and easygoing is great, but may not be for everyone. If your father was very formal and never loosened his tie at dinner, or your mother drummed the old "polite and lady-like" behavior into you, this approach may be hard for you to try. But do it if you can. It's a great icebreaker.

Here are some more possibilities, running the gamut from slightly informal yet professional to a slightly more formal approach. It's up to you to customize them to reflect who you are and what fits the occasion.

But I must warn you, formal is much less in keeping with today's times and styles.

Try reaching into these pockets to find your own great openings:

More Examples of Openings

If it's an audience you know, or an industry you've been in for a while, how about: "Like you, I've been in widgets a long time—maybe not as long as Mike Young over there—but I sure know what you deal with." A comradely approach, with some audience applause for Mike, helps.

How about a little self-deprecating humor? "Who wants to hear a report about bad economic news? And here I am, to open that up again. But not to rub your nose in it. Rather, to explore some ways to make it better." At least you're aware of their discomfort. You're bringing some positive perspective.

Shared Goals? "Jack asked me to give a report about how the new system is working. Like everyone, I'd like to tell you it's great. But since I'm on the floor every day, and you really want to know the truth, my report's going to be mixed. With some great suggestions from the folks I work with." Credible, honest, and purposeful; up front with the audience, with the promise of an upbeat message at the end.

How about the weather on that day and what it took for them—and you—to get there? Snow? Rain? Traffic? Sweltering heat? Try "Maybe we should pack this in and all go swimming." The effect? They think, "Someone with a little humor—understands about goofing off!" Making the first moments a simple, common shared experience.

Is it a conference? What has gone before? "Knowing how many speakers you've heard, what a challenge for me!" Or "Here I stand, the only obstacle between you and lunch" (or "your golf game" or "the cocktail hour"). The effect? They think you're a realist, not an egotist, and you also know how they feel, making your material more credible and probably more succint.

First time in their city? Tell something about what you've seen, what you enjoyed, how much you always wanted to know more about that part of the West. People always love to hear good things about their town.

Was this once your hometown? Ever go to school or live here? Do a little reminiscing about the local high school or things you remember. Great bonding technique.

A Personal Note from Me to You

I want you to notice something: See how many pages I took to explain how to let your audience know who you are.

I heard your possible concerns about revealing your nonbusiness, *human* side: "That's unprofessional." "How could I pull that off?" That's why I took lots of time.

From all my years of experience, I know how hard it is for most people to get informal and personal in a formal situation. We're naturally reluctant to reveal ourselves, especially in public. It's scary for some, strange and unfamiliar for others.

The generational differences are beginning to break this down, but Boomers did not see much informality in their leaders. Therefore, finding a professional-plus-personal model to go by is difficult. I'll just invoke President Clinton's style as a good model to follow. He was enormously successful at speaking of serious matters yet retaining his informal style.

Women do this more easily than men. They are more natural conversationalists, and more accustomed to making personal relationships with friends and colleagues than men are. But for women, the challenge is to be seen as substantive and informed—

a serious major player. Don't think the informal approach is too lightweight. People welcome and prefer listening to an easy style while you say important things.

No matter what, I can't let you off the hook! *You need to relate to your audience personally, as you, first,* before you are Mr. or Ms. Smart Professional. *That's* where you get your audience. *That's* their first impression.

And *that's* why I took so much time to explain, showing you explicit examples to help you find your own way to do it.

The next two aspects of Openings—motivating your audience and outlining the "Agenda"—are left-brained, factual, and logical. They're more *impersonal* and therefore easier to do.

WHY SHOULD THEY LISTEN?

To set the tone for the rest of your speech, this is the time for your Long Shot. Here's where you establish your theme: what you're going to talk about and how your speech will connect with some major issues in their lives and work.

This is the time to use what the television industry calls a "tease." That's a flash of things to come. It's succinct and challenging enough for them to want to hear more but targeted enough to hit their major concerns.

Check out your topic. How can it

- Help them get and stay ahead
- Give them something new they can use
- Make them understand what's happening in their own shop
- Show them what's in the pipeline and what to look for next
- Refocus their energies in a new direction
- Add some perspective on the market, their customer base, or global trends

Here's where you let them know, with a couple of sentences, where you're going with your speech and what's in it for them, clearly and pointedly.

WHAT WILL THEY HEAR ABOUT AND HOW

Your audience needs to know what your agenda is: where you're going and how you'll get there. This orients them and makes them comfortable enough to follow you.

- Giving your agenda at the top tells them the *scope* of what you'll cover.
- Without that, they can dump you at the beginning, not knowing you'll hit something they care about.
- Sharing your agenda, your whole road map, includes them and shares your power.
- Seeing it on a computer slide or written out helps them get it and remember.
- Going back to your agenda each time you change subjects clarifies instantly, renews interest, and makes your speech more organized.

OK. Before we leave Openings and go on to Content, there's still another technique I use that you should know about. You'll like it, because it's interactive and participatory.

Don't Tell: Ask!

Today's audience is accustomed to being independent soloists in getting their information. Here's a way to involve them in your speech right at the top, as proactive participants:

Ask them questions before you start your speech!

How? Start with, "Look, your time is valuable. So in order to make my remarks really useful to all of you, let's talk together a minute to find out who's here and what really matters to you."

Then say, "I want to know who's in the audience."

Even though you prepared your speech already knowing who's there, through the Know-Your-Audience Checklist (right?), this approach hits the mark for several reasons:

How Audiences React to This Approach

The audience is surprised, right at the start. You didn't start by *telling*, you started by *asking!* You gave them a voice, instead of merely presenting your own.

This subtle sharing of power is so important with our self-empowered audiences. It starts your audience out on a partici-patory note, capturing their attention right at the start.

You show your real interest in them. You emphasize how customized and worthwhile your speech will be. And you can use their answers to make points more specific during your speech.

Getting Your Audience to Respond

Get them to shout out their answers by saying, "Tell me!" and ask-ing for it with your hands, beckoning "come on" toward yourself, or cupping your ear. Then select and repeat what you hear.

Get them to answer with a show of hands by just raising *your* hand at the end of your question to indicate you want them to answer that way, and they'll follow.

When you see the show of hands, you can also zoom in on a couple of people near you and ask them some more questions, always repeating what they answer so everyone can hear it.

What Kinds of Questions?

- "Before I begin, let me get to know you a little better. How many of you have ever . . ." to draw a bead on work experience.

- "How do you feel about change (or risk or new inventions or today's market). "How many like it? Why? How many don't?" Let them shout out the answers or follow up with one or two specific audience members.

- Pick up words and repeat them; then take a moment to explain why they're saying that, how people usually respond to change or risk as a lead-in to your speech.

- "What do you think is the biggest problem facing us

today?" Or, name the problem and ask for a show of hands in agreement.

- "How many of you would like to balance your lives a little better?"
- "How many of you would like to get a handle on the amount of stress in your job and find a way to dilute it?"

Your questions should arise from your subject. Use the questions not only to activate your audience and find out how they feel about your subject but also to define their needs and launch into your speech.

CONTENT:
HOW TO EXPLAIN AND PERSUADE

PRESENTING IN AN ORDERLY, ORGANIZED FASHION

Your audience needs to be able to follow the structure of your speech as you move through it. Clear organization is key for the brain to be able to focus and follow. Leaping from subject to subject or wandering down garden paths to get to your point just won't make it.

Now that you've shown it, you must really adhere to your agenda or explain why you're diverging from it. So the first step in presenting your content is to give them the A. head in your outline notes.

Name Each of Your Outline Headings As You Go

Start by naming the heading and introducing your first subject. Here's your Long Shot. Be sure it establishes the context and sets the stage for where you're going next.

Is your first section:

- A brief history of where you've all been in this business?
- The state of the world/your industry/a system or service today?

- Naming the general parameters of a problem, before you go on to give them your solution?
- Simply describing the issue you've come to report on?

No matter what, this first section needs to give the general reasons and/or context for your speech and why they should come with you to points B. and C.

Get into Your Lists and Bullets

Document and explain your A., B., and C. by chunking them down into lists and bullets that break the subject into crisply delivered bite-sized pieces.

No tedious paragraphs. We've got to be able to accumulate the new data you're giving. We can't follow a ramble through the woods. The organized unfolding of bullet point after bullet point is something people can visualize and absorb, because it's incremental and is digested one statement at a time. Lists are easy to follow and the sheer weight of accumulating points is impressive and convincing.

Here's where your "build-slides" exercise from Chapter 5 comes in. Present and show your material one bullet at a time as you talk about it, rather than showing one slide with all your bullets at once, before you even start talking about bullet one.

Remember: we can read many times faster than you can talk. Putting more than one bullet up frees the audience to read ahead and make their own decisions about what you wanted to tell them. At that point you've lost your audience.

Recap and Transition

"Tell 'em what you're gonna tell 'em; tell 'em; then tell 'em what you told 'em."

An old cliché but it's lasted because it works.

When you're finished with section A., don't just arbitrarily leap into section B. We can't see your notes. You have to take us with you as you move on.

First, *recap* what you've just told us, with a line or two:

- People learn at different rates of speed.
- Not everyone gets it the first time around.
- People sometimes drift away for a moment and need to get caught up.

Doing a recap connects the dots for everyone, solidifies what you just said, and allows you *and* your audience to move on together.

As for *transitions,* your audience needs a good reason to stay tuned and come *with* you to your next topic. That means that B. in your outline has to logically grow out of what you've just told us in A. And your audience needs to see and know that.

Your transition should be something like:

- "Now if XYZ is true and that's where we are now, the next question is, what can we do about that? That's the next order of business."
- "What are people in our field doing about that? Let's find out."
- "Now that I've introduced this idea, you're probably thinking 'How does that affect me?' So let me take you to some answers to that question."

Articulate *why* we move on to the next piece of your speech. And did you notice that I did it with a question, rather than a directive or by just starting to talk about B.?

Engage your audience. Make us *want* to come with you, rather than just marching off on your own and assuming we're following.

Another way: go back to your agenda slide to show-and-tell us what the next subject will be. Tell your audience that you're going there now—and why.

One more important point: give us enough background and information in Section A that we're able to go on to B with you and understand it. Always think about what we, your audience, need to know about *before* you can go on to the next level.

TECHNIQUES FOR EXPLAINING NEW INFORMATION

Start with Something They Already Know

Learning something new is fun but it can also be worrisome: "What if I don't get it?" or "This sounds really complicated. I feel lost already."

The best way to explain a new subject or idea, something people don't know and can't picture, is to start with something familiar that they *do* know and can already visualize. Then work up to the new, unfamiliar, information.

The familiar starts your audience out on a solid footing, making them feel comfortable and willing to add new pieces, incrementally. For example:

"Just picture yourself in your car, turning a corner. Easy, right? But what if your steering wheel was square, not round? What would you have to do to turn the corner?"

See how you're picturing this right now? How you're imagining turning a corner and gripping the wheel, making four jerks and adjusting your hands to do the turn? You could then go on to add square wheels and they'd still be with you.

Principle: When the original example is familiar and easy to imagine, adding changes to it is not only possible, it's intriguing and kind of fun.

Process First—Not Detail

The basic process, the bare-bones *essentials,* is all the audience can handle at the start. Once we see the generalities, we're interested in getting more specific. Here's that LS/Med/CU system again. Show the basic general picture before you ever get to the details.

They'll want those once you've got them hooked.

Emphasize Your Points

The most common ways are:

- *Repeat* a word or phrase.

- *Change the pace:* Slow down or speed up to make people notice.
- *Modulate your voice:* sharper, softer, more thoughtful or weighty.
- *Ask them to stop and think:* "How could this affect what you've been doing so far?"
- *Alert your audience:* "This next part is especially important" or "Now I'm coming to a major moment. Just listen to this."
- *Recap in the middle of a subject:* Summarize key points as you go along if it's long and complicated.
- *Create a catch phrase or metaphor* for a certain idea, then repeat it whenever you want to allude to that thought. Remember "if it doesn't fit, you must acquit"? People really remember these.

Of course, save all these big guns for a truly important statement or idea. Don't overstate or overemphasize unimportant points!

Making It Credible

You face an unusual challenge today: How do you get the audience to believe you? With sales resistance at an all-time high; you need to contend with the following issues for your material to be persuasive and accepted:

- *Different generations:* Who do they believe or suspect?
- *The multiethnic workplace:* What is persuasive and credible to different groups and cultures?
- *The many levels of employees:* Do they all automatically take in everything you say, believe, and accept? Who wouldn't and what else would they need?

If you're an outsider who has come to sell a product, an idea, or yourself, what tools can you use to make your audience think that what you're saying is really true, not just a sales pitch?

The answer is *objectivity*. Who *else* says what you're saying?
What *additional proof* can you give, and show, beyond your
words alone? Which of these would sway and persuade your audience? Or *you?* Here are some useful approaches.

- Newspaper, magazine or industry articles, polls, or
  reports
- Comparison with the last three years' figures
- Quotes from a new, groundbreaking book
- Information from a major business guru
- Feedback from customers
- Letters to the company
- Competitor's year-end figures, systems, marketing
- New products on the market
- Senior management directive

These items have no personal bias; they're very credible *outside* sources. To get a handle on what else you need, just ask yourself what else would anyone have to do to persuade *you* about the
theme and points of your speech? Get hard on yourself, and sus-
picious: What would it take to prove your idea to yourself?

SPEAKING AND LANGUAGE SKILLS

Use Easy, Informal Language

Have you noticed that throughout this book, I use informal,
"how we talk" language, not abstract or formal expressions. That's
quite deliberate. I want you to feel that I'm right here, just talking with you—explaining, giving you some new ideas, being helpful and supportive—not some remote expert who pontificates
and sermonizes.

Use words that feel like you're sitting with a member of the
audience, having a cup of coffee and just talking. Feeling
present—easy, relaxed, and conversational—makes for an even
playing field between speaker and listener. Use:

- Short sentences
- Informal, familiar language and expressions
- Recognizable allusions
- An intimate tone

And microphones make an easy conversational tone—even a *whisper*—totally audible.

Become Aware of Your Own Speech Habits

Think about the words you usually use. Ask your friends or family. We sometimes use certain words over and over. For example, by screening my tapes I discovered my special habit-words as a television talk-show host. "Extraordinary" was one. Now how many times can you use that word and continue to be credible? How many things can be extraordinary in one show?

So start listening for your habit-words. You'll soon find alternatives, for variety.

Simplify, Clarify, and Make Your Language Familiar

Edit your word choices. Use familiar synonyms to explain. Challenge yourself to find ways to explain something so others can get it. And be careful not to patronize as you do it. Unwittingly, that creeps in when you're talking about something you know very well that others don't. Share your ideas and message with some enthusiasm.

Know when to use, and not use, insider jargon. Jargon only works when you're with a group of peers who know what you know and talk like that. Otherwise it feels very exclusionary. And when you hear yourself using jargon, stop and explain, with a little laugh and a "That really just means X."

Create Stories or Analogies to Make Principles Vivid

These are some of the best devices for clarifying an abstract concept. Turn away from the usual hard-nosed, pragmatic approach. Find a story or analogy that illustrates the basic *principle* involved. You cause people to be persuaded on much more familiar, pleasant territory. Your audience doesn't have to work too hard to get these, unlike the unfamiliar material you're asking them to reach for. How about this, if you're trying to caution against the dangers of attacking a project without looking ahead to see what the obstacles can be:

> Picture driving your car. A big newspaper flies up onto your windshield. What would you do? Would you keep going, flying blind, or would you stop and get rid of it so you can see where you're going and what's ahead?

Analogies not only provide a change of pace; they also build in a little suspense, as the audience waits for the end to see how the point of your story connects with what you've been saying. Just be sure it does hit the mark and *really* illustrates your idea.

Use Familiar Sayings and Folk Wisdom

Wrap up your ideas with a line from another venue—a slogan, a motto, a quote, a line from literature.

Not only does this give you another dimension, it also gives your ideas much more weight. They become equated with the lines, which have either been in existence for a very long time and are familiar to everyone or capture an issue in a pithy way. "Don't saw on a tree limb while you're sitting on it."

Everything can be used—from some old expression of your grandfather's, whose truth is incontrovertible, to some fable with a great punchy ending.

Ask around, especially among people of other cultures who work with you, to find some of their interesting lines and stories, to add a twist to your speech. Here's a great old Dutch proverb: "A handful of patience is worth more than a bushel of brains."

These sayings can catch listeners with a little extra hit and a moment for musing, unlike the usual speech expressions.

Use Lines from Popular Culture

Lines from TV sitcoms, commercials, recent or classic movies, or even children's literature can be great equalizers before you separate yourself from the group as you tell your new concept.

TV commercial lines like "Where's the beef?" makes your point much faster than 15 minutes of explanation. Invoking scenes from the latest movie hit or some great classic like *Casablanca* or *Star Wars* can also juice up your message.

Facing a tough new road? Invoke "The Little Engine That Could" as a light-handed way of making people feel they can rise to the occasion, adding a little nostalgia and humor. And again, a clear message, given with a twist and a little humor, rather than some trite exhortation like "You can do it."

Use Quotations

Quotations have the same kind of effect. They bring weight and wisdom to back up your various ideas and goals. And using clever, thought-provoking words from prestigious, famous, sometimes surprising sources can give your talk a real lift.

I've collected a number of pithy quotes particularly apt for business communication. They're provocative, often humorous, and said by people your audiences would admire or even be surprised by.

Here are just a few that would be especially apt for your speeches, sorted by subject:

Change

"Change . . . To the fearful it is threatening because it means that things may get worse. To the hopeful it is encouraging because things may get better. To the confident it is inspiring because the challenge exists to make things better."

—King Whitney Jr.

Failure

"I don't know the key to success, but the key to failure is trying to please everybody,"

—Bill Cosby

"Many of life's failures are people who did not realize how close they were to success when they gave up."

—Thomas Alva Edison

Risk

"Great deeds are usually wrought at great risks."

—Herodotus, fifth century B.C.

"The policy of being too cautious is the greatest risk of all."

—Jawaharlal Nehru, former prime minister of India

Success

"Success is the ability to go from one failure to another with no loss of enthusiasm."

—Sir Winston Churchill

For lots more quotations, Google "The Quotations Page." You can choose from zillions of subjects listed there to suit any speech you make.

Talk About People, Not Abstractions

Abstract talk is hard to take. Make images in the audience's minds by getting the *human factor* into anything you talk about. We all relate to familiar images and human situations, instead of just dry, abstract terms and facts alone.

Turn your message into a scene with action. Translate ideas into how people would do that in their jobs. Evoke common work or customer scenes to help audiences identify with what you're talking about.

Contrast these two approaches:

1. "It is now clear that the delivery system in the service department is not operating at the capacity necessary to provide rapid service and cost efficiency. This must end."

Versus

2. "My customer John Q. called me yesterday to tell me how late our delivery was—again! And how he's started thinking we haven't got our act together and maybe he better look elsewhere!"

Use Personal Anecdotes

Something from your own experience or what you recently read or saw that affected you in some way is still another launching pad for bringing your audience with you, visually and personally.

Use Silence

Speakers often have a problem with silence. They're afraid that stopping after a statement looks like they have forgotten what to say next.

Just consider this: Well-chosen words are eloquent, but silence is equally, if not often *more*, eloquent. Eloquent because it gives the audience a chance—actually *compels* them—to think.

When you're delivering a message and the audience is busy absorbing it, you're both moving at quite a pace. Give them a pause in which to consider what you just said. Just a momentary pause is all that's needed. It provides not only relief from your talking at them, but a bubble in which your audience can think for itself.

When to do it? Whenever you deliver a meaningful, surprising or disturbing statement, pausing says, "*That* really matters. Think about it." Or it says, "I know I just shook you up. Let me stop so you can think about it a moment, before we can go on to more explanation."

And when you *do* stop, just stand still and make eye contact. Look directly at them. Show them that it's on purpose, that you're connecting with them in a meaningful way.

Don't Just Tell—Ask!

Open-ended questions starting with who, what, when, where, how—are a truly great technique. Set up what you're going to tell them next by asking first, to stimulate their thinking:

- Is this necessary?
- Why do you need the next step?
- What would it look like if you . . .
- Who would logically be involved in this?
- Where could these changes be made?

We like such questions because, although you challenge me to think about the answer—which I may or may not know—I'm pleased to play along since I know you'll give me the answer in your next phrase. You make me a partner in what you're about to say.

Graphics and Visual Aids

I don't need to say any more about this. Just go to Chapter 6: "Making Your Message Visual" for lots of hints about designing and presenting your ideas graphically.

ACTIVATE YOUR AUDIENCE!

Here are some new ways to involve your audience during your speech—ways to reach out, bring them on board, and keep them there.

Ask Them for Feedback Directly

Generate instant feedback about something you've just said or are going to say. Your request for feedback can net you different opinions and shared concerns. But you also get some really useful information that you can use as reference points or stimulants in your speech, going forward.

What kinds of questions? Well, what's your next topic? Quiz them in advance about where they are now in relation to it. Ask them, "How many of you get frustrated by your computers?" or "How many of you think XYZ is a problem?" Then, when you talk about it, and provide an answer, they'll be doubly interested, since they know you mean them.

Group Questions

Make your questions as inclusive as possible. People don't like to stand out in a group, and if your question is too specific, they won't raise their hands. Always start with a big win—a question that will get a lot of response, even a laugh of recognition. Keep the ball rolling by asking one more. Once they get the idea, they'll like doing it. Remember that I also suggested questioning your audience at the very *beginning* of your speech to find out who they were. This also lays the groundwork for doing it again *during* your speech.

This kind of questioning creates a dialogue between you and your listeners, which is vital for keeping the energy and interest level up.

Get Them to Move!

Here's a novel idea. Your audience needs to move and stretch a little, especially if they've been trapped in their seats and inactive during other speeches before yours. Or perhaps they just need charging up with some renewed energy so they can stay tuned to you.

I do this very often when I speak: Either before I begin, or after a coffee break or even if I feel interest may be lagging (which of course *never* happens to *me!*), I say:

"OK everybody. You've been sitting a long time and need a break. We need to pump up a little extra energy here. So let's get up and take a stretch. Just stand up at your seats, reach your arms up overhead, and S T R E T C H!" And I do it, too.

I don't only tell them to stretch. I ask them to bend over,

touch their toes (if they can!), put their hands on their hips and twist side to side, and finally, "Give me five jumps in place—one, two, three, four, five!" And I do it with them. And then tell them to sit down again.

You know what happens? First of all, they do it *all!* Automatically. No holding back! Everyone's smiling, laughing, buzzing as they readjust themselves in their seats. Faces are flushed. You can absolutely *feel* the energy surge in the room.

Try it. You'd be *amazed* at how much power you have over your audience. You have the mike or the floor, you're in charge, and they positively *will* do what you tell them! And they love it 'cause they need it!

Know what else?

This funny little break shows that I dare to break out of the mold and do an original, and very helpful, thing for them. It also lets me chat them up and do a little small talk as we get settled in again, another great way to connect anew with your audience. And it sure makes people talk about you!

Demos at Their Seats

Build in demonstrations they can do in their seats. Show them something they can try as they're sitting there. This again provides action, a break, a new attention grabber. Whenever I give communication seminars (never lectures, always active lecture-demonstrations), I demonstrate the importance of eye contact this way:

"Everyone turn to your neighbor. Take a partner and just look at each other. No flinching! No looking away! Just a slow and steady gaze." Then I discuss what just happened.

I explain the effects of eye contact and how come they all giggled when they first looked each other in the eye this way. When I explain, I'm talking to *participants* who just experienced it, not just passive listeners who have to take my word for it.

So find *something they can do,* like drawing or writing something, doing something with their hands, to demonstrate something you're talking about. It's fun for them, makes your point, and keeps them active and tuned in.

Volunteers from the Audience

Reach out to some audience members to help you set up or move or hold something. If you have a new process or piece of equipment to demonstrate, a new way of doing something they know, or a little role playing you need to relive a common occurrence at work, go to them for help!

Again, it's an action scene. People love to watch someone from their audience do something, since they identify very quickly with a fellow audience member. So this device really sharpens attention because it's movement, it's fun, it's suspenseful—and it's a surprise.

Troubleshoot with Your Audience

Try finding out where the stumbling blocks to implementing your ideas are before they all go home and find reasons *not* to do what you said. Here are some suggestions about ways to do that.

How to Do It

After you've explained your idea, tell them, "In order to make it functional, viable, and most useful to you, I'd sure like some feedback now. How many of you think it's a good idea? And if not, why not? Let's talk."

Or "Look, it's fine for me to stand here, spinning my ideas. But this is not an ego trip. I'm anxious to hear your response. What do you think of what I've said? Can we do it?"

It's Up to You to Smoke Out the Info

Without your encouragement, the great majority of folks will *not* stand up and say, "Bad idea." People don't want to hurt your feelings or embarrass you before other people. We don't like sounding negative.

So your audience will talk about the speech among themselves, giving all the critique that would be useful to you in making your plan better or making it work. But you won't hear it.

Pose Some Possible Problems After You've Stated Your Ideas

In thinking about your speech, you've surely thought about what people could disagree with. Talk over the ideas in your speech with buddies and see what *they* think could be possible issues. Get them out on the table.

If you're selling, verbalize the objections potential customers would probably voice. Then pose and answer them or ask for more.

Suggesting a change or addition of something in your office? Name the probable objections and encourage their responses before you give solutions.

When *you* name the problems people may have, they're out in the open. And you've encouraged the audience to respond by giving them material they can work with. Otherwise they'll smile politely but won't be straight or bring it up in the question-and-answer period. So go for it! You'll solve issues together and make your speech truly work—*before* they leave.

Avoid the possibility that your idea may not be implemented or even changed drastically because you didn't dare open the door to constructive criticism on your own.

It's a sign of great strength to do what I suggested. People will admire you for it.

Now let's close this chapter, and your speech.

CLOSINGS

The major goals of closings are:

- To recap and summarize what you said
- To leave your audience with an echo—something to think about after they've left
- To end on a high note.

And how can you do all that well?

First, *tell* them that you've come to the end. (That always pleases them!)

Then do a recap, visually as well as orally.

- *Start by reminding them* about your initial premise.
- *Go back* to some of your slides to remind them, section by section, what you covered. Select the pithiest, the ones that make your points best.
- *Give them a call to action:* What do you want them to do now?
- *Be specific:* What should they actually do?
- *Encourage them:* Give them the faith and confidence as well as good reasons to try your great idea.
- *Reinforce why it's a good idea:* Remind them what you proved in your speech to make them know they *should* do this.
- *Thank them* for being a great audience; tell them what a pleasure it was to be with them.
- *Find a last line* that puts the period on your speech. What's the most important thing you said? The most valid, persuasive reason they should accept your idea? Even a pointed quote is a great ender.

You need to be personal and warm in your closing. The old forensic law of "primacy and recency" teaches us that people remember most what they hear or see *first* and *last*. And if you want people to indeed ask questions, you'd better make them feel they're very welcome and you're very accessible.

Now let's turn to the next part: what happens after you've done your closing. The question-and-answer period and how to handle it well.

9

THE ART OF Q & A

WHY DO IT?

Why set yourself up for a public grilling? Is it really useful? For whom?

For you! Inviting questions actually lets you

- Keep explaining in another way
- Add what you left out or didn't make clear
- Dispel problems and straighten out misconceptions
- Discover what doesn't work so you can work on it further
- Make your subject more relevant to this particular group

But Q & As can also be uncomfortable and they have some pitfalls.

Step one on the road to feeling comfortable and becoming good at answering questions is *preparing* for them.

Step two is learning some skills in answering.

PREPARING FOR Q & A

UNDERSTANDING YOUR AUDIENCE

Remind yourself of the audience research you did when you were creating your speech. This helps you begin to predict what these particular people might ask you: what they're most interested in or concerned about.

What was their job level and experience with your subject? What did they expect or need from you? Is this a disparate group who could be asking you questions on different levels about different aspects of your speech?

What to Look for and Expect

Think through what you're telling them or asking them to do:

- What issues and anxieties could your speech bring up for them?
- Is your presentation threatening to the status quo? Will it make more work?
- Does it make them rethink a commonly held belief?
- What about costs? extra training? downsizing?
- Where would the hostility or rejection come from?
- Any built-in opposition in the audience?

Anticipating these makes for fewer surprises and helps you keep your footing.

Understand Who Asks Questions

- Some are really confused.
- Some want specific connections to their own work.
- Some are competitive, more interested in the attention than the answer.
- Some need to criticize and find fault with anything new.
- Some have come to make a statement of their own about your subject.

Gaining insights about the questioning process itself makes it easier for you to field the questions. Putting them in categories helps you keep your balance and decide whether to give them more or less weight and time.

Understand Your Adversaries

Be prepared for disagreement. Know that as impassioned as you are about your idea and your point of view, others are equally impassioned about theirs.

See these folks as misguided or misinformed, not simply as irritants, impediments, or enemies. In order to change their minds, you need a little objectivity. Listen hard to the *heart* of what they disagree with. Take *that* on, not *them*.

Understand Your Feelings

In order to become skilled at fielding questions off the cuff, you need some understanding of the feelings that can arise in *you*. Let's look at what I've found are the most common reactions to being questioned:

Targeted and Defensive

Once you've declared open season on yourself—"I'm ready for questions"—you may begin to feel put upon. This is a dangerous feeling since you then see questioners as antagonists or adversaries rather than simply people asking for more information.

Look at it another way:

- You've said your piece and this is extra—a gift to them.
- You're sharing more information *as they request it*.
- They're clearly interested enough in what you said to want more.

Feeling Loss of Control

Before you were in total control of your subject. But now the agenda is determined by the questioner. Subject, rhythm, and style now belong to him or her, *not* to you. The spotlight also shifts from you to include the questioner, perhaps putting a harsher and more unflattering light on you!

Feeling powerless and defensive erodes your ability to think. It also makes you look for approval as you answer.

Try looking at it another way:

- You have the power to ask questions back.
- You know what you know. You're still *totally in charge* of what you'll say, how *much* you'll say, and how you'll say it.
- You can also deflect, reroute, pass on, analyze, and challenge any question.

So dismiss the feeling that you've lost your power to your audience. It's not true!

Feeling Nervous

You're anxious about whether:

- You'll be as smart, explicit, and clear as you were in your planned remarks.
- They'll ask something you don't know the answer to, right off.
- You can handle the questions well.
- You'll get trapped into saying something you don't mean or shouldn't say.
- Your pride and dignity may be hurt.
- The pace: question (*boom*) followed by answer (*boom*). Will you have enough time to think about the question and come up with a good, carefully edited answer?

Look at it another way:

There is no perfect or prescribed answer to each question. You can make it up, customized to suit this occasion, this question, and this questioner. It is *your* material and you're prepared. You can tell people *where to look* if you don't know the answer. You *can* handle whatever comes your way.

Feeling Exhilarated

Not all your feelings will be negative. If you're a fighter, a competitor, or a performer who likes the spotlight, this part feels exciting. "Let's see how I do with this." But don't get so taken with the performance or the win-lose that you forget to listen and think! Q & A is all about further enlightenment or resolving disputes.

Look at it another way:

You don't need to compete or fight. You've already won. You've had your place in the sun. You *did* tell them what you wanted to, without interruption, from your unique point of view. Your position now is to just help those who fell behind climb aboard.

Bottom Line: Do expect this part of your presentation to actually be more fun! You can banter and chat with individual audience members in an informal way. They're petitioners, asking, and you're in the position of deciding what and how much to give. Feel *flattered* that they want to know more. You must have done a good job!

ANSWERING TECHNIQUES

WHAT USUALLY HAPPENS

You're done. It's over. Now comes that very tense moment. The moderator, chairperson, or you yourself say: "Now we'll open the question-and-answer period. Are there any questions?" And 9 times out of 10, there's a deathly hush! Nothing! No one raises a hand. And your stomach falls through the floor.

"Wasn't anyone listening?" you think. "Didn't they get it? Could they simply have gotten it all and have nothing to say or ask? Were they bored? What do I do now?"

What's left is to smile weakly, say good-bye, and leave with the proverbial tail between the legs, as it were.

Bad stuff—and *embarrassing.* But it surely happens, doesn't it? To help you deal with it and get those questions flowing, here's why this happens and what to do about it.

WHY PEOPLE DON'T ASK

You see, it's not that they weren't listening or aren't curious about something. It's this: people really don't *like* to ask questions! Understanding this helps you get over that initial "deathly hush" and deal with it. Here's what's going on. Here's what they're worried about:

It's Too Exposing

Asking means there's something I don't know and am admitting it, out loud. This could be embarrassing. I'm also asking someone who *does* know! Could set up a little competition here? So most folks opt for not showing their lack of knowledge or understanding. They sit silently, protecting themselves. Result? No questions.

This is raised to the *n*th power when you're in a group or an audience. Here the stakes are so much higher. Now *everyone* will know that you don't know or didn't get it.

But that's not all that keeps people from standing right up and asking you those longed-for questions.

How to Put It

Most folks aren't very articulate when they speak extemporaneously—and they know it. They have difficulty getting their thoughts organized quickly, finding the right words just when they need them, coming to the point, and so forth.

So there's the additional anxiety of standing up to ask and not doing it very well; of bumbling and fumbling a little, looking for the best way to say it. And what if the speaker says, "Could you repeat your question? I'm not sure I get what you mean." Double jeopardy! You may be exposing yourself to extra criticism, or even derision!

Competitiveness

People also worry about how their question exposes them to the group. Will they lose face? Is it smart enough? Do others already know the answer? Will others have better ones? They want to hold back till they see the tenor of *other* questions. Then they'll chime in. Most people are generally a little leery of going first.

So that's what's going on in the minds of your audience. They're being self-protective, and not necessarily bored by you at all!

Here's how to handle this tricky situation.

HELPING PEOPLE GET STARTED

Because I speak everywhere, and often, I've worked out a little scenario. Expecting this to happen and understanding it (as you do now), when the silence falls, I tell the audience straight out what's going on with them:

"Do you know what's going on right now? It's a classic thing and it happens in just about every audience." (This makes them feel good: they're not the only ones, not dumb, not different.)

"Several of you have questions you'd really like to ask. But you're testing your question, thinking 'Nah, maybe others already know this' or 'That's not such a terrific, smart, or insightful question. I'll wait till someone *else* asks one. When I see the nature of *their* question, I'll go second." (This immediately gets head nods and a laugh of recognition. Then I go on with this:)

"So you wait and when you hear someone else's question, you think yours is pretty darn good! And we'll get a flock of hands for the *next* question! But since I think your questions are *all* great because they're about *my* speech, who's going to be brave enough to ask the first question?" And up come the hands.

The key is to *confront what's happening*, not stand there with a vacant smile, just waiting. Don't badger or cajole. Laughing *with it* shows your strength. And they'll *love* the fact that you knew what was happening and shook them out of their paralysis.

The payoff is not just a good discussion. It also relieves you of that long, lonely walk offstage.

Some Other Launches for Q & A

"You've been such an attentive audience and I've talked non-stop for quite a while. So it's my turn to calm down now and change pace. And it's *your* turn to talk, to ask me questions. I *think* I told you everything I could, but there are surely some things I left out or didn't make clear. How about some questions?"

This gets your audience moving because you sound genuinely interested in hearing from them, no holds barred.

Here's another way:

"I know that much of what I talked about is very complex (technical, new). Since I just gave it a kind of basic orientation session, there may be many things that are still not clear. I welcome your asking me anything."

This says, "I won't be insulted if you ask me elementary things. And you're not *dumb* for not understanding the first time out."

Lead the Q & A Yourself

This is an issue that requires a little delicacy. I don't think it's very encouraging or stimulating to end your speech and have a moderator get up and be the one to ask for questions. The rapport you've struck with your audience should make *you* be the one to do it.

Suggest to the moderator you'd like to launch the Q & A directly out of the speech. This gives you the chance to do the little transition I mentioned above.

But since moderators are usually asked to do that job, let him or her start by asking for questions. Then you chime in with your end-the-silence gambit.

The moderator can then help by calling on the questioners, perhaps by name, and you two can play it together.

Frankly, I like to do it all myself if I can. Of course, if the moderator is the *boss,* you need to cede the territory. But if you have any control over this, let the Q & A period grow directly from your speech.

SONYA'S 13 RESPONSES FOR SUCCESS IN Q & A

Now here comes a bunch of how-to ideas for making your Q & A interesting, fun, and useful. And ways for you to shine in this role, too.

1. RELAX AND BE INFORMAL

Set the stage for your Q & A to be an informal one-on-one chat. Be warm, courteous, direct, open, and *conversational*. It's not lecture time. You're basically talking to one person and should sound like you're sitting down over a cup of coffee. It's a rather intimate exchange, except it has onlookers. You should sound collegial, like one of them.

2. LISTEN HARD TO THE QUESTION!

Easy to say, hard to do. We're really bad at listening because we're so afraid of the dead air that might follow if we listen till the end, and don't start preparing an answer while they're still talking!

Because of all those feelings I described earlier, you may still be a little tense and anxious as the questions begin, and want to answer them at once, smoothly, without any hesitation.

The challenge here is to *truly* listen to the question. If you just hear the first half, decide what this is probably about and sally forth, you'll often not really answer the question asked! Instead:

Listen till the end of the question! Take in *all* of what the question is about before you answer.

Ask yourself where it's leading to make yourself tune in more closely. Be sure you understand what the questioner *really* wants to know.

Notice how the question is asked: Hostile? Insecure? Handle that in your answer.

All these techniques will help you formulate better answers that are more to the point. (For lots more on *listening skills*, see Chapter 10, page 276.)

3. CLARIFY THE QUESTION

Don't program yourself to assume you must answer as soon as the question is asked. If you're not sure you've got it straight, ask the questioner until you understand.

People are not great at asking clear, concise, pointed questions. They ask two or three at once, ramble, back and fill. You can end up answering the first part or the last part of a question, or missing the point entirely unless you do something like this:

"Wow, there's a lot to that question! Let me be sure I got it all. I think you're asking . . ." Then rephrase it and ask if that's the one.

Another way: "I want to respond to exactly what you're asking, so could you focus it a little more to be sure I'm on the right track? Do you mean X or Y?"

Be careful not to sound *critical* when you clarify, as though it was a lousy question, poorly asked, something like: "Well, exactly *what* is your question?" Always take the blame on yourself.

4. COMPLIMENT THE ASKER

Nothing feels better than that old saw, "That's a really good question." No, its not corny. It's nice to be acknowledged for having stuck one's neck out or being perceptive. It also says you relish the opportunity to make yourself and your material clearer.

"I'm so glad you asked that. It gives me a chance to say some more about XYZ." This also encourages others to get in the game.

5. TREAT EVERYONE RESPECTFULLY

Audience members have much more in common with each other than they do with you. They are subconsciously bonded and definitely notice how you treat one of their own. Even if the question is dumb, redundant, or off the wall, be *patient*. Answer as though it were as good as any other. Roll your eyes later. . . .

6. AVOID DEBATES

How often have you seen it, or gotten sucked into one yourself; when the Q & A gets derailed into a one-on-one exchange about an ever-narrowing subject? This bores the audience very fast and stops the good flow of questions. Problem: How do you cut this off without sounding like you're running away or being rude? Here are some possible responses:

"You know, that's a great subject and I know there's more to say about it. Let's meet after the program to continue it, OK?"

"Listen, you've got me on the horns of a dilemma. I'd like to keep talking about this, but there are lots of other eager questioners who want the floor. Please see me after the program, OK?"

"That's a really complex, technical point. Let me send you X's article (or whatever) on that. Please give me your email address after the program, all right?"

Speak personally and informally, being sure to save face for the nerd who keeps badgering you. This makes you come off as a thoughtful person, sensitive as well as knowledgeable. Your audience *knows* he's a nerd—and a nuisance!

7. IF YOU DON'T KNOW, SAY IT OUT LOUD!

Nothing else really works. Don't fudge and fumble. You're a much bigger person for admitting fallibility rather than bluffing and letting us see that you're too shaky or embarrassed to admit the truth. And you know what? It's OK not to know! So, how should you say it? Try these:

"I wish I could rattle that off for you, but I can't. And frankly I don't want to bluff my way out of it and be inaccurate. I'd need to go back and look at some data. Please let me know how to be in touch with you and I'll send it to you, if I find it."

"I don't really know but I can tell you where to look."

"Please email me. I have that in my files."

How does that all sound to you? Dumb and unprepared? Surely not. You know where to go and you're willing to help. And you're being very straight with the questioner.

8. HOW TO AVOID A QUESTION

Sometimes you want some advice or need to check with company policy rather than answer. The same tactics as in the paragraph above work well for stalling. But you can also try:

"I knew *someone* would ask me something I couldn't answer right away." Then it's very acceptable to say:

"I'm really not at liberty to answer that right now. We're working on it." Or . . .

"Sorry. You'll hear no public comments from me on *that!* Do you think I want our competition to know those answers? But thanks for asking anyway."

9. TAKING SOME LUMPS IS INEVITABLE

There are times when you can't avoid a question and need to answer it straight and take a hit or two. Do it as gracefully as you can. If you don't, they won't believe *anything else* you've said. Consider in advance which questions those may be and come prepared. But if one comes from left field, save face by answering without excuses or defenses, just flatly and factually: "That's true. Tough, but true." And move on.

10. BUYING TIME

For some of us, the mind-to-mouth route works fast. But for most people, when the question is a tough one, damaging, or difficult to answer, we really want a moment or two to think. You can have it. *You're in charge here!* Say:

"That's a question that needs a moment of thought to answer properly. So give me a sec to think about it."

Your audience will always give you time to do that *if you tell them what you're doing.* Getting red in the face, looking up for inspiration, standing silently—all of these signal that you're stuck. If you tell them *why* you need a minute, they're happy to give it to you. They understand. They've also been there. So, be straight with them. It works every time.

Comment on the question: "Interesting. Never thought of that before." Or "I guess I hit a nerve. Sounds like you have a barrage of questions there."

Take the Question Apart: Asking more about what the questioner really means buys you some time and helps you focus so you can come up with a good answer. "There are two parts to your question. Which shall I answer first?" Or, "Do you mean X or Y?" Or even, "Would you repeat the question?" These all work to give you a little breather.

Comment on how it's asked: "You surely were listening!" or "I hear that you have quite another point of view."

All these little prologues *actually* give your brain a chance to reassemble and think of an answer. They also give you back your sense of power *before* you answer. And they sound responsive, not as though you're stalling.

11. TURN UNCOMFORTABLE QUESTIONS AROUND

Sometimes a question has something in it you'd rather not answer fully or dwell on. You can answer some of it but then take it in another direction.

Make it bigger: "Actually, this affects the whole industry, not just what I've been talking about." *Enlarging perspective* lets you share knowledge about how others are struggling with the same problem. It dilutes issues by making them not so unique.

Focus it tighter: Zoom into a much *smaller* example and get specific about details. "Look, I can't speak for all of it and where it's going, yet. I can only speak about the work *we've* done and what *we've* found so far."

Seize the opportunity: "Thanks for letting me straighten that out." Or, "I have heard that." Or, "You may have read something about that. Here's the way it *really* is." Then go into your explanation instead of staying on someone else's wavelength. Speak only about the points you want to mention, actively taking the conversation to another plane without sounding defensive.

Place it in context: Questions are often asked based on a false premise or insufficient data, or out of context. "In order to answer that, I need to give you some background (or additional information) to know where it fits (or if that is really so)." Then fill in the gaps, setting the question in a proper light and turning the question into a platform for yourself. You'll sound responsive and informative, and actually be more enlightening, by taking the question where you want it to be or where it rightly belongs.

12. CUTTING PEOPLE OFF

This is all about people who take over and go on too long, focus on some nitpicky detail, keep after the same point you have already answered, and so on. It's *always* tough to do. But—*you are in charge!* Don't let it get away from you. The major goal is not to be rude or look like you need to escape. Be very careful to apologize as you interrupt: "I'm so sorry but . . ." "This is really difficult . . ." "Forgive me for interrupting . . ."

Here are some way to do this:

Time or group constraints: "I'm so sorry but others are champing at the bit here. I'm going to have to ask you to tighten your question, OK?" Blaming it on an *objective outside source* saves face for everyone. Or, "Gee, wish we could spend more time on this, but our time is so limited and I have to give everyone an equal chance to ask. So, quick summary, OK?"

Summarize the question: You can interrupt with "I think I hear you asking about X. Thanks. Let me talk about that a little." And then take over and answer. Or, "I see. Your question seems to be all about XYZ. Is that right?" It forces people to tighten up and rephrase.

Keep it on the subject: "Whoa, whoa, hang on just a minute. Yours is a good question but actually it's not my topic." Or, "Sorry to interrupt but could you please focus your question on what my speech was about. That would help the group, I think."

Ask for their help: "Look, I need your help. I have a real problem because I need to be fair and democratic and give everyone a chance. So forgive me when I ask you to end this discussion. And thanks for your question." After an especially garrulous question, say to the group: "Look, folks, I know lots of you have questions and feel strongly about this. But could you help us out by making your questions tight and short so I can answer as many as possible? Thanks."

13. GETTING THE AUDIENCE ON YOUR SIDE

A tricky play but necessary when things aren't going well and someone has just attacked you with a stickler of a question or been nasty. The idea is to come through as human, vulnerable, and straightforward.

Don't pretend it didn't happen: The weakest way to handle something is to avoid mentioning it. Even looking at the audience with a wry smile and saying "No comment" is a powerful move. But since everyone was present at the hostile exchange, you need to show them that you're aware of what happened but you're *not* knocked off your pins and *are* able to continue.

Be real: After a tough exchange, comment on what just happened. Humor is the very best antidote: "Well, you didn't know that you came to a boxing match, did you?" Or, "Is there a doctor in the house? We just had a little bloodletting here." Or, "I'm pretty brave. Let's see what the *next* question will be like!"

Have the last word: *You alone* can say one last thing before you move on. Again, the light touch is the only way to go! It shows you're unscathed and strong enough to have a broad perspective (unlike your questioner). Something like: "There sure seems to be a lot of passion about my subject." Or, "OK, let's just remember my original point before we go on"—and then reiterate what you mean.

Handling hostility in general is tough but I've already told you all about it in Chapter 5. You might want to reread that material. Actually, there's more about this in the next chapter, "Meetings: How to Lead and How to Be Heard." So let's go there now.

10

MEETINGS:
HOW TO LEAD AND
HOW TO BE HEARD

MEETINGS?

"Now what are we supposed to do?"

"Endless!"   "Didn't get anywhere"   "Waste of Time!"   "B o r i n g !"

WHY MEETINGS DON'T WORK

Here are some of the complaints I hear from meeting participants.

- **Passive:** fixed agendas; no input from group
- **Boring:** reports are dull; take too long; aimless talk
- **People tune out:** group is self-involved; only react, don't listen
- **Grandstanding dominates:** a few power-hungry people take over; no room for all

- **Closed-minded:** leader decides; no disagreeing
- **Unproductive:** poor closure; no specific action plan
- **Chairperson power:** run by fiat; dampens open discussion; new ideas
- **Personal issues:** fear of exposure, conflict, competition, retaliation, cliques

The skills you'll learn in this chapter will help leaders and participants overcome these and other unproductive pitfalls. Your meetings will become truly collaborative, involving, and fruitful.

SKILLS YOU NEED TO LEARN AND SHARPEN

Dysfunction arises in several places, but most of all everyone needs to understand more about group dynamics. It's tough to come to conclusions within a group. We all need to know more about how people interact with each other; what gets people on board; what makes conflict; how to persuade, and when to back off.
Meeting leaders need to know how to:

- Design inclusive agendas
- Get everyone prepared before the meeting
- Handle time and fruitful discussions
- Create a productive environment
- Gain attention and keep everyone on track
- Handle conflict, egos, and disagreements
- Come to working conclusions

Meeting participants need to know how to:

- Talk and present
- Prepare for maximum value and place yourself to get noticed
- Enter discussions, stand firm, or yield
- Listen, support, and disagree successfully

- Handle criticism or attacks
- Deal with losing your point or approval of your idea

WHAT MEETINGS CAN AND SHOULD ACCOMPLISH

Team Building and Group Connection

So much work is done in a solo setting these days. People travel incessantly, they work from home, or they hole up in their offices at odd hours. We're used to *sending* material electronically rather than *appearing*. Yet we all need a place to feel connected. Therefore it's vital for coworkers to see each other—to establish a sense of the group, not to feel like disparate individuals.

Seeing and hearing from each other, experiencing joint energies, getting stimulated by piggybacking on another's ideas, forming relationships—all these are powerful team builders.

People also need to see where and how their work connects with the rest of the group. Projects are strengthened when we're all consciously on the same page and can see how the pieces, including the ones you're working on, fit together.

Comparing Notes, Sharing Information

It's reassuring to know that the same knotty problem has also stumped others. At meetings you can hear others' solutions, discover similarities and connections between the work done here and elsewhere. And to not only learn from others, but also to *give* something to the group as well.

Hearing Opinions Openly Discussed

There's always anxiety in any one-on-one with the boss, where your opinions—and you—must stand alone. People have a tendency to hedge their answers when they don't know what others are thinking and saying. Airing ideas in a group gives everyone a little protective coloration, orienting them to the norm and helping decide how far they're willing to go.

Looking for Solutions Together

Two (or more) heads are often better than one! We all get so committed to the sound of our inner voice that it's often a surprise to hear how many *other* ways something can be done. The stimulus you get when you incorporate other points of view and the extra thought that goes into justifying your ideas to dissenters bring everyone's creativity up to a higher level. People go back to their own workspace with some new ideas already percolating.

Developing Consensus

When you agree as a group and set yourself a course of action, everyone in the group becomes everyone else's conscience and spur to action. Conflicts can be resolved in the open and the final product feels right to everyone at once.

Group Self-Criticism

In a group, it's safe to join in on the complaining and nitpicking and even laugh about how badly something's gotten fouled up. The leader can also authorize and direct self-criticism about a project to make everyone contribute, become aware of their difficulties and start solving the problems that emerge.

OK. We've learned the negatives and the positives. Now let's go about learning some ways to build great meetings.

PLANNING A MEETING

DEFINE YOUR OBJECTIVES, LARGE OR SMALL

- Decide on the biggest thing you'd like to accomplish.
- Be clear and get your goals down to three or four lines.
- Edit realistically. You can't accomplish everything in one meeting.
- Know that later meetings can add and refine details or variations.

QUESTION YOUR MEETING

Is this meeting truly necessary? Meetings often get to be a habit, and no one stops to analyze whether a meeting is the best way to go. Perhaps you need a few intimate one-on-ones or a small-group discussion with some key players first, before you bring the whole group together.

Who Should Come?

Consider your issues and who needs to be at your meeting. Do you need anyone else with additional expertise to strengthen the discussion? Should you bring in any key players beyond your group to get them on board? Are updates needed before you can present your issues?

Consider the Timing

Is this the right time to present this subject? Think about what's going on in the workplace; the industry; the money crunch in your shop. Is this a time for a sales push, a new product, a new service? How about management: would they be receptive right now? What is the relevance of your meeting to the ongoing issues of the day?

Meetings are disruptive and affect work schedules. Are there current pressures and deadlines on your group? Take upcoming holidays, events, and vacations into consideration. Ask yourself: Is this urgent or can it wait? Even if it's a regular weekly or monthly meeting, try to stay flexible in light of the above issues.

SCHEDULING A MEETING

There are some often ignored issues that can deeply affect a meeting's success: our energy level, the high and low times of day, hunger, the length of the meeting—these can affect our ability to listen, understand, be productive, or say yes or no.

BEST AND WORST TIMES TO HAVE MEETINGS

We all get cranky and impatient when we're hungry. It's our least generous, least altruistic time. We want *our* needs taken care of. We don't want to *give!* And low blood sugar drops our energy levels and ability to concentrate. So think about this when scheduling.

Here are the good and bad times:

- Right before lunch is not great, unless you arrange a brown-bagger or order lunch in.
- Breakfast and early morning is great, but have lots of coffee on hand. Some people are morning types, but lots of folks' internal clocks don't get going till 10 A.M. Know your group and their work habits.
- Meetings scheduled for midmorning or late in the day call for pick-me ups: provide coffee or suggest bringing a drink because you'll have a snack or sweet waiting.

Consider biorhythms and a little surprise feeding from time to time. This insures a more productive meeting. And care and feeding of the troops makes a much happier shop.

LENGTH OF MEETINGS

- How much time do you actually need? Understand the interruption meetings cause in someone's workday. Make meeting length reasonable.
- Consider attention span and interest in your subject(s).
- Don't try to cover too much. A series of meetings is better.

LOCATION

- Space and environment affect our creativity and responses. Change your environment from the usual when you want something or have bad news.

- <u>Need some team building?</u> Go off-site—it makes people feel special and together.
- <u>Notice the comfort level anywhere you meet.</u> Noise pollution, heat, and cold are real downers. Participants only want to get out of there.

WHICH DAY TO CHOOSE

Know your group. Monday can offer a clean slate and new beginnings, but sometimes it's hard to get the wheels moving again after a weekend. Friday afternoons are the worst times to challenge people to just listen and think. Their heads are full of quittin' time.

- <u>Big-subject meetings:</u> Best done midmorning to give people time to clear their desks.
- <u>Basic information meetings:</u> Tuesday through Thursday.
- <u>Bad news or criticism meetings:</u> Never on Fridays! This gives the person a whole weekend to stew and suffer and blow things all out of proportion. Hold such meetings before lunch or at the end of the day, giving people time to recover.

CREATING THE AGENDA

The four important things you want to think about, since you've already decided what subjects you wish to cover, are:

- Input from the group about their needs and/or new business
- The sheer number of agenda items
- Prioritizing and positioning items
- The time allotted to each item

INPUT FROM THE GROUP

Lack of involvement in setting the agenda is a major complaint. To make the *whole group* feel connected to your agenda and more involved in the meeting, get input from them about the agenda you're planning. You'll also discover other issues or problems that may need attention.

- Whenever possible and appropriate, send an email memo announcing not only the meeting time, date, and place but also your proposed agenda.
- Ask if they have any agenda items *they* want considered.
- You can then choose to put them on this agenda or add them to the next one. Or deal with the issue privately. This is much more productive than just asking if there's any new business at the end of a meeting, when we all want to leave.
- Getting all agenda items *before* the meeting rather than *at* it also helps you decide where all the items should fit and how much time to allot to each one.

NUMBER OF AGENDA ITEMS

Severely monitor this! Remember our attention span. How many items can you realistically cover well, keeping the group involved and the juices flowing? How many levels of intensity can you put your group through—from major subjects to peripheral details? You're better off budgeting yourself realistically than letting a meeting run on and on, leaving unproductive, annoyed meeting-goers.

PRIORITIZING AND POSITIONING

Small Items

- If they're *truly* minimal and if you're well disciplined and can dispose of them quickly, then you can put them first and save the rest of the meeting for major issues. If people get into the second layer of these small items, they use up precious time that should be allotted to major issues.

- When there is both important and unimportant business, consider disposing of the little items by email, or telephone, or saving them for another time. Consider what needs the whole group's input.

- Clumping small items at the end can also mean you never get to them.

Important Issues

- Start with the main agenda items; put little items last, if you need to put them in at all. This is especially true if the meeting is called on short notice or people have to leave at different times.

- Another approach is to call a meeting to discuss one item only. This emphasizes its importance and the amount of time you wish everyone to give it.

- Don't clutter meetings with unnecessary material. This frustrates participants whose full concentration you want. They become unsure what to focus on.

TIME ALLOTMENT

This is tough. We tend to think that the more time allotted to an item, the more important it is. But we don't always have a clear idea how long it takes to discuss things well.

To learn more about how long things *actually* take to discuss:

- Time the items at the next meeting you attend. Yes, use a stop watch. Discover how long is *too* long, how long is *not enough,* how many items before you get bored, and so forth.

- Time TV news pieces and Sunday nonfiction shows to see how long you can stand listening to one person before you get bored.

- Time commercials to see how much can be communicated in 15 seconds!

- Read these pages aloud and see how far you get in 30 seconds, 2 minutes, 5 minutes. It will surprise you.

With these little exercises you will begin to more realistically decide how much time to allot to each item on the agenda. This will help you understand much more about how much time your overall meeting should take. And it will make your agenda times realistic.

Don't forget that you may have a much more intense investment in the agenda than many of your group do. Temper your choices with this knowledge.

Set Agenda Times Together at the Meeting

You will get much better compliance if you put your agenda items up and then ask the group to help decide how much time to give each one. Keeping to the time allotted when people are really into it is very hard. Once it's a group decision, however, you can come down hard on when to end a segment, because everyone has agreed in advance.

OK. Off to the Meeting.

LEADERSHIP SKILLS FOR HANDLING PEOPLE

You know when you sit around the table at a meeting how the same people generally speak up, disagree, criticize, or never say a word? Have you ever stopped to think that they actually fall into types and that their behavior is definable and predictable?

Learning to categorize and understand these types is a key to handling them better and solving many on-the-spot problems. Here is a lexicon for the four basic types to be found in any group or family—wherever people work and interact together—to learn how to handle each one and to add to your group effort, rather than simply being divisive, egocentric, negative or noncontributing.

BASIC PERSONALITIES AT MEETINGS

There are four main types that you'll surely recognize from all the meetings you've attended:*

---

* From *Inside the Family* by Dr. David Kantor.

- **Movers:** initiate action, suggest or develop ideas.
- **Opposers:** react to and oppose movers and new ideas.
- **Followers:** hook on to others' ideas, support or "go along."
- **Bystanders:** watch, stay quiet, and remain noncommittal.

Movers

Movers are natural leaders: They are strong, sure-footed, and very creative. But they are often intolerant of others' ideas and see their own ideas as the best and only way to move forward and get competitive about that. They enjoy power and being in charge. They need and want approval and agreement.

Value at Meetings

They're very creative. They give new ideas and solutions, get the ball rolling, and try to get others on board.

Suggestions to Leaders

Harness the mover to pull ahead in the right direction. Monitor your tendency to single out movers by listening to them first and approving their ideas too soon. Set a course *before* the mover gets started, telling what you want. Say that everyone's input is important and you want to hear and think about *many* ideas. Affirm the mover but encourage others at the same time. Be aware that meeting leaders (you) are generally *movers*, so watch out for competitive feelings or calling on them first.

Opposers

These people create an instant challenge by blocking the mover's direction, and yours. They are competitive with movers, and get attention and importance by *opposing*. They are interested in the "facts" and the "truth." They also oppose in order to become the mover themselves. They can hurt feelings and make enemies, not only of individuals but of the group who can see them as obstacles to progress.

Value at Meetings

Opposers can bring up important issues overlooked in the mover's enthusiasm. They are willing to test ideas, scrutinize data, and find flaws or weak spots. They can actually improve the mover's innovative but flawed ideas and stimulate others' thinking.

Suggestions for Leaders

Though they sound negative, and you want to ignore them, dismiss them, or fight back against their objections, instead, *use* their critique to redirect and even stimulate more ideas or improvements. Give them an assignment; "Find out more and report back with some pro and con examples, OK?" Leaders: Watch your tendency to be an opposer by playing devil's advocate too often. This can dampen the creative drive of the group.

Followers

Followers are *not* uncreative! They need to play it safe, waiting to see the group's attitude before taking an overt stand. They may follow both mover and opposer for separate reasons.

Value at Meetings

They empower others by granting support and creating a constituency, which everyone needs when trying out a new idea. You need followers in your group. You'd choke with a group made up entirely of movers and opposers!

Suggestions for Leaders

Allow the follower to find his or her own level. When you see followers sign on, give them an assignment to help facilitate the project. They're great support staff and are very good at implementing.

Bystanders

Bystanders are interesting characters who need special attention. They're very different from the followers. They stay out of the direct action altogether, making no alliances with the other three types, just watching and keeping their opinions to themselves. They are most comfortable standing apart, offering neutral comments, such as "interesting" or "I'd have to think about that." The commentator role sounds like objectivity and wisdom (often unwarranted) to the group.

Value at Meetings

Bystanders have the power to comfort those they watch by uttering a few asides, making them feel supported and valued. They are seductive to both movers and opposers, who don't know what they're thinking and spend energy trying to get them to sign on.

Suggestions for Leaders

Bystanders aren't that way voluntarily; they've been overshadowed or never given the encouragement or training to try any other role. To help them participate, assign them a specific role, without waiting for them to volunteer. Ask for a private report ("Check back with me") because bystanders are afraid of being judged publicly.

THREE VITAL MEETING SKILLS

The toughest thing to do at meetings is to get people to *work together* to implement a project, and to move forward *as a group*, leaving their own agendas behind.

But individual agendas and personal needs must also be fulfilled before we can focus on the common good. Unfortunately, your needs and mine can often clash. We *each* want recognition and satisfaction, and we *both* want to move ahead—which means ahead of you and the next guy!

Three skills are needed in any group interaction to both feed others' egos and get our message heard:

Listening
Supporting
Disagreeing

These three skills are the absolute *key* to getting your own ideas heard in a group, and building enough support so your ideas are accepted and implemented. Pay close attention to these skills. They spell the secret for success at any meeting. At your next meeting, notice how others do or do not do them and how that affects outcomes.

LISTENING

This Really Matters!

Without listening, there is no flow in the discussion or building of ideas: just random thoughts that don't connect to each other. Vital information and good ideas are lost; we don't explore issues thoroughly.

Because we expect not to be listened to, we repeat ourselves and become redundant, just to make sure. We also notice who's not paying attention and develop some animosity. *Not* listening makes us miss what we're really agreeing to when we vote.

How We "Listen"

Let's get down to a little human nature here. You and I both know that in our zeal to get our own message across, we have little or no patience or interest in really hearing anyone else's idea or opinion. Here's what we do:

You start talking. I hear the beginning, then jump ahead, thinking about where you're *probably* going and what you *proba-*

bly mean without waiting to hear and consider it all. I start working on my countermove, ready to pounce as soon as you're done so I can get myself and my idea heard. I don't really hear or respond to your whole idea because I'm too busy telling you mine.

Nonlistening Costs You!

Nonlistening is obvious. It looks like this:

- Interrupting while someone's talking
- Cutting someone off before the end of a sentence
- Jumping from one subject to another with no connection to what's just been said
- Several people talking at once
- Body language signals: changing positions often, losing eye contact, starting to doodle, drumming fingers, jiggling a leg, clearing the throat

When the group sees that you haven't been listening, just champing at the bit to have your say, your responses to anything are immediately suspect. Seeing how you treat *their* ideas, others will do the same to *yours*.

Techniques for Improving Listening

To make friends around the table and build support for your ideas, try these techniques. Be conscious and deliberate about them. See how much more you'll hear and notice—and actually *learn* from others.

Put Yourself Aside

Wipe your own slate clean while someone talks. Your own word bank won't go dry: when it's your turn to talk, the words will still be there. Just start focusing on another's words for now.

Get Curious

"What's his idea?" "What is she thinking?" Since you already know what *you* think, make yourself find out what someone *else* thinks. It's interesting just to hear how differently people approach the same subject and how many solutions there can be to one problem. Not to mention how many ideas you can pick up and add to your own thinking.

Listen Openly and Noncritically

Suspend judgment while you're listening. We're so good at criticizing, finding fault with an idea, and jumping at why we shouldn't do something. So wait till you've heard the whole thing—*without judging its value*—before you decide what you think about it. Listen wholeheartedly, from the *speaker's* point of view.

Listen Actively and Make Notes

Taking notes forces you to focus on what's being said.

- Discover where the speaker is going.
- Listen to the supporting evidence.
- Keep reviewing and summarizing what you hear.
- Sort out facts from statements unsupported by evidence.
- Make lists and categorize: "This is related to that."

Wait Until the End

Don't jump ahead! This will try your patience, I know, but it's absolutely the key to learning to listen. As you listen, you may imagine what the conclusion might be, but *wait for the end before you speak.*

Look at the Speaker

Eye contact is a major signal to any speaker that you're listening and paying attention. It also gives you lots of information as you see how the speaker is delivering the message. Passionate? Committed? Tentative? Looking for approval? Eye contact really helps you concentrate and listen, and it also gives you a lot of information about the speaker.

Build on Previous Statements

Major proof that you were listening is when you connect what you're starting to say with what the previous speaker or speakers said. This also works to acknowledge the *worth* of someone else's statement, which surely makes friends. It also makes *them* listen better to *you*. Pick up the last few words you heard and use them as you start: "You said, 'A total overview.' You're right, Lynn, we do need some perspective. How about . . .'"

Leaders Can Help the Group Listen

Being alert to the signals of nonlistening, as you now are, leaders can actively intercede when they notice them in the group.

- Say it when you see it: "Hey, this sounds like no one's listening to each other. To get all the ideas heard—and I need *all* of them—let's everyone settle down and tune in to what's being proposed. You can build off each other's ideas and come up with a solution more quickly."
- Summarize what each person has just said, and ask the speaker if that's what he or she meant.
- Comment on what you hear, especially on the most productive or innovative parts.
- Invite a specific person to respond: "Jake, what Linda said is mainly in your department. What do you think about the idea? How could that work for you?"
- Interrupt (benignly) about nonresponsiveness: "Hang on, Andrea. Jerry was just talking about another problem. Let's stay with that before we go on to what you wanted to say, OK?"

Teach your group better listening skills: Actively talk about how tough it is, and show them some ways to improve their listening skills.

<u>Note:</u> This skill is also vitally important in *any* client or customer interchange!

SUPPORTING

This Really Matters!

How you respond to someone else's idea has great consequences. Supporting and building on it helps you develop a team to implement whatever you suggest. Good supporting skills develop better interpersonal relationships in the group as people remember and feel grateful for your support.

Putting down another's ideas makes him respond negatively to yours. Flat-out negative responses in front of a group embarrasses and hurts feelings.

Supporting others' ideas keeps the creative atmosphere alive and makes you emerge as a multidimensional person, able to see another point of view.

Alas, Supporting Isn't Natural

Many of us are competitive at work, so it's hard to be generous. It feels like your position is diminished when you strengthen another's. For some folks, it's threatening to compliment and support because it can sound like you're a follower. Folks also fear that supporting can sometimes be mistaken for sucking up.

Also, criticizing rather than supporting feels like a more proactive and visible role to some. People think that cynicism and negativism sound like strength, demonstrating superior knowledge and experience. Not true, folks.

What Nonsupport Looks Like

- "Here's a good idea!"
  "It'll never work."

- "What about this approach?"
  "Nah, we tried that already."
- "We could do it this way."
  "I'll tell you what's wrong with that."

Talk about cold water!

Techniques for Supporting

Assume Value in Another's Ideas

Put your own ego on the back burner. There can be something of value in *any* idea. New ideas can stimulate your thinking further, send you in a new direction, or make you aware of a basic flaw in your own idea.

Listen for What You Can Support

Quell that competitive spirit long enough to listen and find things you *can* agree with. You don't have to support the whole idea. Just look for the *germ* of a good idea. Comment on a small piece, an addition or departure from the usual.

Discover information or a point of view you don't have. Look for an extension of something you already support. Even notice something that could contribute to the group's thinking and stimulate new ideas.

And find what helps push your own idea forward. Here are some ways to say it:

- "Listen, what Cleo said about X is really good. We ought to . . ."
- "I liked the part about Y. Let's talk more about that."
- "Now this opens a new direction we haven't thought of."

Build On, Add On

"Y'know, using Sue's idea as the foundation, we could add mine about the . . ." This continues the forward momentum.

You're then able to add your own idea to the good part. Connect to what has already been approved. Show how what you're doing or saying is *synergistic* with the new idea. That's where new support for your idea will come.

OK, you've got it. But before I dream up this perfect world where you're all just listening, agreeing, and supporting each other, let's stop. *You also disagree with others!*

And you'd better, since there'd be no yeast or ferment in that other world to make things really grow and be the best that you can be.

So now let's look at skills you can use to *disagree*—without being too *disagreeable*.

DISAGREEING

What's Good About It

Many of us fear disagreeing, thinking it will hurt people's feelings or make an enemy. But disagreement is *good*.

Solutions become stronger if they survive group criticism. Groups are more effective where disagreement is possible because they're conditioned to rethink, even scrap, an ineffectual idea. Constructive disagreement makes people learn to survive critical comment and still keep working together.

Off-the-Track Disagreeing

When your disagreement's personal, not objective or factual, you create discord. Focusing on the *person*, not the *idea*, hurts, and hardly makes friends and future supporters. It also prevents people from dealing with what might be a very legitimate flaw because they're busy defending themselves or a friend. Other no-no's:

- Disagreeing just to grandstand
- Protecting your own idea, thus unnecessarily negating another's
- Finding fault and nitpicking about a whole idea, while much of it actually has validity
- Disagreeing just to protect turf and areas of responsibility

Techniques for Disagreeing Constructively

Honor Divergent Ideas

Major mantra: *Always differ with the idea, not the person!*

Use "it," not "you." Watch *"You've* got that wrong." Use *"It* sounds like there's not enough XYZ in that." Not *"You* didn't think about." Rather, "What seems to be missing is" or "It doesn't quite answer the problem of . . ."

Disagreeing impersonally—based on the objective facts, not the author—makes everyone able to consider the issue.

Listen and Support First, Before You Differ

Build a more unguarded listener by saying something *good, first.* Giving a gift by supporting, before you start deleting, leaves the other with less of a loss. Really hear the whole idea and choose the best part of it first. For example:

"I really liked the part about X. Maybe you can expand on that to solve Y, which still needs work. And then maybe also add Z because . . ."

How to praise before criticizing? Add a suggestion to your criticism:

"That part about the promotion was really a great idea. But you may be taking it too far. How about talking to some customers as a next step?"

Be sure you bring in some objective facts to support your disagreement. Otherwise it's just your word or opinion against theirs.

Ask Questions

Try to get clear about exactly what was said and what it meant *before* you go after it. Sometimes you and another person disagree but you're talking about two different things.

Get more information to support what you will eventually disagree with. Just making the other person clarify his idea can often solve what you were going to disagree with. Ask for examples or if there are any previous experiences with this idea.

"This part is pretty clear, but I'm not sure I understand the other part. Do you mean before or after we close?" "How would it work if . . . ?" "Has this been tried anywhere else?"

Don't just settle for one question. Follow up till you and the group truly understand what's being offered. But do it with straight curiosity, not by cross-examining.

Be Specific and Constructive

After you've said the "agreeing with" part, list everything you disagree with, but in a very organized fashion. Otherwise it sounds like a flood of negatives and no one can use it.

Be sure you specify exactly what you are taking issue with—don't generalize. It's easier to hear if you focus on one or two specific points. Choose the most important ones, and be sure they're relevant to the work you're all doing and the exact issue you're all trying to solve.

Disagree Nonjudgmentally!

Don't characterize any idea. Beware of adjectives! Try:

"Something's troubling me about this" rather than "That's not a useful idea!"

Watch rolling the eyes or looking impatient; unfortunately we're prone to lots of impatience when we disagree. And don't set yourself up as the final arbiter, closer to the truth than anyone else. Even if the idea sounds ridiculous, try to keep the heat or derision out of it because others may actually like her idea better than you or yours!

Always Offer Some Other Solution

Don't just carp about what's no good. Offer a better or alternative idea. Be constructive, ready to add what you think is best: "Maybe not that last part. How about changing that to include Jeremy's idea?" Or, "Could you focus on the printing part? It may be too costly. How can you cut that down?"

Suggestions for Leaders

Leaders can play a big part in ameliorating disagreements, but only if they're hitting a wall.

- Let the individuals discuss a little *before* you enter it; point out what you hear are the missing pieces.
- Interfere by saying, "I hear both ideas and I'll tell you where I think they can fit together" ("complement each other," "take something from each one").
- Mention other aspects that no one has brought up so far; give a reality check of what's possible and what's not.
- Redirect the group: "I think you've taken it a little too far but let's stay with the first thought. Everyone think of how we can use *that*. It's good."

Now to *other* communication skills—for both leaders and participants—that can make a real difference in how meetings go.

COMMUNICATION SKILLS FOR MEETING LEADERS

When you call a meeting, your job description as leader includes:

- Host: The participants are there because you asked them to come.
- Traffic manager: Your job is to make it all work and keep it all moving smoothly.
- Coach: Get everyone on board, working toward a group win.
- Interpreter: Help everyone understand and be clear about the issues.
- Reality checker: Say what's possible, what's urgent, and what are the deadlines.
- Caretaker: Watch out for egos, attention span, interesting presentations, physical aspects of the meeting.

- <u>Referee:</u> Clashes are bound to happen.
- <u>Product and solution developer:</u> End with something tangible.

GETTING THE GROUP'S ATTENTION

- <u>Present each new item</u> first in terms of the effect it will have on the group. The old self-interest theme, in group terms.
- <u>Go around the table</u> at the beginning of a discussion asking everyone's thoughts about a subject (called the Delphi technique); what they already know, have never heard of, have tried, telling how it worked. This is a good icebreaker and catalyst for total participation.
- <u>Focus the ensuing discussion</u> based on what you discover are the main objections or needs.
- <u>Notice which subjects affect</u> only one section or one team or just a few folks. These are potential attention-losers. If you do this, tell the group what's in it for *everybody*. How it will eventually affect the whole group and why you therefore need them all to participate now.

STAYING FOCUSED

- You have to be the watchdog. No one else has the power to step in if a problem develops.
- Keep the group pointing toward solutions or the end product you want from this meeting.
- Notice nitpicking or a negative push-pull and stop it: "Hold on, everybody. This is off the point. Let's get back to where we went off."
- Be aware of tangents but don't just cut them off since they might also have value. Just stop and say, "We need to talk about this, too. We'll make it an agenda item for next week (or at the end, if we have time)."

ENGAGING THE NONPARTICIPANT

Of course you want to involve everyone. The hardest thing for nonparticipants is to be asked for an on-the-spot opinion or a fresh idea without preparation.

"Let's hear from Bill" or "What do you think, Clarissa?" is *not* the way to go. Bill or Clarissa may not be able to come up with something quickly, may have nothing to say on the subject, or may get very intimidated. And in front of the whole group yet . . .

For those who have trouble spontaneously speaking up:

- <u>Give them a heads-up</u> and time to prepare: "Let's hear from David and Diane, and then from Sally (the nonparticipant) on this."

- <u>Engage by asking</u> them a specific question related to something they *know* and have been working on: "Nina, costs are your department. Help us out with that."

- <u>Designate specific reports</u> in advance for those whom you see have trouble speaking up extemporaneously. This gives them time to prepare.

- <u>Assign a task</u> from the current discussion, asking them to check in with you privately at a specific time.

HOW TO CUT PEOPLE OFF

This isn't simple. There's a lot at stake. If you handle it wrong, the other person will lose face in front of the whole group. This isn't good for you as a leader. Saving face for the silenced is key whenever you cut someone off. And your grace and style as a leader—*how* you do the "cutting off"—is also tested.

- At the outset, tell your concern about the time you've all agreed on for each agenda item (see page 271 for how to set agenda times).

- Use a visual for your agenda, with the times allotted written on it. This is a safe, impersonal fallback position for you.

- Say you've got a watch (!) and you'll really time each segment. Assign someone to keep time.
- Give time remaining during each item's discussion. This gives you the perfect excuse to cut someone off.
- Always intro a cutoff: "Interesting stuff, Larry. Want some more about this. Will you add this as an item for the next meeting?"
- Warnings help before you do the cutoff: "Sorry, Sam, but you've got about one more minute on this."
- Cut off with a light touch: "Wow, you're really all wound up about this, Susan. But . . ." Saves face by explaining why she's talked too long,
- Irrelevant-issue talkers can be quickly disposed of: "We just can't go into that now. Why don't you email me about it and let's see how to handle it."

HANDLING CONTROVERSIAL OR TICKLISH SUBJECTS

People may be reluctant to speak about some subjects in public. Participants may worry about consequences if they're identified with unpopular or critical opinions and judgments, especially from you.

- To protect against individual exposure: Break into small groups of three; ask for quick reports on each group's thinking when they rejoin each other.
- Anonymous responses in writing, either written at the meeting or dropped into a designated box or emailed later is another safe way to go.
- Sometimes it helps to start the discussion of a controversial subject with a secret ballot just to see where people stand. It makes holding one opinion or another safer if you find out the majority feels that way.

GETTING AGREEMENT

- Know when to end discussion and go for the vote.
- You or a designate should summarize what happened; it helps to write the points covered on the board.
- Describe consequences; what the yes or no vote means in terms of how you all go forward.
- Get agreement and input for all attending about whether that's what everyone agrees happened.
- If you've discussed the subject to death, the consensus may be very clear and a formal vote is sometimes not needed.
- If the subject has raised some animosity and heat and could be potentially damaging if the vote is visible (like *who* turned down someone's specific report or idea), go for a secret ballot on controversial issues.

WHEN MEETINGS GET OUT OF HAND

Meetings can become unruly, especially when they get over-heated and several people talk at once. This requires a louder voice, with some authority, to be heard and get people calmed down. That's you!

- Set up the rules at the beginning, explaining that it's detrimental and a waste of time when things do get out of hand.
- Use it: "Hey, people." "Hold It." "OK, let's stop now." Whatever is your natural expression. But say it with conviction, like you really mean it. Informal, relaxed, but firm!
- Getting too bossy or angry is a sign of weakness, implying that you can't hold the group by your sheer skill as *leader*—that you need to resort to *overlord*.
- Know that you *can* and *will* control the group. That intention will reflect itself in your voice and how it delivers your call to attention. (The essence of method acting!)

HANDLING EGOS AND CONFLICT

Self-control is the key here. Beware of blowing up at anyone at a group meeting. It reflects badly on your leadership skills. Use your energies to recognize why something negative is happening. Focus on people's inner agenda to understand their outward display.

- Ask yourself, "What is he really saying?" "Why is she so mad about this?"

- In a one-on-one confrontation, *name the anger first:* "I see you two feel very strongly about this. Well, passion and caring are both good things, and I appreciate people who do. But to keep the discussion rolling, let's turn a little passion to some solutions to our issue. . . ."

- Don't just ask people to settle down! They *can't* or they would have! It's painful and also unproductive since you will not yet have taken care of the animosity. And those two people have *already* lost control in front of the group.

- Always think about saving face for the opponents whenever there is conflict. They can't do it for themselves. Give them a graceful way out while you 're getting the meeting back in gear.

- Everyone needs recognition and stroking before their peers at some point. So while you pull on the reins, give an antidote. "Thanks for both of you caring so much about this project. Keep that energy flowing!"

COMMUNICATION SKILLS FOR MEETING PARTICIPANTS

Meetings give you a rare opportunity to emerge in ways others don't normally see at your daily job. You can be seen by the boss as a vital, active, interested group member. You can gain the respect of your peers as they see your capacities for thinking, analyzing and creating. What you say and do and how you relate to them should reflect you at your best.

Since this book is for everybody, more senior people may

already do some of these. But here's a little tune-up for you and an intro for the juniors. Try these:

COME PREPARED

Of course you come prepared. But look at these ideas to see if you can do *more* to widen your scope and sharpen your edge.

- Don't just know the agenda items (usually circulated in advance). Bone up on them. What do you already know? What else can you learn?
- Find out who'll be at the meeting and what they do.
- Anticipate how *they* might feel about the agenda items. What issues would these raise for them?
- Think about how the agenda items affect your department or the firm. Come up with some approach to them from that point of view, not just your personal one.
- Find out about your industry: what's happening in the field?
- Get in the habit of going online to check out professional journals, newspapers, and magazine articles about your business. Consider the global picture and competitors in your field. It gives you a chance for original contributions.
- Print out these articles for show-and-tell at the meeting, or to use in validating someone else's suggestions, even to disagree constructively by using some objective data.

Getting ahead means getting ahead of the pack in how you work and what you know or are interested in finding out.

SIT IN A POWERFUL PLACE

Placement around the table does affect your visibility, how often you're called on to contribute, how hard it is to participate, and people's response to you.

- The power place is, of course, fairly close to the boss, but not right beside him or her. You must be able to make eye contact. Next is in the middle of the table.
- Keep away from the ends of the table, especially on the sides. The boss will not see you there. You'll feel irrelevant and fall out of the action.
- Be very aware of the hierarchy. Don't push too high up the seating ladder too soon. But do make some solid moves to get there.
- In general, and especially if you're quite junior in the organization, always ask if you can sit somewhere *before* you sit down. People do save seats for buddies.
- Sit near the powerful movers or opposite them so you can make eye contact, watch their reactions, and let them see you participate.
- At a big meeting, never sit in the back. Always sit up front, to be seen as interested and involved, *not* looking for a way to stay out of the meeting.

LOOK CONFIDENT AND INTERESTED

No one can ever know how nervous you are or how out of a discussion you feel, unless you *look* like you are. Always walk in knowing you are interested and want to be involved. Accept the fact that you may *feel* nervous. That's OK. Just put it in your pocket and move on to feeling active and involved, on your toes, and looking for the opportunity to contribute or ask a question.

You can *look* as though you're concentrating even though your heart is beating fast. No one can hear it.

- Don't fidget! Don't jiggle around in your seat. Sit still. And no doodling.
- To get rid of extra energy and give your hands something to do, take notes about what's being said.
- If you find yourself being bored or even dozing off (!), get

up and get a cup of coffee or leave the room for a few minutes.

- Movement and a physical change help get you back in gear.

HOW TO SPEAK UP

For anyone to really appreciate you and your worth, you need to *speak up*—to make a contribution at a meeting. If you have trouble speaking extemporaneously, reread Chapters 7 and 8 about making presentations and getting your message across.

Since you know what the agenda's going to be, come in with a few ideas about some items. Prepare and really edit your thoughts in advance till you get comfortable.

- Listen hard to see where there's an opening for you to add something you're comfortable with. The closer you listen, the more you'll find something to add that's uniquely your own.

- Hook into something that's been said, so you don't have to feel that you're boldly plowing fresh ground. Say, "Here's another point of view about that," to hook onto the ongoing conversation and show you're listening.

- Don't just agree with something. Always *add* something or give another good reason *why* you agree. Never speak just to be noticed!

- Always speak in bullet or numerical form: After a very short introductory sentence to alert the group to your point of view, say, "There are two points that might be useful here: 1. Contact the sales team for feedback. 2. Emailing the group with a summary." Then wrap it up with a short conclusion.

- If you want to talk facts and numbers and need to show them, ask the boss: "I think I can explain this best if I write it, OK?" Don't just peremptorily take over and start writing.

- Don't wear out your welcome if you're full of energy and

ideas. Remember you're *part of a group!* Learn to lay back
and listen, too.

- Always speak from the heart—straight, real talk. Never
pontificate, lecture, or get formal in what you say. These
are just your colleagues—folks you know, sitting around,
coffee in hand, doing a job and sharing ideas. Scale your
remarks to the occasion.

ASK QUESTIONS

Another way to be heard and get known is to ask questions.
Ask only *purposeful* ones, for information or clarification; this
makes you sound interested, smart, and insightful.

Asking allows you to participate and be present when you
may not have a major contribution. But be sure your question is
useful, not just for attention. Asking off-the-wall or elementary
questions is harmful.

Be sure, before you contribute, that you're on track with
what's been said and that you're zooming in on a discussed point.
Always anchor your remarks with how they grow out of the previous statement.

IF YOU'RE CRITICIZED OR ATTACKED

Don't get defensive before the group, especially to the boss.
This is a sign of weakness, maybe even guilt! If you're attacked or
criticized, maintain your dignity. Promise attention to the problem and an analysis of the issue. Show an open mind.

- First go for further information: "I see what you're saying,
and I want to look at that. Where can I find it?"

- If there are some other issues the boss may not know
about, don't take the group's time. After the meeting,
give your boss or coworker more data— *in private.*

- Ask questions to make your critic be more specific: "I
appreciate your critique. It would be really helpful if you

explained more about what aspect didn't work. Let me come and see you after the meeting."

- If you were against something that got group endorsement: "Well, you know I wasn't for this, but I will support it since everyone wants it. Since it was your idea, Alec, I'd like to check with you to be sure I understand."

Always be a reasonable person, tuned in to what's being said, willing to listen and fix something. You're strong and unintimidated by criticism.

So there you have it. As much as (and maybe more than?) you ever wanted to know about meetings: how to plan them, run them, make them productive, handle yourself and each other in them. I hope you learned some new ways to do all that.

Is this the end? Not quite. You know how people always like to have the last word. So, here it comes. . . .

THE LAST WORD

How to close? What lasting words can I leave with you that might convey the essence of what it takes to communicate well in your work? Perhaps this story.

A friend of mine found himself seated next to that most distinguished architect, I. M. Pei. My friend is from Boston where Mr. Pei's famous John Hancock building dominates the skyline, growing out of a corner of the venerable Copley Square. The square is also the home of two landmark nineteenth-century architectural marvels: Trinity Church, a medieval-styled wonder of multicolored granite, and the Italian Renaissance-styled Boston Public Library, all Romanesque arches and dignity. The John Hancock building, the newcomer on this scene, is a soaring, rhomboid-shaped tower, completely sheathed in reflective glass.

My friend seized the opportunity to ask Mr. Pei, "Why, flanked by those two old buildings of magnificent stone and granite, did you sheathe, the John Hancock building in glass?"

"Yes. Well, when you look into that glass, what do you see?"

"Why, I—I—see the two magnificent buildings!"

"Exactly."

Mr. Pei's intent was to honor those landmarks by reflecting them first, building his architectural statement around them.

Unless you can build your statement so we can "see ourselves" in your communication, we will have difficulty assimilating it.

To motivate us, your listeners at work, you need to know enough about us to help us see *ourselves* in what you're talking about. Your communication must deal at our level, reflecting our concerns.

Answering questions? Leading a meeting? Selling a product? Disagreeing with a client? Reporting to the boss? In every case, unless you feature us, and we see ourselves reflected in what you're saying and doing, your communication is "for your eyes only."

All the techniques I've suggested to you in this book are variations on this theme. They work because they start by including *us*. That's how to talk so people listen.

So, I end, reluctantly. There are so many more things that I wanted to tell, or show you, not just tell. But if I have stimulated you to rethink how you communicate at work, to start trying some new ways, then I will have reached my mark and can rest easy. Thanks for listening. Now it's your turn. . . .

Acknowledgments

No book happens solely from the writer's own efforts. Along with all my cloistered hours, others were also involved in helping this book come to light. Let me now thank them for their advice and criticism, their support and help along the way.

Many thanks to Marcy Syms, CEO of Syms Corp.; Al Zollar, general manager of Tivoli Software at IBM; Ted Janulis, global head of investment management at Lehman Brothers; Jason Wright, senior vice president, Corporate Communications, at Merrill Lynch; Bryan Simmons, vice president of client and industry communications at IBM; Ida Schmertz, global business consultant; and scientist Dr. Stephanie Leslie. They read the book in process and were helpful, clear, and sometimes painfully truthful in helping me make the book hit the target. . . .

To my lawyer, Bob Levine, for his faith in the book, his vision, and his steadfast support. To Joe Tessitore, whose gracious welcoming of my book and my "brand" have made me a happy and devoted author. To Marion Maneker, who met this book very early on, and whose continued support has made a big difference to me. To my editor, Leah Spiro, my gratitude for holding my feet to the fire. Not pleasant, cutting up my baby, but I do know how necessary it was to shorten and tighten the words, even though I like to set a very full table for my guests (and readers). To Mark Bryant, whose support at the beginning helped me sail forth. To Mareike Paessler, whose great help took this book from edited mark-ups to the finished version. To Bill Ruoto, for being so responsive in designing the book. To Alexandra Kaufman, so helpful in handling so many details, and to Jill Goldstein for her cheerfulness and her chocolate.

Thanks to Barbara Close for her involvement, devotion, and research help, especially for Chapter 2. To Danielle L'Heureux, who came in at the eleventh hour to save a carpal-tunneled Sonya, and helped complete it with so many dangling chores.

And to all my friends and family—you've done it again: given me the love and support you always bring forth when I seem to falter. How could I ever thank you all enough for always being there for me?

Finally, to all the people who have asked me to teach them over the years—know that these words and my conviction about my ideas come from what I've learned from you as I watch you all listen, change, and grow. Thanks.

INDEX